JAMES ALLISON

JAMES ALLISON

A Biography of the
Engine Manufacturer and
Indianapolis 500 Cofounder

Sigur E. Whitaker

McFarland & Company, Inc., Publishers
Jefferson, North Carolina, and London

LIBRARY OF CONGRESS CATALOGUING-IN-PUBLICATION DATA

Whitaker, Sigur E., 1948–
    James Allison : a biography of the engine manufacturer and
Indianapolis 500 cofounder / Sigur E. Whitaker.
        p.   cm.
    Includes bibliographical references and index.

    ISBN 978-0-7864-6165-3
    softcover : 50# alkaline paper ∞

    1. Allison, James, 1872–1928.   2. Liberty engines — History.
3. Indianapolis Motor Speedway (Speedway, Ind.) — History.
4. Industrialists — United States — Biography.   I. Title.
TJ140.A47W45   2011
796.72092 — dc22   [B]   2011000091

BRITISH LIBRARY CATALOGUING DATA ARE AVAILABLE

On the cover: *inset* portrait, James Allison (photograph courtesy
of Rolls-Royce Heritage Trust, Allison Branch); *background poster*
Indianapolis Motor Speedway, 1909 (Library of Congress)

Manufactured in the United States of America

McFarland & Company, Inc., Publishers
    Box 611, Jefferson, North Carolina 28640
        www.mcfarlandpub.com

To my friend and brother,
Joel Whitaker

Table of Contents

Preface

What do the Indianapolis Motor Speedway, Allison Payment Systems, Rolls-Royce Allison Branch, Allison Transmissions and Miami Beach have in common? The common factor is an Indianapolis entrepreneur of the early 1900s, James Allison.

Growing up in Indianapolis, I would occasionally hear references to Allison. I knew the basics — Allison was one of the founders of the Indianapolis Motor Speedway and an engine manufacturer at a company that was then known as Detroit Diesel Allison. I also knew that he was involved in the development of Miami Beach.

On a rainy summer day in 2007, I was at the Indiana Historical Society to do some genealogy research. Not knowing much about James Allison, who was married to my great-great-aunt Sara Cornelius Allison, I typed his name into the computer. Among the historical society's collection was a family photograph album. Thinking it would be fun to see what Allison looked like, I started looking through the album. At first, I was disappointed as there wasn't a single family photograph. Rather, it was an album of their home, Riverdale, which was built between 1911 and 1914 for an estimated $2,000,000. The house with the plain exterior had a richly appointed interior. This piqued my curiosity about Allison.

What I discovered was an entrepreneur who followed his passions. In the 1880s, James Allison was involved with the bicycling craze. When autos were introduced in the early 1900s, he was among the early adapters. He was a self-made man, his fortune being made through his investment in Prest-O-Lite, which supplied the power source for early automobile headlights and was jointly owned with Carl Fisher. The frustration with the quality of the early American automobile led Fisher and Allison, along with two friends, to develop the Indianapolis Motor Speedway. The Speedway led to the creation of Allison Engineering, a high-end machine shop which made automobile parts for race cars for the Speedway. Later, with the sale of Prest-O-Lite,

Allison decided to retire and his life moved on to Miami Beach, where his friend and business partner, Carl Fisher, was a driving force in its development. Allison started an aquarium on Miami Beach which rivaled the leading aquariums of the time and later developed an exclusive private hospital.

Although Allison's name is not widely recognized today, his business interests have continued and have made significant contributions over the intervening years. The Indianapolis Motor Speedway was initially founded with the hope that through racing the quality of the American automobile would improve. During the early years of the Speedway, the progression of the automobile was rapid, with the innovations frequently being either developed for racing or tested at the racetrack. Allison Engineering, the small high-end machine shop for automobile parts in Speedway, Indiana, changed its focus during World War I when it was involved with the development of the Liberty engines. During World War II this company, which was then a part of General Motors, was a primary manufacturer of the V-1710 engine, a significant power source for Allied aircraft. Under General Motors, the company's two primary product lines, engines and transmissions, were ultimately split into two different divisions. The engine manufacturer continues today as part of Rolls-Royce, which makes engines for both airplanes and helicopters. The transmission division today is Allison Transmissions, with its worldwide headquarters in Indianapolis. Allison Payment Systems is the descendant of Allison Coupon Company, the family enterprise where Allison was involved as a young man. Very few people have been so involved with even one company, much less with four entities that have been through numerous business cycles for nearly a hundred years.

This book would not have been possible without the help of the librarians at the Norfolk (Virginia) Public Library. They enabled much of the research on Prest-O-Lite, the Miami Aquarium and Allison Hospital through microform obtained through the interlibrary loan system. The Norfolk Public Library also provided access to the majority of the books utilized in the research. Dave Newill of Rolls-Royce Heritage Trust, Allison Branch, in Indianapolis and his associates John Leonard and Paul Zablonski opened the doors to their archives and photographs. I was also assisted by Dawn Hugh of the Historical Museum of South Florida where I traveled to do some research focusing on Allison's time in Miami Beach.

Others who have been helpful include Sister Rachel West of Marian University in Indianapolis. The Allison home, Riverdale, formed the basis of the university campus when it was formed in the 1930s. Louis Mowbray and Morgan Mowbray provided me with information about their grandfather, Louis Mowbray, the curator of the Miami Aquarium. Also providing help were Carolyn Klepser, Seth Branson, Nicholas Lindberg, Margo Scheuring, Mary Ellen Loscar of the Indianapolis Motor Speedway and Susan Sutton of the Indiana Historical Society.

Introduction

August 3, 1928. It was a hot, humid summer day when a train pulled into Union Station in downtown Indianapolis. Following the passenger cars was the private Pullman rail car (Advance) of Indianapolis industrialist James Ashbury Allison and his bride of four days, the former Lucille Mussett of Miami, Florida.[1] They were met at the train station by Allison's longtime employee Lucien. Climbing into the car, they were driven by Lucien about six miles northwest to their home, Riverdale Springs. Riverdale Springs was the estate built by Jim Allison between 1911 and 1914, at a cost estimated to be over $2,000,000, on 64 acres of rolling Indiana farmland. When built, it was considered a "house of wonders" as it had all of the latest innovations.

The Allisons had married on July 30 at the home of his friend and business partner, Carl Fisher, in Montauck Point, New York. While at Montauck, Allison had contracted a summer cold. After spending a day in New York, the Allisons began their honeymoon, traveling first to Asheville, North Carolina. During the rail trip to North Carolina, the cold had worsened and the honeymoon plans were altered to go to Indianapolis. By the time the Allisons arrived in Indianapolis, the cold had gotten progressively worse and Allison was barely able to walk into the massive entry hall of his home. He rode the elevator up to the second floor where the master bedroom was located and collapsed in his bed. His local physician was summoned.

The cold had developed into bronchial pneumonia. With his bride at his side, and a heart weakened by years of cardiovascular and pulmonary diseases, he was unable to fight the pneumonia and soon lapsed into a coma. Alerted by Allison's physician that his illness was grave, Fisher sent a telegraph to Mrs. Lucille Mussett Allison indicating that he and his wife, Margaret, were leaving New York immediately for Indianapolis.

The next day, Allison was dead at age 55. During his lifetime, the United States was transformed from an agrarian to an industrial economy of which the automobile was an essential component. Indianapolis had also changed from the town of his youth. It continued to be a town where most residents lived in single family or duplex homes rather than the row houses of the East. But the economy of Indianapolis had been transformed along with the United States. Traditionally, that economy had been well balanced and so it continued to be. The automobile industry, in which Allison was closely involved, had added a new dimension and provided employment for thousands, not only in automobile manufacturing but also in parts manufacturing. Allison's life was intertwined with the development of the automobile and auto racing in the United States.

The automobile business was still in its infancy when Allison's longtime friend Carl Fisher, who owned the first automobile in Indiana and opened the first automobile dealership in Indianapolis, showed Allison a long cylinder filled with acetylene gas. This highly explosive device could be used as a power source for automobile headlights. Allison and Fisher, in 1904, bought the device and established Prest-O-Lite Company. Paralleling the automobile industry, Prest-O-Lite grew exponentially. Both Fisher and Allison earned a fortune operating the company, and their wealth grew with the sale of the company within 13 short years to Union Carbide Company for $9,000,000.

Portrait of James A. Allison (courtesy Rolls-Royce Heritage Trust, Allison Branch)

In the early 1900s, the automobile industry was centered in the Midwest, and Indianapolis was a close rival to Detroit in terms of automobile production. Through Prest-O-Lite, Allison interfaced with others in the fledgling industry. Indianapolis was home to several automobile manufacturers as well as numerous suppliers. With the Midwest being the national center for the automobile industry, the quest for improving the automobile led to the founding of the Indianapolis Motor Speedway by four Indianapolis entrepreneurs who were actively involved in the auto industry. One of them was Allison.

During the early years of automobile racing in the United States, racetracks frequently had their own "team cars." Allison purchased a couple of Peugeots which had been involved in auto racing on the European continent. These automobiles along with three specially manufactured Maxwells formed the basis for the Speedway "team cars." These cars needed to be maintained. Responding to this need, Allison began a high-end machine shop originally called the Speedway Team Company.

Shortly after its establishment, the company changed its name to Allison Experimental Company and quickly developed a reputation for high-quality products. With the entry of the United States into World War I, Allison Experimental became heavily involved in the development of prototypes and parts for the Liberty engines. This company continues today as a division of Rolls-Royce and an independent firm, Allison Transmissions.

Upon the sale of Prest-O-Lite in 1917, Allison decided that he would "retire." He had previously visited his longtime friend and business partner, Fisher, in Miami Beach, Florida, which Fisher was crafting from a mangrove and swamp area into a resort. Allison quickly grew to love the area and increasingly spent longer periods of time there. Although not widely recognized, Allison was involved in the early development of Miami Beach, primarily as a financier.

In Florida, he developed a reputation as a sports fisherman and on almost a daily basis he would take trips into the Gulf Stream on his yacht, *L'Apache.* His interest in fishing led to the development in 1920 of an aquarium in Miami Beach. This aquarium developed a national reputation, and reportedly its collection of deep sea fishes and mammals was second only to the aquarium at Naples, Italy. As his health deteriorated, Allison also built a private upscale hospital on Allison Island in the north end of Miami Beach. Just as in Indianapolis, his life in Florida had him interacting with some of the rich and powerful in the early 1920s.

His death was a loss to both the Indianapolis and Miami Beach communities. Among the many giving tributes to Allison, G. Barret Moxley, president of the Kiefer-Stewart Company in Indianapolis, said, "James Allison was a real constructive force and will be greatly missed by his associates in many enterprises. He had a habit of thinking clear through a proposition, was unusually endowed with business acumen and clear vision and was remarkably tenacious in holding to a policy once determined upon. He was unswerving in his devotion and loyalty to friends."[2]

Carl Fisher said,

I don't think he had an enemy in the world. He was never in the courts which is a remarkable thing for a man who handles so much money. Through our close business association and warm personal friendship, I grew to look on him as one of the greatest business men in the United Sates. He seemed to have a business sixth sense, and once he had made up his mind to a plan of action, he followed it through. His judgment was so far reaching that he usually foreseen [*sic*] the end, too. One of the finest things about him was his loyalty to friends. Never were they forgotten. Jim didn't blow hot one day and cold the next. If you were once his friend, you were his friend for good and there was nothing he would not do for you if he could see his way to it.[3]

The greatest tribute to Allison is the continuation of the Indianapolis Motor Speedway, Allison Transmissions and Rolls-Royce Allison to the present day. These companies have impacted the United States and have brought about advances in the automobile and aircraft.

In 1946, Eddie Rickenbacker, World War I flying ace and the owner of the Indianapolis Motor Speedway between 1929 and 1946, said approximately 70 percent of the mechanical improvements to the automobile were either originated or perfected at the Speedway. He believed that the 500 mile race had the same impact as 100,000 "ordinary" road miles.[4]

T.E. ("Pop") Myers, longtime general manager of the Indianapolis Motor Speedway, recounted some of the innovations attributable to the Speedway in its first twenty-five years, including the introduction of a rearview mirror by Ray Harroun in 1911, four-wheel brakes by Jules Goux in 1913, front-wheel drive by Dave Lewis in 1925 and radical balloon tires by de Paolo in 1925. Myers also attributed the development of four-wheel brakes used by Jimmy Murphy in 1921, the straight-eight motor developed by the Duesenberg brothers in 1920, the low-slung automobile bodies with a lower center of gravity making the cars more stable, improvements in suspensions, and the mandatory installation of perfected springs and shock absorbers to the Speedway.[5]

1

The Early Years

James Ashbury Allison was the second son born to Noah and Myra Allison in Marcellus, Michigan, in 1872. He was named for his paternal grandfather, James Allison, and his maternal grandfather, Ashbury Black.[1] Prior to relocating his family to Indianapolis in 1888, Noah Allison was a traveling salesman, first for his father's wholesale grocery business and later for National Surgical Institute.[2]

Indianapolis was a rapidly growing town when the Allison family relocated there in 1880. The population exploded from 45,000 residents in 1864 to 125,000 residents in 1888.[3] Fueling Indianapolis' growth in the 1880s and 1890s was the discovery of gas fields in Indiana which fed an increasingly industrial capital city.[4]

The location of Indianapolis is ideal for a manufacturing center. To move raw materials and merchandise, fifteen railroads radiated like the spokes of a wheel from Indianapolis in 1888. When the Allison family arrived in Indianapolis, industry was dominated by several slaughterhouses, including Kingan's, which would become the world's largest, and various farm implement manufacturers — including Nordyke & Marmon, which manufactured flour milling equipment — and carriage makers.

Upon establishing a home in Indianapolis, Noah Allison, along with Benjamin Nixon, formed a knitting company. Allison knew that many consumers used credit but didn't pay their debts. Responding to a need, Allison and George Abell started the American Creditors Association, a collection company, in 1885. Three short years later, Allison began publishing the *Indiana Trade Review*.[5]

At American Creditors Association, Allison helped creditors collect receivables. In 1888 he founded Allison Coupon Company. The company printed coupons merchants could accept for services rather than extending credit. The coupons came in books that could be purchased for cash on payday or, in some instances, given in lieu of payment of wages by the employer.[6]

9

By selling the coupons at a slight discount, the bearer could get more supplies than if he had paid cash. Coupons could be used for the purchase of merchandise from commissaries, for board at hotels and for ice purchases. They also simplified bookkeeping and merchandise charges. In foreign lands, such as the Panama Canal, the Allison coupons became a form of circulating currency. In order to prevent fraud, the coupons were printed on special watermarked paper.[7] Although Noah Allison died two brief years after the founding of Allison Coupon, his widow, Myra, and her children, including Jim, grew this company into the largest of its type in the world, with operations throughout the United States and in foreign countries, including Canada, Cuba and Central America.[8]

As a teenager, Allison dropped out of school, which was not an unusual thing to do in the 1880s. Most able-bodied boys were expected to contribute to the family income rather than to graduate from high school. Most people in those days believed that a higher education was needed only by those entering a profession.[9]

As Allison came to maturity, the face of Indianapolis was changing. With a significant German population, Indianapolis had beer gardens, concert saloons and variety theaters. In 1888, a new state capitol was constructed and Union Station was completed. The station had an enormous clock tower and a 70 foot high vaulted ceiling with skylights. At either end of the building were rose windows. Also gracing the skyline was the Civil War Memorial on the Circle.[10]

Allison began his business career as a messenger in Indianapolis. With the death of their father when Allison was 18, the Allison brothers became involved in the family business. Jim's first venture into business other than with Allison Coupon Company showed his mechanical tendencies. Frustrated with the fountain pens then available, Allison decided to reinvent the fountain pen. After examining several different types of fountain pens, he took the best features of each. The Allison Fountain Pen was well received. Expressing praise for the Allison Fountain Pen, R.G. Fiel of the American Express Company said, "Of the many different fountain pens I have used in the last 15 years as money delivery clerk ... none have given the satisfaction yours has."[11]

There were many activities for a young man in Indianapolis in the early 1890s. In the summer, Allison could swim, boat or canoe in the canal, Fall Creek or White River or bicycle along the Central canal towpath.[12] In cold weather, popular activities included ice-skating, sledding and tobogganing. There were also several private amusement parks, including Fairview Park, which was at the end of the Illinois Street line.[13] Sara Cornelius, who was to become Allison's wife, recalled picking violets with Allison in the fields on warm spring days.[14]

In the 1890s bicycling swept across the nation. Bicycling opened a new world as an alternative to walking or, if you could afford it, traveling by carriage. By 1893, there were one million bicycles in America.[15] By 1895, Indianapolis was fully engaged in the bicycling craze sweeping America. Bicycle shops and bicycle riding schools lined the west side of Pennsylvania Street between Market and Ohio streets. The largest was the Waverly Bicycle Company, which employed approximately fifteen hundred men as machinists, saddlers and rubber makers. By 1900, bicycle manufacturing was a $1 million business in Indianapolis.[16]

Although Allison was not employed in the bicycle industry, he was bitten by the craze and became an active participant in the Zig Zag Cycle Club. Zig Zag Cycle Club members were known for their bright bicycling uniforms and frequent rides on the weekends, including a Century Ride, a round-trip journey to Bloomington of approximately 100 miles, or the distance to Cincinnati. Although unknown at that time, Allison's interest in cycling and friendships made through the Zig Zag Cycle Club would become pivotal in his life.

Among Allison's friends in the Zig Zag Cycle Club was Arthur Newby. Newby, who was born in Monrovia, Indiana, spent most of his childhood in Kansas. Returning to Indiana when he was fifteen years old, he gained employment as a bookkeeper with Nordyke & Marmon, a producer of milling equipment, and later rose to office manager there. His association with bicycles began when he worked for Hay & Willits Manufacturing Company, which made Outing Bicycles. Along with Charles Test and Edward Fletcher, Newby started a bicycle chain manufacturing company. In 1890, as a result of his passion for bicycle riding, he also started the Zig Zag Cycle Club.[17] In addition to organizing rides, the Zig Zag Club would host bicycle races, including the August 24, 1893, one mile race at the Indiana State Fairgrounds. The prize for winning this race was a gold and diamond encrusted cup worth $1,000.[18]

In 1898, Newby and Allison developed the Newby Oval, a quarter-mile wooden track on the north side of Indianapolis at Central Avenue and 30th Street, to host the League of American Wheelmen's national championship, which was held in Indianapolis the week of August 9.

Designed by Herbert Foltz, an Indianapolis architect,[19] the racetrack had a 2,000 seat grandstand on the south side of the track. Directly opposite the grandstand was a 2,500 seat amphitheater; bleachers circled the remainder of the track. The track attracted up to 20,000 people for some races. It was built from white pine boards dipped in preservative and then nailed down with the rough side up to provide traction. Arc lights were used to illuminate the track at night. It was dedicated over the July Fourth weekend.[20]

The Indianapolis Wheelmen's Club, which included participants of many Indianapolis-based cycle clubs, boasted 25,000 local bicycle riders out of a population of 187,000. The national championship was the biggest event of the year and the Newby Oval was lauded by cyclists as well as race officials. The Newby Oval was successful in all aspects except for one: attendance at the national championship was lower than expected.

Another friend in the Zig Zag Cycle Club was Carl Fisher. Fisher, born in Greensburg, Indiana, was the driving force behind a bicycle repair store in Indianapolis which he owned and operated with his two brothers. Obsessed with speed, Fisher was active in the bicycle racing circuit throughout the Midwest. A born promoter, Fisher soon began selling bicycles at his shop.

Around the turn of the century, the popularity of bicycle racing gave way to a fascination with automobiles. Allison and his friends, Fisher and Newby, became early adapters to the automobile. Fisher led the pack and was the first in Indianapolis to own an automobile. He also converted his bicycle shop into the first automobile dealership in the city. Newby and Allison weren't far behind. Newby quickly became the president of the National Motor Company, which was a leading automobile manufacturer in Indianapolis, while Allison's close association with the industry began in 1904 with the development of Prest-O-Lite.

2

The Birth of the Automobile Industry

The development of the automobile began in Europe with Joseph Cugnot's mechanical vehicle in 1765. By the early 1800s, heavy steam-driven coaches had been developed which provided seating for only four or five persons.[1] The development of the internal combustion engine as an efficient alternative to the steam-powered coaches was the link to the development of the auto we know today. Although the first documented "explosion engine" was in 1784 by R. Street, the first practical engine was developed by Etienne Lenoir in 1860.[2] Two years later Lenoir attached one of his engines modified to run on liquid fuel to a vehicle. He drove this vehicle from Paris to Joinville-le-Pont, a six-mile journey that took between two and three hours.[3] This rudimentary vehicle was a predecessor of today's automobile, as it was the first vehicle not powered by steam.

In 1862 Alphonse Beau deRochas, a French scientist, proposed a four stroke, compression ignition engine. This engine was successfully made by Gottlieb Daimler, an employee of Otto and Langen. Otto and Daimler patented the engine in 1876 and it was marketed as the "Otto Silent Gas Engine." By 1885, the Daimler engine design had been modified to have the valves placed one above the other.[4]

Another milestone in the development of the automobile occurred with the introduction of the Daimler engine into France by Edouard Sarazin. He approached a friend, Emile Levassor of the firm Panhard et Levassor, to build and market the engine. Sarazin died in December 1887 before the engine business was underway; the rights to the engine passed to his widow. Sarazin's widow subsequently married Levassor in May 1890.[5] By 1891, Panhard et Levassor were building cars on a "systeme" which became the prototype for the development of the twentieth century motorcar. The engine was placed vertically at the front of the car. Instead of a belt drive, a transmission was developed which could provide a choice of different speed ratios.[6]

The fledgling industry gained speed when Karl Benz exhibited one of his vehicles at the Paris Exposition in 1887. Powered by a three horsepower engine, this vehicle could achieve a maximum speed of 14 mph. Benz's vehicle was marketed to the public in France by Emile Roger either as a "Roger" or a "Roger-Benz."[7] Between 1885 and 1901, over 2,300 cars were manufactured by Roger and Roger-Benz.[8] There were other companies which also produced vehicles using the Benz design. At this point, automobiles were the domain and novelty item of the very rich.

Also contributing to the early development of the automobile was Comte Albert De Dion (later a marquis), who was a shrewd businessman. An amateur mechanic, he was interested in developing a horseless carriage. In 1881 he saw a tiny model steam engine with the cylinder made of glass so that the movement of the piston could be seen. The model was made by Trepardoux and his brother-in-law, Georges Bouton; the two who were barely making a living. With the promise of a 20 percent pay increase, to 10 francs a day, Comte De Dion enticed Bouton and Trepardoux to work for him. Between 1883 and 1894, De Dion's interests expanded to include the development a petrol motor. De Dion and Bouton have been credited with producing the first high speed internal combustion engine. Their first high speed engine was ¾ hp with an output of 4 hp per liter of petrol and had a normal speed of 1,500 rpm.[9] This compared favorably to the Daimler engine with a normal speed of 750 rpm. De Dion and Bouton attached this engine with an electric ignition apparatus to a bicycle. The first bicycles outfitted with this engine began leaving the factory in 1895.[10]

Peugeot's first vehicle with a light tubular frame and wire wheels was developed in 1891. The engine, which was cooled by water running through the tubular frame, was placed at the back of the vehicle. A Peugeot vehicle followed the long distance bicycle race from Paris to Brest — some 1,500 miles — at an average speed of 10 mph.[11]

Compared with Germany and France, England and America were slow to develop an automobile. In England, archaic laws that hindered the development of the automobile included a law that "locomotives" of less than three tons had to have an attendant walk in front of the vehicle in town, thus limiting the speed to three or four mph. Vehicles were also limited to a maximum speed of 14 mph on the open roads. Influential men such as Hon. C.S. Rolls, Hon. Evelyn Ellis and Sir David Salomons had encountered private carriages in France and could foresee the development of the new industry.[12]

Ellis purchased a Panhard et Levassor in 1892 to use when traveling around the continent. In 1895, he brought the vehicle to England. Hoping to highlight the absurdity of the law and as a challenge to be prosecuted, he frequently drove it around England. Also pushing for the overturn of the laws were Charles Rolls, who purchased a Peugeot and brought it to England, and Evelyn Ellis, who not only brought a vehicle to England but also established the Self Propelled Traffic Association with the hope of focusing public attention on the law. By 1894 and 1895, several men had established agencies (franchises) for motorcars, including Henry Hewetson for Benz and Gascoigne L'Hollier for Roger.[13] In November 1896, the law requiring an attendant was overturned.

In the United States, the development of the automobile was virtually nonexistent as the country did not have a network of roads. The initial settlement of the western wilderness was by covered wagon. Later, due to the expanses of land between cities, a wide network of railroads was used in the westward push. By the early 1890s, there were several Americans tinkering with a petrol engine vehicle, including Duryea, Olds, Ford, Maxim and Winton. There were also a few electric vehicles being used in town.[14]

Races were significant in the development of automobiles, both in Europe and in the United States. In July 1894 a distance trial of 79 miles between Paris and Rouen was organized by Pierre Giffard, editor of *Le Petit Journal*. This trial was the precursor to the first automobile "race."[15] Shortly after the trial, the Comte De Dion suggested to Giffard that a race would be a real endurance test of the vehicles. De Dion proposed a round-trip race between Paris and Bordeaux, a distance of 732 miles. Fearful of the reaction if there were any serious accidents, Monsieur Marinoni, the proprietor of *Le Petit Journal*, did not support the race. De Dion formed a committee with his friends and they raised 3,000 pounds to cover the race expenses, including prizes. The response to the proposed race was overwhelming, with 102 entrants.[16]

One of the requirements of the race was that the prize would be awarded to the first *four* seat vehicle to complete the course. Despite a large group of entrants, there were only 18 vehicles and three motor-bicycles which started the race on June 11, 1895.[17] Emile Levassor's car was first to complete the circuit, in 48 hours and 47½ minutes at an average speed of 15 mph. Despite this feat, the Panhard et Levassor vehicle had only two seats and did not win the prize. The official winner of the race was a Peugeot, which completed the course in 59 hours and 49 minutes.[18]

After the race, the De Dion committee developed into the Automobile Club of France, which by 1896 had almost 2,000 members. The effect of the race was long reaching. It transformed the hobby of a few wealthy eccentrics into something the masses desired. Racing also was an essential part of the rapid improvement in the automobile.[19]

The French led the way in the development of the early vehicles. Panhard et Levassor, Peugeot and De Dion were regularly leading the pack in various races. Although Daimler had been inventing motorcarriages, German vehicles were not competitive. Aware that their vehicles were not competitive, Damlier in 1899 introduced a 24 mph racing car (the "24"). Unfortunately, the weight in front was below the center of gravity while most of the weight behind was above the center of gravity, making controlling the car at higher speeds or on wet roadways difficult. It was geared to run at 46 mph and the maximum speed was 52 mph.[20] The first appearance of this vehicle was in the Nice meet in 1900. Despite the improvements, it still was not competitive.

In the subsequent Paris–Marseilles race, this vehicle developed a reputation as a killer when one vehicle ran into a ditch and a second broke two wheels trying to climb the Turbie hill. The "24" was owned by various nobility, including Emil Jellinek, the Austro-Hungarian consul in Nice.[21] Driving one of the Daimler cars in the Paris-Nice race, Jellinek took as a pseudonym the name of his daughter, Mercedes. After the race, Jellinek appointed himself as the unofficial agent for the Daimlers in the south of France and urged the Daimlers to produce something lighter and more controllable than the "24."[22]

The new resulting vehicle had a pressed-steel chassis, a forward mounted honeycomb radiator, and a gate gear change. Its mechanically operated inlet valves could be operated either by hand or by pedal control, effectively acting as a throttle. This made it possible to reduce the speed of the engine over a much wider range. By the driver pressing the accelerator, the motorcar immediately picked up speed. Letting up on the accelerator caused the vehicle's speed to immediately decrease.[23]

To overcome the French dislike of German products and to differentiate it from the "24," this model was called the Mercedes (25). The Mercedes was acclaimed as the most advanced design of the times and bridged the nineteenth century horseless carriage to the twentieth century motorcar.[24]

3

Development of the Automobile in the United States

Imagine life before the development of the automobile. The primary modes of transportation were foot, horse-drawn carriage or train. Those who could not afford a carriage and the horses to power it were limited by how far they could walk. The costs associated with the maintenance of a carriage further limited its use to the middle and upper classes. The development of trains probably limited the development of a highway system, which was integral in the development of European and British automobiles.

Although many attribute America's automotive roots to 1893 when Charles Duryea and his brother, Frank, test drove a rudimentary vehicle outside Springfield, Massachusetts, the groundwork for this feat had been underway for some time. As in Europe, the development of the automobile in the U.S. was dependent upon the development of an engine.

In 1772, Oliver Evans of the Delaware Colony heard about a blacksmith's son who, using water and wadding stuffed in a long-barrel shotgun, had produced a shot as if it had been from gunpowder. This news spurred Evans to action: "It immediately occurred to me that there was a power capable of propelling any wagon, provided that I could apply it, and I set myself to work to find out the means of doing so."[1]

Evans went to work developing a power source. By 1787, he was granted a patent by the House of Delegates for the State of Maryland based upon drawings and a model steam engine. His work continued and by 1792 he had a variety of engines, including a reciprocating engine as well as a rotary engine.[2] Evans continued to innovate, developing a steam engine adapted for use in grain mills. His thoughts continued to be focused on improving transportation. On September 26, 1804, he made a proposal to the Lancaster Turnpike Road Company to form an experimental company to build steam engines.

Evans was commissioned by Philadelphia to build a river dredge. It was built with wheels so that it could run on land at 3 to 4 mph. The dredge led to the development of a rudimentary steam-powered wagon. Evans drove the wagon, which was capable of carrying 100 barrels of flour over the sixty-two mile Lancaster Turnpike, covering the distance in two days. It would have taken five horse drawn wagons three days to transport 100 barrels of flour the same distance.[3]

Evans wasn't the only one developing an engine-powered vehicle. Colonel John Stevens built a steam engine–powered carriage in 1802, and Samuel Morey built and obtained a patent for an internal combustion engine.[4] Stuart Perry also built an internal combustion engine similar to that developed by Morey; however, it utilized turpentine as the fuel source.

Between 1860 and 1880, the development of the steam powered carriage reached its zenith. Sylvester Roper of Roxbury, Massachusetts, developed a two-person, 650-pound steam carriage. Over the next two decades, Roper built ten of these carriages. He also built steam powered bicycles, a predecessor of the motorcycle. One of his steam powered bicycles was timed at two minutes on a one mile run.[5]

George Brayton developed an internal combustion engine that was patented in 1872. This engine was used in a streetcar as early as 1873 and by 1879 it was used in an omnibus.[6]

Wisconsin actively encouraged the development of vehicles powered by means other than horses or other farm animals. In 1876, the state legislature offered a reward of $10,000 to any Wisconsin resident who developed "a machine propelled by steam or other motive agent" as a "practical substitute for the use of horses and other animals on highway and farm." On July 18, 1878, a test was held for two machines developed as a result of the reward that pitted the "Green Bay Machine" against the "Oshkosh" on a 201 mile run. The "Oshkosh" won the challenge, covering the distance in 33 hours, 27 minutes, with an average speed of 6 mph.[7]

Charles Duryea, a 27-year-old Peoria, Illinois, bicycle manufacturer, read an 1889 article in *Scientific American* about an internal combustion engine–powered vehicle developed by Karl Benz. Joined by his brother, Frank, a machinist, they set to work to build a vehicle. By the summer of 1893, they were ready for a test drive of the vehicle outside Springfield, Massachusetts. The trip was a mere 200 feet, but the American automotive industry had been born.

There were others who were fascinated by the idea of a motorized vehicle, including Elwood Haynes of Kokomo, Indiana. "One afternoon, or night, rather, while driving home after a hard day's work, I thought to myself that it would be a fine thing if I didn't have to depend on the horse for loco-motion," he recalled years later. "From then on my mind dwelt upon the subject of a self propelled vehicle, that could be used on any country road or city street." Haynes was successful in developing such a vehicle, the "Pio-neer," which was driven along Pumpkinville Pike on July 4, 1894. Haynes also vied for the title of having first created the vehicle type, maintaining that the Duryeas had merely attached an engine to a buggy. Two years later, in 1896, Haynes-Apperson automobiles began production. By 1900, Haynes-Apperson was one of the few car manufacturers in the United States to pro-duce more than 100 cars a year.

Another person who was obsessed with building a horseless carriage was Henry Ford. Growing up on a farm outside of Dearborn, Michigan, he showed a mechanical bent, repairing watches at an early age. At age thirteen in 1876 on a trip with his father, William, to Detroit, Ford saw a steam engine mounted on wheels which was used for powering threshing machines and sawmills. Ford recounted years later that it was this sighting which ulti-mately led him to the automobile industry.[8]

By 1879, Ford had left the family farm. He began working a series of jobs in Detroit, increasing his knowledge of mechanical works, first for the Michigan Car Company, which built streetcars, then for Flower Brothers, which made brass and iron castings, and then for the Detroit Dry Dock Company, which manufactured a variety of iron ships.[9] Ford returned to the Dearborn area in 1883 and for the next two years he was a repairman for Westinghouse machines, which gave him exposure not only to their engines but also to those made by Mills and Daimler. In 1885, on eighty wooded acres received from his father, Ford spent his winters operating a sawmill and his summers working on portable farm engines for the Buckeye Harvester Company. His talk had turned to building a "horseless carriage" and by 1885 he had sketched a design.[10] Feeling the need to understand electricity, he returned to Detroit in 1891 and began working for the Edison Illuminating Company as an engineer and machinist. Ford built a "horseless carriage" in a shed behind his Detroit home. The first test run of his "Quadricycle" was on June 4, 1896.[11] The Quadricycle wasn't suitable for production, resulting in Ford's building a second automobile. He obtained financial backing and started the Detroit Automobile Company, which failed within a couple of years. His third attempt to produce automobiles, the Henry Ford Company, failed within three months, as his interests had turned to the new sport of automobile racing.[12]

Just as rudimentary auto racing was essential in auto refinements in Europe and England, it was also the case in the United States. In 1895, the publisher of the *Chicago Times-Herald*, Herman Kohlsaat, read an article about the French race from Paris to Rouen sponsored by the French publication *Le Petit Journal*. He decided that the *Times-Herald* could benefit from the sponsorship of a similar race in the United States. Kohlsaat sponsored "The Race of the Century" on Thanksgiving Day 1895. The vehicles were to travel a 54 mile route from Jackson Park in Chicago to Evanston and return. The rules were simple: a vehicle had to have at least three wheels and two passengers (a driver and an umpire).

On the bitterly cold race day only six vehicles showed up from the eleven entrants in the race. There were three gasoline-powered Benzes, a two cylinder gasoline-powered Duryea Motor Wagon and two battery-powered electric vehicles. The race course had a foot of mushy snow from the previous day. A Benz powered Roger driven by R.H. Macy, the department store magnate, had a series of accidents, including a collision with a horse cart, a collision with a sleigh and a collision with a taxi. On the fourth collision, which was with a carriage, Macy called it quits.

Another competitor, H. Mueller, in another Benz was gaining ground on the leading Duryea when Mueller blacked out from the bitter cold and the car ended up in a snow drift. Of the six contestants, only two finished the race. Frank Duryea won with an official driving time of seven hours and 53 minutes and an average speed of 5 mph. The actual time of 10 hours and 23 minutes included time for repairs and other stops. For winning the contest, Frank Duryea collected $2,000. The other finisher was the relief driver for the Benz driven by H. Mueller.[13]

This race ignited automobile racing in the United States. Historian Rudolph Anderson said, "All of the different types of motorized exhibitions were to grow out of this event — road races, speedway bowls, high-speed demonstrations, endurance tests, reliability runs, hill climbs, transcontinental tours, automobile shows and the mammoth displays at the World Fairs."[14] Another aspect of this race, which helped to establish both racing and the automobile, was the decision by P.T. Barnum to have Duryea's car join the Barnum & Bailey Circus, where it shared top billing with the trapeze acts and elephants.[15]

The first closed track race was held in 1896 at the Rhode Island State Fair and drew 50,000 spectators.[16] Automobile fever was starting to spread across America. Thomas Edison, in November 1896, predicted the future of the automobile when he said, "Ten years from now you will be able to buy a horseless vehicle for what you have to pay today for a wagon and a pair of horses."[17]

In February 1896 the Duryea Company went into production and built

13 identical cars, establishing the first "brand" in the United States. From this small beginning, the growth of the automobile industry in America was spectacular. Just four years later, in 1900, there were more than 100 different manufacturers. All of the vehicles were produced by hand. Given the very expensive nature of the manufacturing process, only the very rich could afford a vehicle.

Ransom Olds was another early adapter and manufacturer of an automobile. His first efforts were with a steam-powered vehicle. He realized that a gasoline-powered internal combustion engine was the power plant that should be put into the vehicle. He also realized that the auto needed to be both functional and reliable. By 1899, he had started the Olds Motor Works, which produced a car with the nickname of the "Runabout." Within a year, there were eleven different models being produced, all with different styles and price points. The runabout could go 20 mph on a one cylinder engine.

Between 1896 and 1899, automobile registrations had increased from 16 to 3,200. Additionally, in 1899, the United States War Department purchased three automobiles for the use of officers. The inventory listing included a notation that the vehicles were "equipped so that a mule may be hitched to it should it refuse to in case they didn't run."[18]

Olds displayed his vehicles at the automobile show held at Madison Square Garden in New York City in November 1900. Fisher, who had gained notoriety when he drove a De Dion motor tricycle through the streets of downtown Indianapolis in 1898, was also in attendance. Fisher met Olds at the auto show and when Fisher returned to Indianapolis, he was an "agent" for Olds.[19]

After fire destroyed the business and all but one prototype in 1901, Ransom Olds realized that for his business to thrive it needed standardized parts that would enable the mass production of vehicles. He subcontracted out the production of the parts to individuals who would later become household names: John and Horace Dodge for transmissions, Henry Leland, the founder of Cadillac and Lincoln, for engines, and Fred J. Fisher, whose family became the body maker for General Motors.

Ransom Olds was also a marketer. He promoted his Runabouts to the owners of horses and carriages by talking about the advantages of the gasoline-powered vehicle over the horse. The auto was more convenient. At $650, it was less expensive than a carriage with a horse since it didn't have to be fed and stabled. And unlike a horse, it could go all day without tiring out. He sent his assistant, Roy Chapin, on a promotional tour of 800 miles, from Detroit to New York, in the fall of 1901. Chapin didn't have the luxury of gasoline stations or someone to repair the vehicle if it broke down. Also, the roads were basically dirt paths. Upon Chapin's arrival at the Waldorf Astoria in New York City, he was feted by the local press. The publicity had the desired impact. In 1902, 425 Runabouts were sold. In 1903, 2,500 Runabouts were sold; and by 1904, sales had increased to approximately 5,000 vehicles.

In 1902, Ford Motor Company was begun by Henry Ford. It did not take long for Ford to become the industry leader. By 1908, the country's first mass produced car, the Model T, was unveiled. Over the next 19 years, there were 15,500,000 Model T's sold, which outstripped the production of all other manufacturers combined.

In the early 1900s, Ford Motor and Oldsmobile dominated automobile manufacturing because they were mass produced and more affordable.

4

The Early Races

The development of the automobile and auto races went hand in hand both in Europe and on American soil. An immigrant from Scotland in 1878, Alexander Winton, was active in the early races both in France and in the United States. Upon arriving on American soil, Winton started a bicycle company in Cleveland, Ohio. In 1897, he had built an automobile and established the Winton Motorcarriage Company. His automobile was the first American built vehicle to be sold in the United States. Winton drove his automobile from Cleveland to New York.[1] By 1899, the Winton Motorcarriage Company was the largest manufacturer of gasoline-powered vehicles in America.

Automobiles were very much a novelty for the rich at the turn of the century, and outside of the cities they were virtually unknown. America was still the land of the horse and carriage. Winton believed that through competition an automobile could prove its durability and speed, thus attracting potential customers. In 1899, Winton challenged Fernand Charron, the leading Panhard racing driver. From this challenge arose a series of contests, the first of which was from Paris to Lyons. The Winton car looked very old-fashioned and did not complete the race. The Panhard et Levassor easily won the challenge. The next American entry into continental racing did not occur until 1903, when Winton participated in the Gordon Bennett race held in Ireland. Just as in the previous race, the American's car wasn't competitive and soon dropped out of the race.[2]

Although the investors in the Henry Ford Company thought Ford was constructing a passenger automobile, he was busy building a racing machine. Ford believed racing would promote his passenger automobile. The racing car, which was completed by the fall of 1901, weighed 2200 pounds and could generate up to 26 horsepower. Ford, while testing his racing car, harbored the desire to break the world's speed record for one mile then held by Winton.[3]

In October 1901, promoters held a series of short races in Grosse Point, Michigan. The short races would become the standard format for racing days during the early 1900s. With Winton participating in the races, Ford would have his opportunity for direct competition. The interest in the racing was strong, as evidenced by eight thousand spectators showing up for the event. The day, by and large, was a disappointment for the crowd, as the speeds failed to meet their expectations. By the last event, which was a ten mile contest, only two of the five registrants ran. Ford in his 26 horsepower racing machine would compete directly with Winton.[4]

Winton's car led during the early laps of the race. Although Ford apparently had greater speed on the straightaways, Winton's superiority in the curves provided an advantage. When Winton developed engine trouble on the seventh lap, Ford roared to the lead and won the contest by three quarters of a mile.[5]

One of the people in the crowd at the 1901 Grosse Point races was Tom Cooper, a successful bicycle racer during the racing craze of the 1890s. Cooper was very interested in getting involved with the development of racing cars and in 1902 provided capital to Ford to build two racing machines. The racing machines had four cylinders with a reported seventy-five horsepower. Ford's vehicle was painted red and was named the "999" after the New York Central train that had made a record run from New York to Chicago. Cooper's vehicle was painted yellow and was called the "Arrow."[6]

Cooper and Ford test drove their new racers around racing tracks in Detroit. With 1,080 cubic inches of displacement, the cars were so powerful that both Ford and Cooper were afraid of them. A previous business partner of Cooper, Barney Oldfield, was invited to look at the cars. Oldfield, who had been a bicycle racer, had already established a reputation for being fearless. The "999" and the "Arrow" represented to Oldfield the opportunity to transition to automobile racing, which he correctly believed was the future of racing.[7]

In October of the same year, Carl Fisher arranged an exhibition in Dayton, Ohio, and asked if Cooper and Oldfield could bring the vehicles to the contest. Cooper, Oldfield and Spider Huff went to Dayton and despite their best efforts were unable to get one of the two vehicles to run. The other car eventually started running, then it promptly stopped. Oldfield diagnosed the trouble as a problem with getting fuel to the engine. After making a modification to the vehicle, they got it to run well enough to give the crowd at Dayton reasons to cheer as it picked up speed and slid through the corners. As they were sliding through a turn, Cooper yelled to Spider Huff, who was driving the vehicle, that he should slow down or else they were going to crash through the fence on the turns. Huff responded that "she sure goes like '999.'"

At a horse racing track a week later on a cold, rainy October 25, 1902, Winton and four other automobile enthusiasts met for a five mile competition at Grosse Point, Michigan, called the Manufacturer's Challenge Cup. The diversity in the vehicles underscored the newness of the automobile. Winton would drive his automobile, called the "Bullet," which had a forty horsepower engine. Also participating was the largest car in Detroit, a Geneva Steamer, driven by Buckman. The Geneva Steamer was powered by four large boilers. Also entered were a Winton "Pup," a white Steamer and the automobile simply known as the "999," which had been entered by Tom Cooper.

As the cars lined up for the start, an unknown driver was at the wheel of the "999." As the drivers started accelerating for the running start of the race, the "999" was behind the others, as it was being driven by Barney Oldfield, then a novice driver. Accelerating to catch up to the other drivers, he shot ahead of the field as they started the race.[8] By the conclusion of the first lap, the "999" was ahead of the field. With an aggressive driving style, Oldfield ran away from the other cars and completed the five mile race in a record 5 minutes, 28 seconds, a new world's record. The Geneva Steamer was second, a full lap down, and the Winton "Pup" placed a distant third. The Alex Winton Bullet, which had experienced mechanical difficulty, didn't finish the race.[9]

After the "999" won the Manufacturer's Cup Challenge, Henry Ford was quick to make sure that he got credit for the design of the car. The race resulted in Ford's obtaining financing for his motorcar company, which was started in November 1902.[10]

On June 20, 1903, Carl Fisher was a copromoter of a meet at the Indiana State Fairgrounds. Fisher challenged Oldfield with a prize of $250 if he could drive the one mile oval dirt track in less than a minute. Driving the "999," which had the largest engine displacement of that era at 1,080 cubic inches, Oldfield roared around the track with an estimated speed of 80 mph.[11] Watching Oldfield set the new mile record, Allison was bitten by the automotive bug.[12]

Henry Ford believed that he needed some additional publicity for his new car, the "Model B." This new car would later be known as the 1903 Model A.[13] He set his sights on establishing a new world's record. Ford acquired the "Arrow," which had been wrecked in 1903, and rebuilt it with a Model B engine.[14] In January 1904, this car would set a world record when Ford drove the race car at 91.370 miles per hour on frozen Lake St. Clair outside of Detroit.[15]

At the end of 1902, Oldfield left his friend and business partner, Tom Cooper, and signed on to drive for the Winton racing team. Several other manufacturers, including Oldsmobile, Knox and Packard, had started racing teams in order to prove the reliability of their vehicles.

One of the first series of auto races in the United States was the Vanderbilt Cup. William Kissam ("Willie K") Vanderbilt II, the heir to the Cornelius Vanderbilt fortune, hoped that by establishing the Cup, American automobile manufacturers would improve the quality of their vehicles and make them competitive with European autos.

Vanderbilt was the grandson of Commodore Cornelius Vanderbilt, who had amassed a fortune of greater than one hundred million dollars through various railroad and shipping interests. Upon his death Commodore Vanderbilt was believed to have been the richest person on earth. A substantial trust fund and the presidency of the New York Central Railroad gave W.K. Vanderbilt II the funds to actively pursue his two passions — fast automobiles and yacht racing. In pursuit of the automobile, Vanderbilt had more than one hundred autos in his garage and employed twenty mechanics. In 1904, he had set a land speed record of 92.3 mph driving a Mercedes at the Daytona Beach Road Course at Ormond Beach, Florida.

The Vanderbilt Cup was held on a twenty-eight mile stretch of a windy road on Long Island.[16] Up to two hundred fifty thousand spectators lined the race course, often within touching distance of the speeding automobiles. Held in 1904, the first Vanderbilt Cup was won by George Heath in a French Panhard. The second, run in 1905, was won by Victor Hemery in a Darracq.[17] The Vanderbilt Cup was particularly dangerous in the 1906 race; four people were killed. Underscoring the weakness in American built automobiles, an American built entry would not win the Vanderbilt Cup until 1908.

In the early 1900s, Indianapolis had two significant automobile manufacturers, Nordyke & Marmon and National Motorcar. Begun in Richmond, Indiana, Nordyke & Marmon manufactured flour milling equipment which was shipped throughout the world. Its entry into automobile industry was a result of the passion of the owner. With strong engineering in its blood, Nordyke & Marmon developed a demonstration vehicle in 1901/1902 and a prototype Model A in 1903/1904. The first Marmons were the most unique car on North American roads. They were "System Engineered," with the driver, the car, the road and the tires all interfacing in the design. They had a unique crankcase/crankshaft interface and the company pioneered the pressure lubrication system via a drilled crankshaft and connecting rods.

To show off their engineering prowess, Nordyke & Marmon made sure Marmon vehicles were frequent participants in the early endurance races.

They achieved perfect scores in the Glidden Tours of 1906 and 1907. In 1908, Marmon vehicles were entered into several endurance contests, including the 1908 Glidden Tour, the two-day Indianapolis–French Lick Springs sealed hood endurance run, the Chicago 1000 mile four-day sealed endurance contest and the Boston–Mount Washington twenty-four hour nonstop sealed contest. Through these endurance meets, Nordyke & Marmon established itself as a progressive, well engineered automobile builder.

In a promotional brochure in 1922, Marmon proclaimed, "Long before the motorcar came into being, the Nordyke and Marmon Company was an institution devoted to the manufacture of flour mill machinery and had established a worldwide reputation for manufacturing integrity and business vision. Marmon flour mill machinery had long been going into every corner of the world, carrying the message of a work well done. Today Nordyke & Marmon company stands as a vision realized. Its mills are to be found in every country where wheat is raised and flour made. Its motorcars represent the highest degree of mechanical excellence yet conceived."

Yet another company had entered the field of auto manufacturing. By 1905, Arthur Newby was the president of National Motor Vehicle. Founded in 1900, the company manufactured electric automobiles. By 1903, at Newby's urging, the company had begun manufacturing gasoline-powered vehicles.[18]

The Indianapolis Automobile Racing Association was founded in 1905 and had participation from several Indiana manufacturers. Most racing was done on dirt tracks at county fairs. In the early 1900s, the county fair was an opportunity for farming families to get together for a weekend of fun as well as an opportunity to show off the farmers' prized animals. Frequently, auto races were the big event which followed the horse races. To prepare the soft dirt track for the heavy vehicles and to cut down on the dust, the racetrack would be dampened by a horse drawn water wagon.[19] The Indiana Automobile Racing Association sponsored races at the state fairgrounds on the north side of Indianapolis.

The association had scheduled races to be held over the Labor Day weekend in 1905. Due to postponements, the races weren't held until November 4, 1905. The schedule for the day featured a 100 mile race as well as six shorter runs. For the 100 mile race, Allison, Fisher, Newby and Wheeler were in the grandstands at the Indiana State Fairgrounds. The race started with nine participants. By lap fifty, the two National vehicles driven by Charlie Merz and W.F. ("Jap") Clemens were battling each other for the lead. The other racers were running far behind the two National entries. Clemens, driving a car owned by Newby, won the race in one hour, 53 minutes and

21.8 seconds. This drive shattered the international record for dirt tracks by almost five minutes.[20]

The shorter races on that day included both Fisher and Allison as participants. Fisher attempted to break the one mile record driving a 100 horsepower Premier. He also won in a five mile contest. Allison participated in two contests driving a Pope-Toledo. The first was a three mile race which he didn't finish. The second contest was a five mile owner's race. This race was won by Charlie Merz in a National. Allison finished second with a time of 6:31 minutes.[21]

Enthused by the race on that day, the four friends began discussing a race which would test the endurance of the vehicles. They decided to hold a twenty-four-hour race and Allison took on the responsibility for organizing the race. One of the challenges to a twenty-four-hour race was that the Indiana State Fairgrounds did not have lighting around the race course. This provided an opportunity for Allison and Fisher to showcase Prest-O-Lite's lighting ability. Allison arranged for the racetrack to be fitted with five hundred Prest-O-Lite lighting devices spaced every twenty-five feet on both the inside and the outside of the track. This provided lighting for the race to continue through the evening hours.[22]

The twenty-four hour race at the Indiana State Fairgrounds was held on a cold November day. A 1917 brochure for National Motorcar hearkened back to this night at the Indiana State Fairgrounds. "It was around the campfire, watching the all-night run, that the National founder and his friends conceived the possibility of a great motor speedway, and as a result, those same four men built and own the world famous track at Indianapolis."[23]

Only two participants, Jap Clemens and Charlie Merz driving National Motorcars, circled the track trying to break the twenty-four-hour record set by Guy Vaughn at Yonkers, New York.[24] After 152 miles, the steering knuckle on Clemens' car broke. The car careened down the racetrack, taking out a number of fence posts before breaking through the inside fence and destroying the car.[25] Clemens, who was not injured, shared the driving responsibilities with Merz for the remainder of the 24 hours. It was so cold that night the mechanics had to help the drivers from the car. By the end of the twenty-four-hour mark, a new record was set at 1,094.56 miles having been driven — some 79 miles more than the then existing record.

Closely related to the auto races at county fairs were barn-storming tours by various race drivers, including Barney Oldfield. These were staged events in which Oldfield would ultimately prevail although the races were generally close enough to maintain interest.[26] Barnstorming Barney Oldfield thrilled the crowd with the racing events. Writing in *Collier's* magazine,

American Automobile Association official Fred Wagner said, "Oldfield pioneered the 'circus style' of racing. At close finishes he was an artist, often managing to win by less than the width of a tire."[27]

The American Automobile Association (AAA), founded in 1902, joined forces with the Manufacturers Contest Association in 1909 to combat the negative image being given to auto races by the multiple deaths at the Vanderbilt Cup. The mechanism chosen was the AAA Contest Board, which became responsible for the policing of racing events. The racing teams, drivers and mechanics had rules to obey and the Contest Board provided timers, referees, starters and scorers who enforced the rules. The Indianapolis Motor Speedway agreed to the regulations of the AAA Contest Board.[28]

In 1909, the AAA Contest Board established a racing series. The initial tour consisted of twenty-six events, which would be supervised by board officials. Fred Wagner, AAA Contest Board starter, was the most well known official. He was charged with not only starting the race but also enforcing the Contest Board rules and eliminating gambling that followed the tour. A driver or a racing team that broke AAA Contest Board rules risked suspension from the national tour.[29]

5

Prest-O-Lite: The Early Years

Carl Fisher began his business career selling magazines and candies on commuter trains. By the time he was 18 years old, he and his brother had started a bicycle repair shop in Indianapolis. Recognizing that there was more money in selling bicycles than in repairing them, Carl very quickly began offering bicycles for sale. From his earliest working days, he had a gift for promotion. Although his eye sight was severely limited, he loved to race bicycles in the Midwest.

At the inception of the development of the automobile in the United States, Fisher was quickly hooked after attending an automobile show held in 1900 in Madison Square Garden. He was the first in Indiana to own a vehicle, a French De Dion Bouton. By 1903, Fisher had started his Oldsmobile dealership in Indianapolis and was already showing an interest in the fledgling sport of auto racing.

One day in 1904, an elderly man approached Fisher at his shop with a small metal cylinder about a foot long with a three foot length of copper tubing and a forked tip attached to a valve at one end. Percy ("Fred") Avery explained that he had obtained the rights to a French patent for converting compressed carbide gas into a bright light. Although this system was already used for buoys and lighthouses, he thought it could also be used for headlights. Between the acquisition of the patent and the development of the device Avery had used all of his capital. With no money to bring the device to market, he had been visiting various automobile manufacturers in Michigan, Ohio and Indiana trying to interest them in the invention. Avery was turned down because the automobile manufacturers weren't willing to invest in the technology as they realized the danger.

Avery demonstrated the apparatus to Fisher by striking a match on his shoe and putting the flame up to the end of the coupling. Poof! There was a flame emanating from the coupling brighter than anything then available. At that time, automobiles primarily used oil-powered coach lamps to light the way. They frequently went out due either to the bouncing of the vehicle or to the wind. If this new device could provide a steadier and brighter stream of light, it would revolutionize the early headlights. The issue was the instability of the acetylene gas.

Fisher asked Avery to let him keep the invention so that he could further investigate it. Not terribly excited about the idea but with no other prospects for its sale, Avery acquiesced. Fisher put the tank on a shelf at his dealership and went off to meet Allison for lunch. Over lunch, Fisher told Allison of the invention and offered him a third ownership in this new venture for $10,000. Knowing that Fisher's capital was tied up in the new dealership, Allison was suspicious of the proposal. Allison inquired as to how Fisher was going to come up with his share of the monies, to which Fisher replied that he had "discovered" it and that Avery would also be a third partner. Had Allison accepted Fisher's proposition, he would have effectively bankrolled the venture. But like Fisher, Allison didn't have $10,000 to gamble on this new invention.

But the allure of the lighting system had hooked Allison, and, like Fisher, he thought that the invention had great promise. Understanding that the greatest obstacle to the device was the explosive nature of the gas, Allison proposed that he would try to determine whether or not the canister was safe.

Taking the canister from the shelf at Fisher's dealership, Allison took it to the West Washington Street bridge spanning White River. Looking from the bridge, Allison hypothesized that if the canister did not explode upon the impact of hitting the rocks below it was probably safe for automobiles. Not knowing what the result of this impromptu test would be, he threw the device onto the rocks. The canister did not explode. Allison collected the canister from the rocky shore and returned to Fisher's dealership, where they agreed to start the new company.[1]

The business, called the Concentrated Acetylene Company, was started on September 6, 1904, "for the purpose of manufacturing, assembling, handling and selling lamps, reflectors, receptacles and gas for automobiles, carriages, mines, buoys, and all other machines and things in which artificial gas is necessary or required to be used."[2]

In a dilapidated shed on the north side of Indianapolis, Avery and an assistant, Jack Noble, began experimenting with the canisters. Noble had the unenviable task of filling the cylinders from a hand pump. Although the canister had survived being thrown from the bridge, the men quickly learned the danger of acetylene gas. The frequency of explosions resulted in complaints from nearby residents.

In filling the canisters, they had to balance the need to have a cylinder small enough to fit on the running board of an average sized vehicle but also large enough that it wouldn't have to be refilled too often. The containers also had to be leak-proof and reasonably safe to operate. An additional concern was determining the type of tubing and valves needed to feed a steady supply of gas to the headlights. Slowly the invention was perfected.

With Fisher's marketing ability, the men enticed Packard to use their system of lighting on its 1904 vehicle. With the lighting source being far superior to other sources, the business expanded quickly.

6

The Marriage

Upon moving to Indianapolis, the Allison family became active members of Roberts Park Methodist Church. This downtown church traced its roots back to the early days of Indianapolis, with the latest church being built in 1876. By the early 1900s, it was one of the largest and most influential churches in Indianapolis, with a congregation of 1,350.[1]

Another family in the church was the Cornelius family. George Cornelius was a highly regarded Indianapolis businessman with interests as a merchant, a chair manufacturer and an insurance executive. He and his wife, Melissa, had three daughters, Sara, Jessie, and Mary. Melissa Cornelius was a Sunday school teacher. It was at Roberts Park Methodist Church that Jim Allison met Sara Cornelius, who was two years younger. Sara and Jim were good friends during childhood and this friendship continued as they became teenagers.

Around 1890, when Allison's career was beginning, Sara Cornelius left Indianapolis to attend Northwestern University in Evanston, Illinois. While there she met Andrew Parker, the son of a Chicago banker and in 1895 Sara became Parker's wife. Allison apparently had hoped to make his friend, Sara Cornelius, his wife. "Everybody expects me to go to the dogs now. Well — I'm not going to. I'm going to make a success of my life. And — I'll have her yet."[2] These words were told to Sara Cornelius, upon the occasion of her wedding to Parker, by Myra Allison, Jim Allison's mother.

The Parkers initially settled in Chicago where he was employed as a banker. After a couple of years of marriage, Parker became very ill with typhoid fever. Unable to work, he resigned his job. During his convalescence, the Parkers moved back to Indianapolis and became part of the Cornelius household.

Upon recovering sufficiently from typhoid fever, Parker found employment at the insurance company owned by George Cornelius. He stayed at the insurance company for a year and a half, but was unsatisfied with the position. Then, to seek his fortune, he went to Puerto Rico. The trip was financed by Sara Cornelius Parker from monies left to her from her grandmother. When the funds ran out, Parker returned to Indianapolis. Once again he found himself employed at a Cornelius company and once again it was not to his liking.

At home, although he and Sara were in the same household, the marriage was showing the strains of Parker's inability to provide for his wife in a manner to which she was accustomed and expected. Additionally creating strain in the marriage were Allison's frequent visits to the Cornelius household where he would consult with George Cornelius as a mentor. It was a surprise when Sara discovered that she was pregnant. The Parkers' daughter, Cornelia, was born in 1901.

Having a child did not change Parker. His next attempt to find himself was to go to Saginaw, Michigan. Just as with the previous adventure to Puerto Rico, Parker was not successful in Michigan. He returned to Indianapolis for a short time and then decided to once again seek his fortune, this time in Panama. After he left, Sara Parker filed for divorce in the fall of 1905 after ten years of marriage.

On the day the divorce was finalized, Sara Parker tells the story that she and Cornelia were walking back from the court when an automobile approached. In those days, automobiles were novelties and attracted attention. This car had one occupant and it stopped near Sara and little Cornelia. The occupant of the car leaped out and slammed the door. As he turned to speak to them, Sara saw the man was Allison. Sara Allison told the tale of the meeting.

"Hello, Sadie," came his invariable first greeting.

"Of all things — to meet you — like this," Sara replied.

"What's so strange?" he asked. But before Sara had time to reply, he was bending down to greet Cornelia with his hand outstretched. "How do you do, little lady?" Cornelia timidly pressed against Sara's skirts and hid her face. She cautiously peeked at the stranger before saying hello back. When she did, she was smiling in response to Allison's broad smile.[3]

Allison, still a bachelor, was free to pursue the newly divorced Sara Cornelius Parker. By this time, Prest-O-Lite was rapidly growing and he had the money to woo her.

In December 1905, Sara Parker became seriously ill and lost a great deal of weight. The physicians quickly diagnosed the cause of the weight loss as tuberculosis and prescribed that she should go to Phoenix, Arizona, to regain her strength. Allison had business on the West Coast and arranged to accompany Sara, Cornelia and Sara's mother, Melissa Cornelius, to Phoenix on the train. They arrived in Phoenix on Christmas Eve and Allison made sure that the ladies were settled before continuing on his business trip.

After several months of recuperation in Arizona, Sara returned to Indianapolis against doctor's orders. She quickly relapsed and was then sent to Colorado Springs in June 1906. When Allison could make arrangements, he would visit Sara in Colorado Springs. In December of that year, he took a little red plush box out of his pocket. He opened it and lifted her left hand and slipped a beautiful ring on her third finger: "Sadie, my love, I want you to marry me."[4]

They were married on July 16, 1907, at a Methodist church in Colorado Springs. The wedding was a family affair with Sara's mother, Melissa, and sisters, Jessie and Mary, in attendance along with Allison's mother, Myra Allison. After the exchange of vows, the wedding party went to the Broadmoor Hotel for breakfast. After a short honeymoon in Colorado, Sara continued to recuperate in Colorado Springs and Allison returned to Indianapolis. When he could, he would travel to Colorado to be with his bride. She did not return to Indianapolis for another year.

7

Prest-O-Lite Expands — and Explodes

As the growth in the automotive business took off, so did the fortunes of the Concentrated Acetylene Company. The complexity of their product had grown from a simple acetylene canister to feed a lamp and had developed to the point that the "Prest-O-Liter" automatically regulated the pressure and was able to feed two, three or five lamps providing for automatic lighting. Not only could up to five lamps be lit, but also, by slightly turning the knob, the driver could change the brightness of the lamp.

Having expanded beyond the capacity of the shed, the business was relocated to a three story building owned by the estate of Frederick Ostermeyer. The building was located in a mixed usage neighborhood on the southeast side of Indianapolis, which provided a labor source that could walk to work. Located near the stockyards, it had quick access to the railroad station, which was beneficial as the filled canisters were shipped to various parts of the country by train on a daily basis. The building also allowed the company to consolidate its operations.

The ground floor was used for filling and storage of the acetylene canisters. In the filling area they had a dozen large leak-proof tanks filled with calcium carbide. In the filling process, the calcium carbide was combined with water to make the acetylene gas. This gas was then put into the Prest-O-Lite canister. Until the time for transport to the train station by horse drawn dray, the canisters were stored on the first floor in close proximity to the filling area. The second floor was used for the assembly area, which would allow for the refurbishment of the canisters when they were returned for refilling. On the third floor an office area was located. Normally a clerical staff of three plus the plant engineer and head sales person could be found on the third floor.

About the time of relocating the business, the partners decided that the corporate name didn't have much pizzazz and searched for a new name. Thinking of how quickly and easily it lit headlights, the new name, Prest-O-Lite, was adopted.

On a sultry August day in 1907, John Luckey was filling canisters on the first floor. Between 200 and 300 filled canisters were waiting for shipment. Outside, Mr. Young was loading a Fry Transfer Company dray with filled canisters of gas for transport to the train station. Suddenly, Luckey saw a fire break out. His first thought was to cut off the electricity flowing to the filling machine. In his rush for the switch to the filling machine, he fell over a can of gas. Although his leg was bruised, his hand was cut and his knee was sprained, he reached the switch and stopped the electricity. Then, he scrambled to his feet and rushed outside.

Outside Mr. Young saw the room enveloping in flames. He instinctively knew that this was a very dangerous development. Jumping onto the driver's seat of the dray, he attempted to drive it away from the danger. But the horse had also sensed the danger and was "trembling like a leaf." Despite Mr. Young's urging of the horse, it wouldn't budge. Some employees of Prest-O-Lite seized the horse by the reins and led it away from the building.

Suddenly, the tanks inside the building became heated to the point they began exploding. The employees on the first floor were able to escape the flames and the exploding canisters. But on the second and third floors, the employees had greater challenges in escaping the building. There were 12 employees on the second floor who were able to escape through windows using a rope.

When the fire broke out, there were three office workers — Emma Brown, Kate Metz and Mayme Clemons, the manager, Frank Sweet, the Prest-O-Lite chemist, O.H. Skinner, and a contractor, W.H. Bass, on the third floor. Mr. Skinner was the first to see the fire and was able to escape down the interior steps of the building. But the fire was spreading quickly. The women, who wore dresses down to their ankles, and Sweet and Bass had to escape the fire by going out a window to get onto a fire escape. Thankfully, none were seriously injured. Emma Brown suffered a sprained ankle and Kate Metz had a bruised arm and slight lacerations. The one fatality was an old mongrel dog, Jack, a favorite of the Prest-O-Lite employees.

It was fortunate that the employees were able to escape from the building quickly. For the first half hour, exploding tanks became jagged pieces of steel hurtling through the air. Other tanks were like missiles being propelled from the building. One 2 to 3 pound tank flew about 150 feet and impaled a railroad car. Another part of a tank bottom flew across East Street and hit the side of Frank O'Brien's restaurant.

Prest-O-Lite fire following the explosion in August 1907 (courtesy Indiana Historical Society, W.H. Bass Collection).

Rushing to the scene, fire chief Charles E. Coots could see from a distance the neighborhood where the fire was raging. He told his driver that he knew the fire was at the Prest-O-Lite plant. He had long been concerned over the location of the plant given the explosive nature of the gas. With the barrage of exploding cylinders, Chief Coots' initial focus was to keep his men from risking their lives. "In fact, it was necessary for me to warn the men several times that they were running too great risks and to order them away from the more dangerous positions," said Chief Coots.

The firemen prevented catastrophic damage to the building and other nearby structures by providing a stream of water to the retaining tanks which held the calcium carbide and kept them from exploding. If water had gotten into the tanks, when it combined with the calcium carbide the resulting explosion would have caused significant severe damage to the surrounding area and there probably would have been a significant loss of life.

Mr. Sweet, the Prest-O-Lite manager, estimated that the damages totaled $25,000, with $10,000 in damage to the building and the remainder to the equipment. Not included in the total was the loss of income while the filling machines were idled in the busiest part of the year. The business did not have insurance as the cost was prohibitive.

Following the fire, Chief Coots and the building inspector joined forces to encourage the city council to adopt an ordinance prohibiting the filling of gas canisters inside the city limits. This action, if taken by the city council, would have caused Prest-O-Lite to cease operations until a new building was located and the operations were relocated.

Although the only victim of the fire was the dog, the public realized that the outcome of the fire could have been significantly different. Prest-O-Lite announced that they would be building a new location on South Street, which was near St. Vincent's Hospital. Given the location of the proposed new factory, public sentiment was that the operations of Prest-O-Lite should not be in the city limits.

Although the building inspector, Thomas A. Winterrowd, agreed with the public that the Prest-O-Lite operations should not be within the city limits, there were no city ordinances prohibiting businesses with a "hazardous characteristic" from being located within the city limits. Despite misgivings, Winterrowd's hand were tied by the lack of an ordinance. The proposed building was of concrete and steel and met all of the codes of the city in terms of construction and fire safety. Reluctantly, he approved the building plans. Prest-O-Lite agreed that after filling the gas canisters, they would be stored in a concrete vault and they would limit the number of large tanks of calcium carbide, the key element of acetylene gas, on the first floor.

As construction was proceeding on the new location, Prest-O-Lite continued operations in the previously damaged building. Due to heavy damage to the top two floors, the business had the filling operation and the refurbishment of the tanks conducted on the first floor, which led to very crowded conditions.

Suddenly, on December 20, 1907, history repeated itself. This time, between 10 and 12 employees were in the building. John Luckey was working on the gas generator while fellow employee Elmer Jessup was working on the buffing machine polishing the brass cylinders as part of the refurbishment process. Employees later indicated that, unlike the first fire, this time the explosion was simultaneous with seeing the flames. Very quickly, the flames were waist deep and spreading towards the ceiling.

Unlike the fire in August, this fire had serious injuries. Elmer Jessup was located the farthest from the door when the explosion occurred and was almost immediately surrounded by flames. When he finally reached the East Street door, almost every piece of clothing was burned from his body. Outside, Mr. Feasley, a transfer man who had been waiting for a load of canisters, sprang from his wagon and threw a blanket around Jessup, extinguishing the flames. Being severely burned and without the modern knowledge of treatment, Jessup died later that day of his injuries. Lesser injuries were suffered by chemist O.H. Skinner and employee Charles Hall. True to his name, Luckey escaped from the building without a scratch.

Most of the Indianapolis Fire Department was at the scene of the fire trying to contain it. The exploding tanks sounded as if there was a bombardment. Just before the arrival of the first firemen, a cylinder was blown from one of the windows of the plant across East Street and struck a window on the second floor over Frank O'Brien's saloon. Mr. O'Brien had been cooking sauerkraut. The force of the explosion blew the lid off of the sauerkraut, ruining the batch.

Despite the efforts of the Indianapolis Fire Department, the two-alarm fire completely consumed the Prest-O-Lite building.

The repercussions of two explosions at the Prest-O-Lite factory within a four month period began with the presentation of an ordinance at the January 1908 city council meeting. This ordinance would prohibit the manufacture or storage of gas within the city limits and effectively banned Prest-O-Lite from conducting operations at their existing facilities. The ordinance further required that the location of the building be at least fifty feet from any public highway and sixty feet from the line of any abutting property. The proposed ordinance was passed on April 6 and was approved by Mayor Charles A. Bookwalter on April 8.

Prest-O-Lite had been anticipating this action and had found property outside the city limits at River Road and White River which met all of the parameters established by the city council. Construction of the new facility had begun but was not yet completed. If the new ordinance was strictly enforced, this would have shut down the Indianapolis operations. The owners negotiated with city officials to allow Prest-O-Lite to continue operations, including the charging of gas cylinders, until the new plant was constructed.

On the home front, Sara Allison was well enough to return home from Colorado. Allison had purchased six acres adjacent to the Prest-O-Lite factory being constructed on Three Notch Road, on the south side of Indianapolis. With her return to Indianapolis, they established their home in a yellow frame structure.

8

Prest-O-Lite Explodes—Again

After negotiations with the City of Indianapolis, Prest-O-Lite continued its operations at the recently built South Street facility as the construction of the new River Road facility continued. As part of the agreement to continue operations, Prest-O-Lite agreed not to have a large number of calcium carbide tanks located near the filling area. The large tanks were relocated to the second floor and had an asbestos filter through which the gas would percolate. The gas then traveled through tubing down to the first floor where the gas was fed into the charging machine. As an additional precaution, the cement building had dividing walls between different sections. The first floor had two rooms which were separated by an iron door.

On June 5, 1908, approximately thirty employees were in the building. Summers in Indianapolis can be hot and humid and on this day the iron door separating the two sections on the first floor was open, probably to provide some air circulation. The back part of the first floor had a long row of automobile canisters which were being filled with the gas. Suddenly, the plant was wracked by an explosion for a third time within a year.[1]

Although the cause was never determined, it was believed that an employee on the first floor was burnishing one of the acetylene-filled canisters. The heat generated by the burnishing process caused the gas to expand and then explode. The force of the first explosion set off a chain reaction with other canisters on the first floor. The chain reaction continued with the large drums of gas on the second floor beginning to explode.[2]

As the four drums exploded, the percussion could be heard throughout the surrounding area followed by a series of smaller explosions as the cylinders exploded. A large fireball erupted with the ensuing smoke being visible throughout the city. The explosions sent debris flying throughout the neighborhood, and downtown Indianapolis was blanketed with little fragments of asbestos. Windows as far as a half mile away were shattered by the force of the explosion. All of the employees were able to escape from the building,

41

including the women office employees on the second floor, which was attributable to the construction of the building.

The force of the exploding large tanks resulted in a hole being torn in the roof of the building. One piece of heavy iron was blown over the roof of the Big Four Railroad freight house across South Street from the Prest-O-Lite building and landed on the Union railway tracks, severing a railroad tie. Another heavy piece of iron shot through the open door of the freight depot and landed a half block away. A third piece of iron weighing more than a hundred pounds fell near Delaware Street, narrowly missing an automobile in the street.

St. Vincent's Hospital, which was within 100 feet of the Prest-O-Lite plant, was rocked not only by the force of the explosion but also by a heavy beam. It struck St. Vincent's Hospital and severely damaged the east corner and roof on the third floor, causing the shattering of windows and the falling of plaster in the facility. The force of the explosion knocked patients from their beds on the east side of the building. Panic ensued inside the hospital and some patients fled from the building. Several women left the hospital and ran to a saloon across the street from the hospital.

In the kitchen on the first floor, the cooks were busy preparing dinner. Lena Ryan, a pastry chef, was putting the finishing touches on an apple pie when the explosion occurred. The pastry chef reported that she was thrown ten feet and did a somersault in the air while holding the pie. Although the pie was still in her hand when she landed on her feet, it was no longer edible. Like the other food being prepared, it had been showered with shards of glass.[3]

One patient at St. Vincent's, a driver of a brewery truck, had broken both legs in a fall from the truck. He had been at the hospital for some time and his legs had healed to the point where he could slowly walk with the use of two canes. At the time of the explosion, he was resting in his third floor room. Within seconds of the explosion, forgetting his pain, he descended the stairs to the first floor of the hospital without either cane.[4]

Also located in the neighborhood was Indianapolis Fire Station #2. Since fire trucks were pulled by horses, the design of fire stations had stables for the horses and equipment on the first floor while the second floor was the housing for the firemen. After completing their morning duties the firemen were relaxing. Firemen William Steinhauer and George Schick were resting in a rear room on the second floor. Outside, Captain Ike Rosengarten and firemen Andrew Miller and John Keating were seated in the alley between St. Vincent's Hospital and the fire station.

When the explosion occurred, a huge piece of twisted sheet metal became airborne and landed about three feet away from the men seated outside. The firehouse itself was severely damaged, the roof of it having been picked up by the force of the explosion. When it settled, the roof was several inches out of alignment.[5] William Steinhauer, who weighed 230 pounds, was sitting in an overstuffed chair. The force of the explosion lifted him from the chair and he landed on the floor.[6] On the first floor the horses, spooked by the loud kaboom, charged from their stalls and out of the fire station. As they turned eastward and charged down the street, firemen Andrew Miller and John Keating and Captain Ike Rosengarten gave chase. When the horses stopped, the firemen were able lead them back to the fire station. Two of the horses were hitched to the chemical engine that had been rolled out into the street by William Steinhauer and George Schick.

The horses in the firehouse weren't the only ones startled by the explosion. There were several other horses on the streets which bolted when the explosion erupted. One woman was driving a buggy with several small children by the front of the Prest-O-Lite building when the explosion occurred. The woman was so startled by the loud explosion that she fainted, dropping the horse's reins. The horse ran a block and a half down the street before it stopped.

The damage to the fire station was severe. In addition to the damage to the roof, the walls were bowed and a large piece of steel had crashed through a gable. Additionally, all of the windows had been blown out. Prior to the explosion, the city had been considering consolidating this firehouse with another one on Virginia Avenue.[7] The severity of the damage to the fire station led to the abandonment of the location.

The homes in the neighborhood were also impacted by the force of the explosion. One nearby residence had nearly all of its windows broken in the explosion. At home at the time of the explosion, Mrs. James Clune was in the dining room, which had a canary in a cage and a glass globe filled with goldfish. The large dining room window was broken by the first explosion and reportedly a flash of fire shot through the broken pane. Mrs. Clune was so startled by this occurrence that she ran through the living room to the front door which was locked. Rather than unlock the door, she climbed through a window, dragging her bulldog with her. Neither the canary nor the goldfish were injured.[8]

Amazingly, although the explosions were heard all over the city and caused significant damage from the flying debris and broken windows, there were no serious injuries to either the employees of Prest-O-Lite, the patients and staff at St. Vincent Hospital or those in the neighborhood. Just one employee who had jumped from the second floor of the plant suffered a broken leg. Others suffered minor injuries and after treatment at St. Vincent's were sent home. Despite the explosions and the fire within the Prest-O-Lite building, it sustained less damage than did either St. Vincent's Hospital or the fire station.[9]

With three explosions in less than a year, public outrage ensued. Many of the residents of the area condemned both the owners of Prest-O-Lite and city officials. Led by Emil Dietz, the local citizenry complained that their earlier concerns had been summarily dismissed by the city council:

> The City Council was not willing to listen the other time [said Dietz]. We presented the opinion of expert chemists and others to prove our point, but they preferred to wait until it happened. At the time, the Prest-O-Lite people were declaring they would resist any action by the city to make them move, if they had to take it through every court in the country. That was their principal argument — that they would fight the case so long that the property owners would gain little by their efforts. Barnard Korbly and John Welch who were looking after the interests of St. Vincent's Hospital, insisted that it would be better to accept the amended ordinance than to go through the long legal fight.[10]

Some of the crowd urged that action be taken against Fisher and Allison, as they were violating the city ordinance recently passed that prohibited the charging of acetylene tanks within the city limits. In response to the public outcry, the city council called for a special meeting.

At the special meeting, the council voted that Prest-O-Lite's manufacture of gas and filling of cylinders be prohibited by ordinance. Mayor Bookwalter said, "I feel sorry for the men who have made their investment in these two plants but these three costly experiences have proved that the stuff is too dangerous to have in the city under any circumstances. Why, the company assured us, with every protestation of certainty that the South Street plant was absolutely safe; that it was so constructed and such measures of safety in operation had been enforced, that an explosion could not occur, even when manufacturing the gas there. But it has."[11]

Fisher and Allison had anticipated this response from the city council and had already begun to disassemble the charging equipment to move it to the new facility on White River. Fisher told the *Indianapolis News*, "Operations will not be resumed in South Street, and there is therefore, no occasion for public alarm. All pumps and connections have been taken down and the room which was used for pumping will be utilized in our copper plating business."[12]

The new plant on River Road used a different method for filling the canisters with acetylene gas. Filling the small automobile canisters as the gas was manufactured reduced the potential for a massive explosion. Additionally, the plant on River Road had a concrete room about half way down the river-bank for the generation of the gas. Fisher explained that if there was an explosion during the filling process, the explosion would occur pointing towards the river.[13]

Fisher also made a plea to the city council and the public to allow the business to continue: "We employ 100 people and have a business which concerns many thousands of automobile owners, and we ask nothing more than a chance to keep it going for the few days necessary to remove else-where."

Fisher acknowledged the responsibility of Prest-O-Lite: "We recognize our liability in this explosion, and expect to settle all claims against us on an equitable basis."[14] One unusual suit was brought by a German citizen who had three barrels of sauerkraut in his yard, which was located three blocks away from the plant. The force of the explosion, according to the man, knocked the lids from the barrels. The exposure to the air ruined his sauerkraut. When Fisher asked what he thought the damages were, he replied that he thought $2 would be sufficient. Fisher provided the funds and the claim was settled.[15]

The city council passed an ordinance which made it illegal to store more than 50 tanks in any one place. Additionally the ordinance limited a tank to containing no more than one cubic foot of gas. The ordinance also prohibited an operation of the plant on any acre of unplatted ground within the city limits, a provision aimed specifically at the new plant located on Missouri Street. The new law required publication for two successive weeks prior to going into effect.[16]

The owners understood that if the law was enacted, it would "be a great hardship upon us and a great business loss if we are compelled to get outside of the city limits. We will not only lose the new plant now about completed but will lose our customers during the interval which must elapse before we can buy and build in a new location." During that time, the company filed an appeal which would test the validity of the ordinance.[17]

To insure the long-term viability of Prest-O-Lite, Allison and Fisher knew they needed to relocate the filling plant away from the city limits. A benefit of the move would be the consolidation of multiple plants around Indianapolis. Within several months, a new location was located northwest of Indianapolis. By 1913, a new plant had been built in the area of the Indianapolis Motor Speedway, which was near the Ben Hur railway spur.

9

An Indianapolis Racetrack
Becomes Reality

The story of the Indianapolis Motor Speedway is closely tied to the belief by the owners of it that American-made automobiles would benefit from a racing circuit. There were already several well known races, including the Vanderbilt Cup, the Grand Prix type and the Targa Florio on the continent. As early as 1905, Carl Fisher believed that the dirt tracks which were used in the United States weren't conducive to improvements in the automobile.

Fisher, along with Tom Taggart, a former mayor of Indianapolis,[1] began formulating a plan to build a 5 mile racetrack in French Lick, Indiana, a well known Midwest resort. French Lick had a grand hotel which catered to the financially well off of the Midwest who went to escape the summer heat and humidity. Another draw was that French Lick and nearby West Baden, Indiana, had mineral water which had curative power. Taggart owned significant land in the French Lick area and believed that the racetrack would be another attraction.[2] Fisher felt that since auto racing was a pastime of the wealthy, the demographics of French Lick were supportive of a racetrack.

In what probably turned out to be a blessing in disguise, the topography of rolling hills wasn't conducive to the construction of the track. The cost of building a racetrack would have been excessive. Additionally, having a racetrack at French Lick would have limited its draw of spectators as it was not easily accessible from the major population areas of Indianapolis, Chicago, Louisville, Detroit and Cincinnati.

At the same time in England, Hugh Fortesque Locke-King, a wealthy British landowner, attended both the Grand Prix and the Italian Targa Florio, which were both run on public roads. At the races, Locke-King saw that the British carmakers were uncompetitive, a result of the 20 mph speed limit on the British roads. Passionate about the burgeoning automobile industry in

46

England, Locke-King decided that an off-street track was needed to improve the quality of automobiles. With a fortune inherited from his father, he had the financial capacity to develop an off-street racing venue.

From a 700-acre property inherited from his father, Locke-King carved out approximately 300 acres of swampy woodland to develop an off-street racing track. Additional challenges to developing a racetrack included a railroad track bordering it on the west side and the River Wey flowing through it.

In September 1906, Locke-King convened a meeting of fellow motoring enthusiasts including E. deRodakowski, Charles Jarrott and Selwyn Edge. Jarrott was both a race car driver and an auto dealer, while Edge owned the agency (dealership) for Napier cars. Edge believed that the racetrack should be built so that the cars would be visible to the spectators for as much of the circuit as possible. The conclusion of those at the meeting was that the racetrack would be 100 feet wide and would be banked. In some areas, the banking ended up being nearly 30 feet high. The track would be called Brooklands.

The plans for the Brooklands track were drawn by Colonel Holden, a Royal Engineer, and John Donaldson supervised the construction of the track. For nine months, over seven hundred men worked to create the racetrack. The River Wey was diverted, small landholders were relocated and thirty acres of woodland were cleared. The overall length of the track was 3.25 miles (5.23 km), of which two miles were level and the remainder banked. The track had 200,000 tons of gravel and cement. For the steeply banked segments, the concrete was laid in sections from the bottom of the banked segments to the top. Spectator stands were constructed for 5,000 people. Upon completion, the track had a capacity of 250,000 spectators and occupied almost 340 acres.[3]

While the Brooklands track was under construction, Carl Fisher traveled to England and visited the site. Upon returning to the United States, he again began to think about building a racetrack.

In late 1908, Fisher and one of his real estate associates, Lem Trotter, took a day trip to Dayton, Ohio. On this trip of approximately 120 miles, his car had frequent mechanical breakdowns. On the return trip, the car overheated twice and just inside the Indiana border a tire blew for the third time that day.

The frustration of the day pushed to the forefront Fisher's idea of a grand American racetrack. He kept complaining to Trotter about the unreliability of American cars and how if things were going to improve, a huge test track was needed. Trotter challenged Fisher to stop griping and start acting: "You've been talking about a racetrack ever since you got back from

Europe. If you think it would make money, why don't you just build it yourself."

Having been goaded by Trotter, Fisher again began formulating plans
for a racetrack. He turned to Trotter to locate a piece of suitable land. Trotter
knew of the "perfect" spot — the old Pressley farm, which was about 5 miles
northwest of Indianapolis. The Pressley farm had been subdivided into four
eighty-acre tracts, three of which were owned by Daniel Chenoweth, an
insurance executive. The fourth parcel's location was key to having train
transportation available. The owner of this tract, Kevi Munter, was a livery
stable owner.[4] Not only was this 320-acre track available but it also had
other benefits. It was located on the Ben Hur Interurban line, which ran
from Indianapolis to Crawfordsville and could easily transport spectators
from downtown Indianapolis to the racetrack. The property was also adjacent
to a railroad track.

Another highly beneficial aspect of the property was its proximity to
Indianapolis, which at that point was second only to Detroit in the manufacture of automobiles. With so many people of Indianapolis involved in the
manufacture of automobiles, its population intently followed the racing circuit, most of them pulling for the hometown manufacturers. On December
12, 1908, an option on the property was obtained for $72,000. The Cheno-
with tracts were acquired for $48,000, or $200 per acre, while Munter negotiated a price of $24,000, or $300 per acre, for the final tract.[5]

When Fisher, who had been conspiring with Allison about the racetrack,
told him about the property, Allison was also excited about the idea. They
approached three friends, Arthur Newby, president of the National Motorcar
Company, Frank Wheeler, president of Wheeler-Schebler Carburetor Company, and Stoughton Fletcher, president of the Fletcher National Bank. The
five men agreed to form a company to build and operate a motor speedway.

Before the articles of incorporation were filed on February 9, 1909, as
the Indianapolis Motor Speedway Company, Fletcher withdrew from the
group due to pressure from the bank's board of directors, who thought participating in this venture would not convey a conservative image to their
depositors. The initial capitalization of the company was $250,000, with
Fisher and Allison both contributing $75,000 and Newby and Wheeler each
subscribing $50,000. Fisher was named president, Newby first vice president,
Wheeler, second vice president and Allison, secretary and treasurer.

Park T. Andrews, a New York engineer, was hired to design the track.
Although the topography was relatively flat, there was a stream running
through the southwest corner of the property. The original track design was
a three mile oval with an inner loop that would extend the racing surface to

a five mile track. Andrews suggested that the track be shortened to two and a half miles, as the larger sized track would be very close to the property lines while a smaller track would give more room for grandstands. Each straightaway would be five-eighths of a mile long and the four corners a quarter mile in length. The two short stretches between the turns would be an eighth of a mile. The straightaways would be fifty feet wide and the width in the turns sixty feet.[6] Final estimated cost of the speedway was $220,000.

The total cost of the project was financed through $184,000 contributed by the partners and the remaining $32,000 from a bank loan. At that time, Arthur Newby could raise only $25,000 in cash rather than his share, which was $46,000. He suggested that, rather than his borrowing the difference, Allison and Fisher each take one-fourth of his share. The final stock distribution at $100 per share was that Allison and Fisher each had 575 shares (31.25 percent of the ownership each), Frank Wheeler had 460 shares (25 percent ownership) and Arthur Newby had 230 shares (12.5 percent ownership).

From the beginning the partners wanted the track surface to be something better than dirt. They explored various alternatives and, believing that the cost of a concrete or brick track was prohibitive, decided on a crushed stone track bound together by asphaltum oil to be laid on a firm clay base.

With an ambitious schedule to have the first auto races on July 4, King Brothers began building the track on March 15, 1909. The work crew consisted of nearly 500 men and approximately 300 mules along with several road scrapers and rollers. Grading of the land produced a smooth, firm surface on top of which two inches of creek gravel were spread then rolled by a 15-ton roller. This was followed by a second two-inch layer of crushed limestone rolled with an eight-ton roller and then two gallons of taroid per square yard poured on top. One to two inches of crushed stone chips were applied followed by another coat of taroid at the rate of 8 to 10 gallons per square yard. Finally, a thin layer of crushed stone ranging from dust to two inches was applied with a final rolling by a three-ton roller.

Also constructed was a 12,000 seat grandstand on the main straightaway (500 feet long, 82 feet wide and covered) and two sets of bleachers, one of which was 500 feet by 50 feet and the other 350 feet by 65 feet. Other structures included a superintendent's residence, cafes, refreshment stands, garages, stables, the Aero Club clubhouse, press stand and restrooms. A pedestrian bridge spanned the track near the main grandstand and an auto bridge by the northwest corner of the track.

While the track was under construction and with automobile races being planned for the July Fourth holiday, Arthur Newby took on the responsibility for discussing the rules with the manufacturers and officials of the Automobile Club of America and the American Automobile Association. In April 1909, a meeting was held to draft the rules.[7]

Not only were the partners busy with their individual businesses and the construction of the Indianapolis Motor Speedway, Allison, Fisher and Newby, along with Robert Hassler, a mechanical engineer for National Motor Vehicle Company, also announced the formation of Empire Motorcar Company in the early summer of 1909. The vision for Empire Motorcar was to develop a low-priced, four cylinder, 20-horsepower auto which would retail for $800 beginning in 1910. The men were able to take over the struggling Mohawk Cycle Works, with a factory at 29th and Elmira streets. The business plan centered around producing between 1,000 and 2,000 six cylinder runabouts a year. The press releases were quintessential Fisher, stating that the Empire had "been under development for a year" through which "long and careful experimental work it has reached a very high state of perfection." They also announced that the Empire would have two entrants in the first races at the Indianapolis Motor Speedway.[8]

The Empire Motor Company's first car was called the Twenty and was offered in two different models. The "A" model was a conventional runabout with a rumble seat for a third passenger and priced at $800. The "B" model, which was known as the "Little Aristocrat," had two bucket seats, a longer hood and higher gearing and retailed for $850. The advertising for the "Little Aristocrat" promised that, although it was not an expensive car, it would "look as classy and perform as well as the most costly car you can buy." The car couldn't deliver its stated maximum speed of 35 mph. Although it was stylish, it was in reality a low priced vehicle with a maximum 20 mph engine.[9]

10

The Indianapolis Motor Speedway Opens

With significant capital contributed to the construction of the Speedway, the partners were interested in getting a return on their investment. Although the Midwest was experiencing industrial development, the primary economic driver continued to be farming. With planting in the spring and harvesting in the fall, the season for the racetrack was relatively short and spanned the period from Memorial Day to Labor Day. Also to be taken into consideration were the other racetrack schedules, including courses in Savannah and Chicago. The question before the partners was how to maximize use of the Speedway without saturating the market.

Informal discussions by the owners as to the format for the first year of operations frequently were held around the big round table at "Pop" Haynes' restaurant, which was adjacent to Fisher's automotive showroom on North Pennsylvania Street. Allison suggested that the racetrack be used for things other than auto racing and proposed motorcycle races and other special events.[1]

The idea of a balloon race was promoted by the ever adventurous Fisher, who had experienced balloon flight while in Europe. As a preliminary step to bringing the national balloon races to Indianapolis, Fisher started the Aero Club of Indiana in January 1909 to stimulate interest in lighter than air travel.[2] He also knew people in the ballooning community, including George Bumbaugh, a well known balloon pilot in the Midwest. Earlier, Bumbaugh had piloted a balloon over Indianapolis with an unusual gondola — a Stoddard-Dayton car owned by Fisher. This was one of many publicity stunts by Fisher, who enjoyed this unusual balloon ride.[3]

The schedule announced by the owners included motorcycle races, a balloon race and two weekends of auto racing. With the track under construction, the first event to be held at the Indianapolis Motor Speedway was a balloon race on June 5. The first automobile races were scheduled for the 4th of July weekend. The National Motorcycle championships were to be held on August 13 and 14. The closing event for the year was another weekend of automobile racing over the Labor Day weekend.[4]

As the partners were involved in other business interests, they realized that they would need a publicist who had connections in the auto racing world to promote the events at the racetrack. Ernest A. Moross was the publicist for the very popular barnstormer Barney Oldfield. As Oldfield was frequently involved in races across the United States, Moross had developed many acquaintances among sportswriters and automobile editors. Of benefit to the partners was that Oldfield had been put on probation for unsanctioned races. Moross accepted the partners' offer of employment.[5]

The first publicity event for the Indianapolis Motor Speedway targeted the local citizenry. Oldfield was in town applying for a job with the National racing team. Also in town were three members of the Buick racing team: Louis Chevrolet, Bob Burman and Lewis Strang. This was the perfect opportunity to seize upon the celebrity of these auto racing legends. Moross invited the local press representing the three Indianapolis newspapers (the *Morning Star*, the *News* and the *Sun*) for a tour of the racetrack on May 1, along with Oldfield and the three members of the Buick racing team. After touring the track, which was under construction, Lewis Strang pronounced that he believed new world records would be set at the Indianapolis Motor Speedway. This statement created the desired buzz among the local citizens.[6]

The creek flowing through the southwest corner of the property created a design issue. In hard rains, a culvert would not be capable of handling the water flow. Andrews recommended to the owners the building of two bridges over the creek.[7] The construction of the bridges over the creek in the southwest corner of the property caused the construction to slow. By mid–May, it became clear to the owners that the auto races for the July Fourth weekend were in peril. Fisher wanted the completion of the Speedway to be expedited. With men and equipment working during the daylight hours, the only means available to increase the number of hours worked was to provide lighting for the evening hours. Gas lines were extended from Indianapolis to light the inside of the track and Prest-O-Lite also provided some tanks for lighting the outside of the track. Despite these efforts, the partners soon realized that the track would not be ready for the July Fourth auto races. The race schedule was modified so that the first races would be held several days after the motorcycle championship and the Labor Day races would be rescheduled for the fall.[8]

When a balloon race was secured for the Indianapolis Motor Speedway,

Fisher wanted to be a participant. To qualify, he needed to have ten flights, including one at night. He had already completed six flights in Europe and two in the United States. To help him meet the qualifications, he turned to George Bumbaugh. On May 22, with Captain George Bumbaugh in the 40,000 cubic foot balloon *Kathleen*, they sailed to the southwest at approximately 3,000 feet in altitude. The second flight was made in the brand new 80,000 cubic foot balloon, *Hoosier*, which was built by Bumbaugh for the Indiana Aero Club. This trip lasted approximately 40 minutes. With this flight, Fisher had not only qualified to participate in the balloon races[9] but also became the 21st person to qualify as a balloon pilot.[10]

There were nine entrants in the National Balloon Championship. To qualify for participation, a balloon had to be between 60,000 cubic feet and 78,000 cubic feet in gas capacity. Because three of the entrants did not meet the qualifications, the partners scheduled a handicapped race for these three balloons. To generate interest in the balloon races, the partners had prizes for both the handicapped and the National Balloon Championship.

Ever the optimist, Fisher had high expectations of a large crowd turning out for the balloon races. He was hoping for 20,000 in attendance. Meanwhile, Ernest Moross was expressing concern that not many people would pay to watch the balloon race when they could be outside the gates and see it for free.[11]

The day of the balloon race turned out to be perfect for flying. The partners were successful at generating interest in the race, with an estimated 40,000 people watching it. Unfortunately, a large number of these decided that they could see the activities just as well outside the gates to the Speedway. They clogged the arteries surrounding the Speedway, limiting access to the gates. Among those caught up in the large traffic jam was Indiana governor Thomas R. Marshall, who would later become vice president of the United States. Marshall was scheduled to participate in the preliminary activities. So as not to delay the lifting off of the balloons, the partners did not await for his arrival, which was delayed nearly an hour. The gridlock was so bad that Governor Marshall finally parked a mile from the entrance in a farmer's field and then walked the remainder of the distance. When he finally joined the race officials at the judge's stand, all but three of the balloons had already departed.[12]

The handicapped race began at 3:50 P.M. in a southerly wind. The first balloon to lift off was the *Ohio*, a 40,000 cubic foot balloon. Following in five minute intervals were the *Indianapolis* and the *Chicago*, the largest balloon in the world at 110,000 cubic feet. As the *Chicago* rose to around 500 feet, Mr. Coey unfurled a large silk American flag, resulting in a thunderous ovation from the crowd.

Balloons waiting for the start of the balloon races starting from the Indianapolis Motor Speedway, 1909 (courtesy Indianapolis Motor Speedway).

The *Ohio's* trip was very short. They landed just two and a half hours later one mile west of Nashville, Indiana. Taking both the Merchant's Cup given for the longest flight and the cup given by Carl Fisher for the longest time in the air was the *Indianapolis*, which flew 235 miles over a 19-hour period with a maximum altitude of 13,000 feet. The crew of the *Indianapolis* reported being shot at by farmers in Kentucky on two occasions. The *Chicago* landed at a fairground in Scottsburg, Kentucky, about 16 miles north of where the *Indianapolis* landed.

The order of liftoff for the championship race had been determined by a draw the previous evening. As the luck of the draw would have it, the favorite to win, the *New York,* lifted off first. With six American flags attached to its basket, the *Indiana*, with Fisher on board, lifted off approximately five minutes later. As it ascended into the blue sky, the band started playing "The Star-Spangled Banner" as Fisher threw roses to the crowd below. The *St. Louis 3,* which some believed exceeded the 78,000 cubic feet of gas, ascended third. Race officials had not addressed the eligibility issue and said they would make a determination after the conclusion of the race. Fourth to lift off was the *Cleveland*, followed shortly by the *Hoosier*. Capt. Thomas Baldwin stood on the top edge of the basket shouting his good-byes through a megaphone to the crowd below while Charles Walsh lost his hat waving it to the crowd. The last balloon to leave was the *University City*.[13]

As the balloons were carried by the prevailing winds, the spectators could only watch the first few minutes of the race and then quickly dispersed. With the exception of the *Cleveland*, which was the first casualty of the race, it would be several days before the adventures of the balloonists became known. The *Cleveland* landed about eight miles west of Columbus, Indiana, close to sunset, around 8:00 P.M. The short flight was caused by a 4-inch tear in the balloon about 20 feet from the top.[14]

Just as with the handicapped race, there were trophies for the winner of both the Indianapolis Merchant's cup and the cup given by Fisher. The *Hoosier* sailed to Greenbriar, Tennessee, about 25 miles south of the Kentucky/Tennessee border.[15] Fisher and Baumberger were in the air 49 hours and landed in the Cumberland Valley. The *St. Louis 3* landed after sailing 320 miles to Kelso, Tennessee, in 36 hours and 30 minutes.[16] The distance prize was awarded to the *University City*, which traveled a total of 382 miles, landing just south of Ft. Payne, Alabama. The *New York* was a close second, landing just south of the Tennessee/Mississippi border near Corinth, Mississippi. It had crossed into Alabama when a north wind reversed its course. Its total distance flown was 355.5 miles. The *New York* was awarded the cup for the longest time in the air.[17]

Ernest Moross' concerns were justified, as the Motor Speedway's official attendance at the balloon races approximated 3,500.[18]

Indianapolis had attracted the seventh annual convention of the Federation of American Motorcyclists (FAM). The four-day event included a parade, a business meeting and several receptions as well as short races and endurance runs on Friday and Saturday.[19] As the Newby Oval, which had been used in the late 1890s for bicycle races, had been torn down, the Indianapolis Motor Speedway played host for the racing events. It was an unlikely place to hold motorcycle races due to its construction. Most motorcycle races were held on wood tracks, which resulted in a fairly uniform texture.

Prior to the start of the convention, there was an endurance run in Cleveland. Several of the motorcyclists on their way to Cleveland stopped by the Speedway to get some practice laps in. Imagine their surprise, when, instead of a wooden oval, they saw a very large track with a surface of crushed stone and taroid. They immediately expressed concern about the condition of the track, particularly the edges, which had exposed sharp angles from the crushed stone.[20] In an effort to reassure them, Fisher promised them the track wouldn't look the same after the final coat of oil had been applied and an additional two or three days of work by the heavy rollers. Fisher also promised them time to practice on the completed track upon their return from Cleveland.[21]

Work on the track went on at a fevered pitch, as the motorcyclists would be in Indianapolis on Wednesday to begin the convention. The last application of oil for the track was dependent upon the arrival of five railroad tank cars. By Tuesday, these tank cars still had not arrived in Indianapolis and Fisher ordered that a replacement for the missing tank cars be sent immediately to Indianapolis from Chicago.[22] When the riders returned from the trials in Cleveland the next day, they found that construction on the southwest corner of the track still was not completed. The estimated time to finish it was 12 to 15 hours. Incensed with the condition of the track and the inability to practice on it, some members of the group pressed FAM president Earl Ovington to cancel the championship. Others wanted the championship to be moved to the mile dirt oval at the Indiana State Fairgrounds. Fisher promised that the track would be finished the following morning in time for a practice period prior to the beginning of the race.[23] Although Mr. Ovington made the decision to hold the championship at the motor speedway, several of the riders continued to express concerns about the surface of the track.[24]

Friday dawned a rainy day. With publicity having been compromised due to the lack of practice time and rain impacting the anticipated turnout, Speedway management decided to postpone the Friday races until Saturday.[25] This pushed the Saturday races back to Monday. By mid-afternoon, the rains let up and the track began to dry. By late in the afternoon officials thought that the track was dry enough to allow a practice run. Al Givne of Indianapolis was the first motorcyclist to take a practice run around the racetrack. On the third turn, he hit a wet spot and lost control of his motorcycle. Skidding out of control, he suffered serious head injuries and was rushed to the hospital. His injuries only reinforced the angst of some of the riders about the condition of the track. Shortly thereafter, the rains returned and the practice time was closed for the day.

By Saturday morning, the weather had cleared and a full day of racing by both amateurs and professionals was anticipated. The day was very hot and, combined with the rains the previous day, there was a high level of humidity, not ideal conditions for an outdoor spectator event. The opening race was a five mile amateur event. The second race was an FAM national championship for a one mile run. Although there were 29 entrants, at race time there were only 10 participants. Additional races included two five milers.[26] Disgruntled with the lack of action on the racecourse, some of those in attendance started to leave before the start of the 10 mile professional championship run.

With dissatisfaction growing among the crowd as well as the motorcyclists, Fisher believed that if they switched the race program around and ran the championship race, the events of the day might be salvaged. He approached Ed Lingenfelder to see if he was willing to race. Lingenfelder agreed to the race if another racer was willing to join. Jake DeRosier of Springfield, Massachusetts, finally agreed to the duel. DeRosier was dressed in red tights with an American flag stitched to the back of his shirt. Lingenfelder was in an all white uniform. When the signal was given to begin the race, both motorcyclists roared down the straightaway. Coming out of the fourth turn at the end of the first lap, DeRosier's front tire blew out. As the rubber separated from the rim and lodged in the fork of the motorcycle, he was thrown over the handlebars and turned a half flip, landing on his back near the inner edge of the course. Lingenfelder completed the second lap as a solo run.[27]

After the race, management made the decision to can the Monday program.

The motorcycle races were a disappointment. Attendance was a paltry 3,500. Having had to cancel the second day of races was a negative. The concerns of the motorcycle riders over the condition of the track were a harbinger of things to come. Their concern was over the sharp edges, but as the owners of the racetrack would soon discover the choice of construction materials would also be detrimental to auto racing.

11

Indianapolis Motor Speedway Racing

There was an intense rivalry between the car manufacturers in Indianapolis and those in Detroit. Detroit had taken the route of automation to produce vehicles while the manufacturers in Indianapolis had chosen to continue to handcraft their automobiles. It wasn't long before the much higher cost of the handcrafted automobiles could not be sustained as long as the masses could purchase autos made in Detroit. Ultimately, the Indianapolis manufacturers closed shop.

These two geographical areas also had more racing cars and drivers than any other area in the United States. Although Indianapolis stood number two to Detroit in the total number of vehicles manufactured, it ranked number one in the number of cars entered into races. For the first few years of racing at the Indianapolis Motor Speedway, the highly competitive races were concentrated in a handful of companies which then were household names in the Midwest. But today most (except Buick) have vanished from memory: National Motorcar, Stoddard-Dayton, Marmon and Buick. Indianapolis had several automobile manufacturers (National Motorcar and Marmon) that not only were well represented in the early years of the Indianapolis Motor Speedway racing but were also hometown favorites.

The first race weekend, in late August 1909, had 65 entrants.[1] Buick dominated the field with 15 vehicles and 40 drivers. Arriving at noon on Monday, August 16, the Buick drivers Bob Burman, Lewis Strang and Louis Chevrolet were favorites among the racing circuit.

Also with a strong showing at the Speedway were the Indianapolis-based Marmon and National teams. Although there were some professional drivers, most drivers were employed by the manufacturers in various capacities such as engineer or mechanic. Two hometown favorites were Ray Harroun and Johnny Aitken. Harroun was an engineer at Nordyke & Marmon and Aitken, nicknamed "Happy Johnny," was employed by the National Motor Vehicle Company.[2] Practice on the track provided a glimpse of the upcoming races. By Thursday, under the heat of the August sun and the weight of the cars, the track began to breakup. It was repaired that evening.

As publicity for the upcoming weekend of racing, Bob Burman took Betty Blythe, a reporter for the *Indianapolis Morning Star*, for a few laps around the Speedway in his Buick. For the first lap, he drove the vehicle at 60 mph. By the second lap, the speed had reached 70 mph. She published her thoughts in the *Morning Star*:

> Don't get the notion that riding in a racer is anything like gentle dalliance in a touring car. First you hold hard and guess if you will land on the biggest pile of rocks. You turn up a disgusted nose at the oil that rains from the machine and wraps you in a cloud. You try to find another foothold for the foot that you are sure the red-hot engine is burning to a cinder. You observe with deep distaste that your hand is reeking with nasty oil and you suspect that what is left of your face is likewise decorated. You find yourself inquiring sarcastically of the driver how he knows precisely where all the roughest spots are. The fact that the driver is completely oblivious to the fact that you are talking at all does not make any difference.[3]

Also creating publicity was Barney Oldfield. He created quite a buzz by breaking the two minute barrier for the 2½ mile oval with a time of 1:58. With strong racing teams representing National Motor, Marmon and Buick, as well as the record setting drive by Oldfield, the weekend of racing was shaping up nicely.

Opening day for the Speedway was August 19, 1909.[4] To accommodate the crowd that descended upon the Speedway, Cleveland, Cincinnati, Chicago and St. Louis (commonly known as the Big Four) ran special trains from Union Station in Indianapolis on a 15 minute schedule while the Ben Hur Interurban provided additional transportation. Parking inside the Speedway could accommodate almost 10,000 cars and had 3,000 hitching posts for horses. Entry to the track was $1 at the main gate and 50 cents at the east gate, which had balloon bleachers on the south side of the track.[5] Speedway management was pleased with the 15,000 in attendance on opening day.[6]

Entering through the main gate, visitors saw a row of tents that housed cars on exhibit by the various auto manufacturers. Overland Automobile Company's exhibit gained a lot of attention with a gold-plated automobile to be awarded to the driver with the fastest mile time obtained in 1909. The drivers would be permitted to make two attempts, each electrically timed for the kilometer and mile records on Friday and Saturday.[7]

Henry Ford and the four founders of the Indianapolis Motor Speedway, 1909. From left to right: Ford, Arthur Newby, Frank Wheeler, Carl Fisher and James Allison (courtesy Indianapolis Motor Speedway).

Earlier in 1909, Marmon had introduced the "32," which was a relatively small car. They entered two of the 32s in the Glidden Tour. As with the tours in 1906 and 1908, one of the Marmons finished the Glidden Tour with a perfect score. The second car was also driven by Ray Harroun in the Frank A. Munsey Reliability Tour in Washington, D.C. But all was not perfect in the Marmon world. Prior to the opening of the Indianapolis Motor Speedway, a new track had opened in Atlanta. Participating in races at that track were teams from Nordyke & Marmon as well as National Motor. Nordyke & Marmon engineers were disappointed with their vehicles' performance in a 200-mile event and decided to make improvements. Ray Harroun, Nordyke & Marmon's number one driver, felt that the cars needed to have more "horses" under the hood.

Marmon had adopted the racing colors of yellow with black striping. For the first weekend of racing at the Indianapolis Motor Speedway, Nordyke & Marmon had three entries driving the new Model 32. The 32 car driven by Ray Harroun was nicknamed the "Yellow Jacket" (or the "Yellow Peril"), given the prowess that Marmon vehicles had shown on the racetrack and in various reliability runs. With employee interest in the race being very high, Nordyke & Marmon hired a train to bring about 500 workers from the plant in Indianapolis to the racetrack.

During the early days of auto racing, riding mechanics were an integral part of the team. With the noise from the loud engines preventing verbal communication and no rearview mirrors, the riding mechanics alerted the driver to traffic around him through a series of hand signals. To alert the driver of an approaching car, the mechanic held up one finger. If two fingers were displayed, a competitor was close behind. When a car was very close, the mechanic would hold up three fingers, while four fingers meant that someone wanted to pass. If the car was out of oil, the signal was the thumb and 1st finger in the shape of an "o." Additionally, the mechanics monitored the engine's oil pressure and took care of any emergencies that arose. There were stories of mechanics climbing out on cars to put out fires and working as relief drivers.[8]

Festivities began when the Indianapolis Military Band entered the track area in front of the grandstand at 11:30 A.M. and played music until the start of the first race. Unlike the Indianapolis 500 mile race, which began in 1911, the first weekend consisted of races of various lengths with the vehicles segregated according to the cubic inches of displacement (CID). This theoretically paired the vehicles so they had approximately the same capacity.

In the first race the five entrants were to begin the race with a rolling start. As the five cars approached the starting line, rather than being in a straight line across the track, they were spread out. The drivers anticipated seeing the red starting flag as they approached the starting line. What they saw instead was a yellow flag, which was a signal for them to stop. Rather than try for another rolling start, the racers were lined up across the track.[9]

At the dropping of the red flag signaling the start of the race, the racers roared off from a dead stop. Louis Schwitzer in a Stoddard-Dayton quickly took the lead followed closely by his teammate, Carl Wright. In the second lap, Schwitzer and Wright continued in the one/two positions. The 1,200 employees from Stoddard-Dayton who had been brought to Indianapolis from Dayton, Ohio, on a specially chartered train were cheering wildly for their drivers as Louis Schwitzer took the checkered flag.[10] Stoddard-Dayton was founded in 1884 as a manufacturer of hay rakes and other agricultural implements. Charles Stoddard, the principal of Stoddard-Dayton, announced the design of his first car, in 1904, by H.S. Edwards. Entering the production of automobiles, the company ceased making agricultural implements. Its output of autos expanded rapidly from 125 vehicles in 1905 to 385 vehicles in 1906 and 1,200 vehicles in 1907.[11] By 1911, the company had 20 different models, including the 70 horsepower Stoddard–Dayton Knight at a price of $6,250.[12]

The second race was a 10 mile event that Art Chevrolet, driving a Buick, led from the beginning. He set a blistering pace and completed the four laps, setting a world record of 66.93 mph. In this event, Buick scored a trifecta, as his teammates Louis Strang placed second and Bob Burman placed third.[13]

After the fourth race, all eyes turned to Oldfield, who was attempting to break the world's record for a mile held by Webb Jay at 48.20 seconds.[14] By 1904, Oldfield had broken every record of races from one to fifty miles. Always known for aggressive driving, Oldfield was in a spectacular crash in 1903 at the Detroit Free-for-All. When his rear tire blew on the seventh lap of the race, he wasn't able to handle the barreling car. It skidded out of control and smashed through a wooden railing before heading down an embankment and crashing into a tree. Thrown from his car, Oldfield was fortunate to survive. In the crash, he broke several ribs and several molars. After the crash, Barney always drove chomping down on a cigar.[15] Roaring down the straightaway and chomping on his trademark cigar in this fourth race, Oldfield shattered the record, covering the mile in 43.10 seconds as the crowd cheered.

The fifth race was the Prest-O-Lite Trophy Race, a 250 mile event (100 laps). Nine cars were entered in the event, including three Buicks. On lap 37, Lewis Strang in a Buick pulled into the pits with flames shooting out of the back of his car.[16] The fire was quickly extinguished. He got ready to pull back out onto the racetrack to continue his quest for the Prest-O-Lite trophy; however, he was disqualified as some people not from his team had helped to extinguish the flames. He protested this decision and after reconsideration, the decision was reversed. Although he was able to continue the race, he had lost considerable time and was five laps down. His hopes of winning the trophy were dashed.[17]

For the first 125 miles (50 laps), Buick drivers Bob Burman and Louis Chevrolet were setting the pace. After 125 miles, while attempting to pass Tom Kincaid's National for a second time on the backstretch, a stone flying up from the track hit Louis Chevrolet in the goggles, breaking them. After safely stopping the car, his riding mechanic led Louis to the track hospital a half mile away where he had slivers of glass as well as dust and tar removed from his eyes.[18]

On lap 58, Wilfred Bourque, in a big Knox, was being closely followed by Jap Clemens, in a Stoddard-Dayton, who wanted to pass. Bourque's riding mechanic was giving him the signal of an approaching car. When

Bourque tried to sneak a peak at the approaching car, his car swerved slightly to the right and hit a pothole. This caused Bourque to lose control of the car, which darted into a ditch on the outside of the track and then flipped end over end, ultimately slamming against a fence post. It stopped upside down on the ground. Hundreds of people rushed to the scene. Both Bourque and Harry Holcomb, the riding mechanic, were killed in the mishap.[19]

The inaugural Prest-O-Lite race was won by Bob Burman, a salaried Buick factory driver, with an average speed of 53.77 mph. Finishing a distant second almost eight minutes later was Jap Clemens in a Stoddard-Dayton.[20]

With the surface breaking up badly in places, particularly in the turns, officials from the American Automobile Association were very concerned about the condition of the track as well as the design of the course, which had ditches on the outside of the track in the turns. They considered canceling the remaining two days of racing. Fisher assured them that the racetrack would be repaired overnight and would be safe for racing on Friday. He also agreed to put heavy planks over the ditches.[21]

An estimated crowd of 25,000 enjoyed the second day of racing. Several drivers decided not to participate in the races this day, including Burman, Chevrolet and Ellis, who had experienced difficulties the previous day as a result of the track deterioration. As promised, today's was a safer event. The day started with several drivers participating in trials to set new kilometer and mile world records. In the 100 A & G Trophy race, Strang in a Chevrolet set a new American record for cars with less than 300 cubic inch displacement.[22]

The excitement of the day was when Oldfield, driving a new National called "Old Glory," had his engine catch on fire. Rather than abandon the car, he attempted to drive it back to the pits. As he drove, the fire burned through the leather straps which held the hood in place. As the fire weakened the straps, they finally lost the battle and the hood flew off of the car. His quick reaction of shielding his face and head with his right arm resulted in his avoiding a potentially catastrophic accident.[23]

Saturday, the final day of racing, was highlighted by the 300 mile Wheeler-Schebler Trophy Race. Wheeler-Schebler Carburetor Company had commissioned Tiffany's to create a seven-foot-tall silver vase at a cost of $10,000 to be presented to the winner of the race. With over 35,000 in attendance, the grandstand was filled to capacity.[24]

At 1:25 P.M., the Wheeler-Schebler Trophy Race began with 19 entrants. These heavy cars once again subjected the track to lots of pressure. By the 41st lap, the track began breaking up again.[25] Driving an Apperson, Lytle hit a rut in the southwest turn and lost control of the vehicle. It was heading for a group of small private stands. Fighting to regain control of the vehicle, Lytle cut the wheel sharply to the left to avoid a catastrophe. His vehicle careened across the track where, in the infield, it ended up in a pile of dirt, throwing his riding mechanic, Joe Betts of Kokomo, free of the car. After checking to make sure that Betts was not injured, Lytle grabbed a shovel and began digging his car out. After freeing the vehicle from the dirt, he rejoined the race.[26]

For the first 100 miles, Johnny Aitken, a member of the National racing team, set a world record at one hour, 31 minutes and 41.90 seconds. Aitken's record setting pace did not last long. At 105 miles, his car experienced a cracked cylinder head, ending his day of driving.[27] Aitken and his riding mechanic, Charles Kellum, returned to the pits. Upon arriving in the pits, Aitken predicted that someone would surely get killed if the race continued.[28]

As the race continued, Charlie Merz, another National team member, experienced battery failure on the backside of the racetrack. His riding mechanic, Herbert Lyme, ran across the infield to get a new battery, arriving at the pits out of breath. As a member of the National team, Charles Kellum, Aitken's mechanic, delivered the new battery to Merz and continued with him for the remainder of the race. At 175 miles, Merz blew a right front tire, which caused his car to spin out of control. Sailing through the air for over 100 feet, the car ripped through five fence posts, and hit the crowd standing at the fence. Eventually, the car bounced on its tires, flipped upside down and landed on the other side of the creek. Kellum, the riding mechanic, was killed instantly. Merz crawled out from underneath the vehicle with only minor injuries. Two spectators, James West of Indianapolis and Homer Jolliff of Franklin, were killed and several other spectators were injured.[29]

The carnage continued when Bruce Keene, driving a Marmon, rounded the southeast corner of the track and hit a hole. Spinning out of control, his car hit one of the pedestrian bridge supports. Although he was not hurt, his riding mechanic, Jim Schiller, jumped from the car and had lacerations to his scalp and a possible skull fracture. With this occurrence, starter Fred "Pop" Wagner stopped the race and declared it "no contest." Leading when the race was called was Leigh Lynch with a one-lap lead over Ralph DePalma. He had run 235 miles.[30] Since the race wasn't completed, the Wheeler-Schebler Trophy was not awarded.

The AAA Contest Board was very concerned about the condition of the track and rumors circulated in Indianapolis that there would be no more racing at the Indianapolis Motor Speedway.[31] The partners at this point realized that the rush to complete the track and to have it made of crushed stone were significant issues. Fisher again promised that the track would be repaired, even if it cost $100,000. The final weekend of racing scheduled for later in the fall was canceled.[32]

The partners consulted with Park Andrews, who, after spending three weeks studying the issue, suggested that the track be rebuilt with either concrete or bricks.[33] Andrews estimated that the cost of a concrete track would be $110,000. Although bricks were 50 percent more expensive than concrete, they would last longer, provide better traction and had the potential benefit of having higher speeds, estimated at a mile or two more per hour.

Before making a decision about the material to be used on the track, the owners tested the bricks to make sure that they were worth the extra money. In early September, several hundred yards of bricks were laid on the Speedway's racing surface, as well as wood block that had been treated with creosote, an oily liquid obtained by the distillation of coal tar. Aitken, driving a National, made several high speed runs over the bricks. To further test the durability of the bricks, the wheels of Aitken's car were secured by a rope to two posts anchored into the ground. One of the posts was behind the car and the other in front of the car. After securing the car, which was sitting on the bricks, he ran it at full throttle, causing the wheels to churn on the brick surface. After running the tests, the owners decided to pave the track with bricks, thus leading to the track's being affectionately called the "Brickyard."[34]

Resurfacing the track began the next month; Newby covered the cost of the bricks.[35] To have an adequate supply of bricks, the partners contracted with Veedersburg Brick Company, which subcontracted with an additional four firms. Each of the 3,200,000 bricks used in the resurfacing weighed 10 pounds and measured nine inches long, four inches wide and four inches deep. They were placed on their sides on a two inch sand cushion. After the bricks were laid, they were compressed into the sand base with a three ton roller. Filler, composed of equal parts of sand and concrete, was mixed to the consistency of a thin batter and applied with shovels and then spread between the bricks with squeegees. To make sure that the racing surface was smooth, inspectors checked the level with straight edges 12 feet long. Any variation over three-eighths of an inch in any 12 feet of track resulted in the bricks being relaid. Construction of the track concluded the week before Christmas, in a remarkable 63 days.[36]

After the reconstruction of the Speedway using bricks as the pavement was completed, a number of city officials from both Indianapolis and points farther away inspected several Indianapolis streets as well as the Speedway. They were very interested in the process used in the construction of the

Speedway. Key to the quality was a properly built concrete foundation and a uniform sand cushion upon which the bricks were laid. The uniform application of a well mixed cement filler applied between the bricks prevented the edges of the bricks from chipping. C.H. Rust, a Toronto, Canada, city engineer, proclaimed, "Indianapolis ought to have as good brick streets as that brick track out at the Motor Speedway." Agreeing with this comment was an Indianapolis city engineer who proclaimed that the streets in Indianapolis would be built using the same process as had been used at the Speedway.[37]

In addition to bricking of the racetrack, other improvements were made to the physical plant, including a 33-inch-high retaining wall with a 9-inch thickness around the outside turns as well as in front of the grandstand. Also installed was an improved automatic timing device made by Warner Autometer Company that registered the exact instant when a car's tires touched a small wire stretched across the track. Along each side of the straightaways and around the inside of each turn, a 5-inch by 24-inch concrete footer was poured, the top of it flush with the racetrack. A one-inch expansion joint was placed between the brick and the concrete strip.[38]

On the infield, a course for airplanes was constructed which was 150 feet wide and one and ½ mile in length. The world's largest aerodrome was built, providing space for 10 airplanes and two inflated dirigibles. Additionally, the owners purchased generators, gas holders, fittings and reflectors to provide night lighting of the entire track at 20 foot intervals.

The cost of the improvements was far beyond Fisher's pronouncement that they would make them even if they cost $100,000. The investment in the racetrack had risen to $700,000.

While the improvements were underway, Fisher, who was then 35 years old, married Jane Watts. Their honeymoon consisted of a business trip to California. Later that year, as Christmas approached, they took a boat trip down the Mississippi River. Fisher's yacht ran into mechanical trouble and the Fishers returned to Indianapolis. After the repairs were completed on the yacht, John Levi, the boat captain, took the boat around the Florida Keys and was headed to Jacksonville. He pulled into the small town of Miami and wired Fisher that it was a town worth seeing. Based upon Levi's urging, the Fishers traveled to Florida and became enamored with the climate. In a few years, Fisher would be living most of the year in Miami and starting the development of Miami Beach.[39]

In Indianapolis, with the racecourse finished, the partners wanted to have a day of racing, in part to recoup some of the expenses associated with the track. Additionally, they hoped showing the improvements to the Speedway would have a positive impact on the 1910 racing season. Fisher estimated that this day could bring in between $15,000 and $20,000. His partners, however, disagreed that a day of racing would bring many people. It was very close to Christmas and there was the possibility the day could be bitterly cold. There was also concern that if the day was cold it could adversely impact the race cars. Allison suggested a compromise that was accepted by the partners. The manufacturers would be invited to the track to race for records but no prizes would be offered. The public was welcome to come and there would be no admittance fee. The reopening of the track was scheduled for December 17 and 18.[40]

As publicity for the reopening of the Speedway, Fisher drove the popular retired heavyweight boxing champion James J. Jeffries around the track, which event was photographed and run in various newspapers across the country. This was good publicity not only for the Indianapolis Motor Speedway but also for Jeffries, who was planning a return to the boxing ring in an effort to regain the title from James Jackson. The story goes that while riding around the track with Jeffries, Fisher had another promotional idea. One brick from the finish line would be removed from the racetrack and replaced with a "gold" brick. This brick was manufactured by the Wheeler-Schebler Carburetor Company from a carburetor and was made of brass and copper. Prior to being installed, the brick was displayed in a downtown storefront.[41]

December 17 was bitterly cold. It was 9 degrees when Indiana governor Thomas Marshall laid the gold brick in place while members of the press snapped pictures.[42] The first racers back on the renovated track were four motorcyclists riding Indian and Thor bikes. These four hearty souls made one trip around the oval before calling it quits.[43]

The first car on the track to try for a record was an Empire. Driven by Newell Motsinger, the Empire was the only car competing in its class of 160 cubic inches and under. Its performance that day was disappointing, as it was the slowest car on the track. In the 20 mile free-for-all, it finished 6th of seven entrants. The seventh-place car, a National, had run out of gas.[44]

Saturday was even colder and only three drivers decided to participate in the record runs. The drivers, Lewis Stang in a Fiat, Newell Motsinger in an Empire and Christie in a Marmon tried to dress for the cold. They were wrapped up with special face masks and fur lined gloves. The drivers stored their fuel and oil in heated rooms and filled the cars shortly before attempting the record breaking runs. A small crowd of 500 watched as Lewis Strang in the Fiat achieved a one mile speed of 111.86 miles per hour and a five mile average speed of 91.813 miles per hour.[45]

12

The Town of Speedway, Indiana

Nineteen hundred nine was a watershed year for Fisher and Allison. The racetrack which was to lift the engineering of American motorcars had become a reality. Prest-O-Lite was thriving and expanding. The partners were involved with the new Empire Motor Company. Individually, Allison continued to be involved with Allison Coupon Company and Fisher continued with his dealership.

Prest-O-Lite's success and growth continued to push the partners for an answer to how long the new factory on River Road in Indianapolis would be adequate to support the operations. They also had the challenge of operating small multiple facilities in Indianapolis. Eventually, they would need to address the need for new facilities.

Fisher, the dreamer who consistently pushed the envelop, started dreaming once again. The new dream was for an industrialized town. He told William Herschell, an Indianapolis journalist, about his newest project:

> I'm working on a new idea, Bill. The automobile is at the dawn of a great development. Airplanes are in their infancy but you will live to see them familiar travelers across the sky. We are coming into a fast moving age and the old horse can't go the pace. Wouldn't it be a great idea to build a horseless city just opposite the Motor Speedway, an industrial city devoted to motorization of all traffic? Electricity and gas would be the motive powers. Every business house, industrial plant and home would have the most modern equipment. The homes would be homes and not the kind of shacks that usually infest an industrial center.[1]

In 1912, the land surrounding the Indianapolis Motor Speedway was purchased by Fisher, Allison and Newby. Most of the property acquisition was done by Trotter through Globe Realty. Speedway City was being developed by Speedway Realty, and the use of Globe Realty allowed the purchase of property without disclosing the end purpose.

Trotter was hired to lay out the town Fisher had envisioned several years before. After taking a drafting course at night, Trotter laid the town out according to a block pattern very similar to that of Indianapolis.[2] The primary east-west street, 16th, was laid out so that the width matched that of Washington Street, the primary east-west street going through downtown Indianapolis. Trotter later regretted that the lots on 15th and 16th streets were more spacious than those on 10th Street.

The town developed as envisioned by Allison and Fisher. In addition to the Indianapolis Motor Speedway, Prest-O-Lite relocated its factory to the town in 1912. Electric Steel Company started operations in Speedway in 1913. With the relocation of Team Speedway from downtown Indianapolis to Speedway in 1917, Allison Engineering became a significant employer. Also relocating to Speedway, Indiana, was Esterline Angus in 1923.[3] Allison was on the board of Easterline Angus from 1914 until 1922. He was influential in the relocation of this company, initially from Lafayette, Indiana, to the former Prest-O-Lite location on South Street and in 1923 to Speedway, Indiana.[4]

Speedway, Indiana, which continues to be a separate town, is now surrounded by the City of Indianapolis. The town honored its heritage from the founders of the Indianapolis Motor Speedway by naming the four elementary schools in their honor.

13

The Second Year of Racing

With the investment in the Motor Speedway having increased substantially, the partners decided to have three weekends of racing in 1910. Capitalizing on long weekends would enable three days of racing. The races were scheduled for Memorial Day weekend, the 4th of July and Labor Day weekend. Also scheduled was a 24-hour race for August 12 and an Aviation Week.[1]

The racing circuit began in the warmer climates of California and Georgia. As the weather turned warmer and the days grew longer, the racing circuit moved northward. The 1910 racing season began on the Los Angeles dirt racing track, Ascot Park, in March. Continuing the trend set in 1909, the engineering strength of the Marmon team resulted in a strong showing. Marmon race cars finished a close one/two in the 100 mile race. Punctuating this victory, Harroun also won the Ascot 50 mile and 20 mile races.[2]

Having shown well at the Ascot Park races, the Marmon team then faced tests at the Los Angeles Motordrome, a new board track, the following week. As with the races at Ascot Park, Harroun, in different Marmon vehicles, displayed prowess on the track. On April 8, Harroun won the 100 mile race. In the fifty mile race, the Marmon vehicles took first and second. A week later, the Los Angeles Motordrome hosted a two hour free-for-all. Once again, Harroun set the pace. In the two hour run, he covered 148 miles at an average speed of 75 mph. Showing flexibility, the next day Marmon entered the smallest car in a 100 mile race. Once again, Marmon won, sending the Grand Prize Trophy, which also had a $1,000 cash award, back to Indianapolis.[3]

By early May 1910, the racing circuit had traveled to the Atlanta Speedway. The strength of the vehicles manufactured by various companies based in Indianapolis, including Marmon, National, American, and Cole, was underscored in these races. Out of ten total races, Indianapolis drivers won nine of the contests and in many races also finished with a one-two-three sweep of the race. Harroun continued his winning ways in his car named

70

"Yellow Jacket," winning three races, including the 10 and 12 mile free-for-all events. Capping off the Atlanta races for Marmon was a victory by Harroun in the 200 mile race driving a 4 cylinder Marmon. Spectators adopted the moniker of "Wasp" for the vehicle.

After the Atlanta races, the racing circuit went to Indianapolis. For those drivers of Indianapolis-based teams, it was good to be back home and in front of the hometown crowd.

Allison, Fisher and Newby understood the importance of showing well in races; it was good advertising for the cars. They entered the Empire "Little Aristocrat" in a three day carnival in late May 1910. Once again, the car's performance was disappointing. In a one mile flying start, Newell Motsinger covered the distance in 107.3 seconds. Other cars participating in the carnival had times in the 41 to 46 second range. The "Little Aristocrat" was also entered in a ten mile free-for-all. Howdy Wilcox won the race driving a National. The Empire entry finished four minutes behind all other entrants except for Herb Lytle's car, which crashed.

The local citizenry had high expectations as Memorial Day weekend approached. They had been intently following the feats of the Marmon team and were proud of the results from the Atlanta Speedway. Additionally generating interest in the races were the prizes and trophies to be awarded. The Memorial Day weekend meet was billed as one of the richest auto racing events ever scheduled, with trophies and prizes valued in excess of $22,000. The three days of racing included a 50 mile Remy Grand Brassard Race, a 100 mile Prest-O-Lite Trophy Race and a 200 mile Wheeler-Schebler Trophy Race.

The 1910 season opened Memorial Day weekend with events being held on Friday, Saturday and Monday. The Speedway Helmet Race, a five mile free-for-all, was held on Friday, the first day of racing. The prize for winning this race was $100 plus a $100 weekly salary to the driver as long as it was defended. There were six racers vying, including four Indianapolis manufactured cars. Ray Harroun was driving a Marmon, Herbert Lytle was in an American and the National team had two cars involved driven by Johnny Aitken and Tom Kincaid. Bob Burman, a salaried factory driver for Buick, won the race.[4]

The final race on May 27 was for the Prest-O-Lite Trophy, valued at $1,400. Hourran, driving a Marmon, was favored to win the race. He led the first twelve laps on the way to establishing new 20 and 30 mile records. On the 13th lap, the car broke a valve. With Harroun heading to the pits, the lead was taken over by his teammate, Joe Dawson, who set five new records for 40, 50, 60, 70 and 80 miles. He had built a lead of 2½ miles (one lap) on the second place car driven by Tom Kincaid in a National Motorcar. With only five laps to go, a spark plug went bad and Dawson limped into the pits. The lead was then assumed by Tom Kincaid, who won the race. As with the Atlanta races, the Indianapolis drivers made a strong showing, winning four of the eight races on the first day of racing.

The Wheeler-Schebler Trophy Race of 200 miles was the feature event for Saturday, May 28. The trophy, a Tiffany art piece with a value of $10,000, was highly desired as it was the largest and most valuable of any trophies offered in the racing circuit. Additionally, there was a $10,000 cash prize. This race attracted one of the greatest fields of cars and drivers in America. There were nineteen entries. Marmon's entry was a six cylinder version of the Marmon 32, driven by Harroun, who won the race.[5]

On the final day of racing, the premier event was the Remy Grand Brassard Trophy Cup. This fifty mile race had an award of $2,500 to the manufacturer plus a small silver armband and $75 per week in salary to the driver as long as the Brassard was defended. The majority of the race was a two car duel between Harroun in a Marmon and Frank Fox in a Pope-Hartford. Harroun led the first two laps and Frank Fox led the next two laps. Then the drivers changed the lead on each of the next four laps. On the ninth lap, Fox began having tire failure and Harroun took the lead. Harroun finished the race, setting new records for 20, 30 and 40 and 50 miles.[6]

The Memorial Day weekend events were considered to be a resounding success. The new track had held up well to the punishment of the vehicles. With forty-two different races, the only accident was Herb Lytle, whose car spun out and overturned. He sustained a broken leg.[7] Additionally, many new records were set.[8] Pleasing the hometown crowd, the Indianapolis drivers won 12 of the 24 races, Harroun and Aitken winning four each and Caleb Bragg winning three races in one day.[9] The partners were also pleased, as the crowds were the largest to date. Allison estimated the paying gate to be 60,000. With a successful racing weekend, the partners looked forward to the upcoming July Fourth weekend races.[10]

In between the short four weeks between Memorial Day and the 4th of July, the Speedway played host to an "aviation" week featuring Wilbur and Orville Wright, who were credited with the first sustained powered flight (at Kitty Hawk, North Carolina). The Wrights, based in nearby Dayton, Ohio, were naturally among the leading aviators of that time.[11] The Speedway partners anticipated a large turnout for the events. However, the opening day of the aviation week was a disappointment in terms of crowd support — a mere 1,000 spectators. But those spectators were thrilled with the display of flying exhibited by Walter Brookins, who flew a Wright biplane to an altitude of 4,384 feet, a world record.[12] The next day, attendance soared to 19,000. Of the 11 entries in the aviation meet, six were on the Wright Brothers team and four were from Indianapolis. One feature of the event was Carl Baumhofer's wind wagon, which was a regular stock Overland automobile aided by a wooden airplane propeller. This contraption, in a race against an automobile, obtained a speed of 53 mph.[13] On the fourth day of Aviation Week, Brookins set a new world's record. His instruments indicated he had reached 5,300 feet, but engineers determined that the actual height was 4,938 feet.[14]

In June 1910, management of Empire Motorcar Company announced that for 1911 they would produce only one model (the "C"). Designed as a two seat roadster, it was priced at $950 and had extras such as a "racy type top" for $50, a folding glass front for $25 and a Prest-O-Lite tank fitted to the car with the gas line installed for $20.

In contrast to the success of the Memorial Day races, the racing events over the July Fourth and Labor Day weekends were disappointing. Joe Dawson of the Marmon team won the Cobe Trophy Race, a 200 mile event. His effort clipped 10 minutes, 28 seconds off of the previous record.

The Empire Motorcar participated in the July events and turned in its best performance. Charlie Merz drove the car in a one mile flying start with a time of 63.38 seconds. It also participated in a 10 mile free-for-all and finished 16th out of a 20 entrant field. After having proclaimed for the past year that the Empire could run with any other car and not having the performances measure up to the promotion, Allison, Fisher and Newby stopped the promotion. The Empire's racing days were over.[15]

With attendance estimated at 20,000 people over the July Fourth weekend, management reconsidered both the 24-hour event scheduled for August 12 and the Labor Day races. They decided to cancel the 24-hour race and reduce the Labor Day races to a two day event rather than the original three.[16]

During the Labor Day races, there was a very exciting five mile race. Although there were ten participants, the race quickly became a four car contest. In the first of two laps, less than one second separated Aitken, Harroun, Dawson and Greiner. During the second lap, each of these drivers had a time at the lead of the race. As the cars came thundering out of the fourth turn, all four cars were in the race. The winner of the race was Aitken in a National, followed closely by Dawson, Greiner and Harroun; less than a second separated the cars.[17]

One of the motivators for automobile companies to maintain race cars was the advertising value of winning. Marmon was taking full advantage of the publicity factor of their wins during the 1910 racing season. By the end of the season, Marmon had entered 93 contests and won 25, finished second in 24 and third in 13.[18] To capitalize on this success, their ads frequently resembled a newspaper sporting page extolling the success of their cars and drivers. Disappointing to both Nordyke & Marmon as well as the Indianapolis fans was the announcement by Harroun of his retirement from the sport.

Although the track was profitable in 1910, the partners were disappointed with the declining interest as the season progressed. In evaluating the 1910 season, Allison, Fisher, Newby and Wheeler discussed potential causes. Ultimately they decided that there was nothing to differentiate the races at the Indianapolis Motor Speedway from those at other tracks. Given the proliferation of tracks featuring short races, unless there was an overarching reason to be in attendance many people wouldn't journey from a long distance to see the races in Indianapolis. They could view the same types of races closer to home. Thus began the quest by the partners to find a formula which would differentiate the races at the Indianapolis Motor Speedway from all other races.

14

The Inaugural Indianapolis 500

In the discussions among the partners about the format of the races in 1911, Fisher hearkened back to his European travels. He had attended several races which attracted tens of thousands of spectators. He proposed to Allison, Wheeler and Newby that they differentiate the Indianapolis Motor Speedway by establishing a one of a kind event that would bring the best of the world's racers to Indianapolis.[1] Fisher felt that a 24-hour race would be an ultimate test of both man and machine. Allison believed the solution would be to offer fewer races and raise the prices.[2] The owners discussed the pros and cons of a 24-hour race and a 1,000 mile race. Newby interjected his opinion that both a 1,000 mile race and a 24-hour race would not be well received by the spectators. They were just too long. He felt the maximum length of the race should be six to seven hours, which was about 500 miles.[3] In making the decision about the 1911 racing format, one of the questions the owners asked was what the drivers and the manufacturers thought about either a 24-hour or a 1,000 mile race.

By the time the owners met again, Allison had talked with various manufacturers. He had learned that, although they were willing to go along with whatever the owners decided, the manufacturers favored a 24-hour race. The manufacturers understood that winning this type of race would prove the durability of the vehicles which would increase the demand for their product.

The race drivers didn't have a preference over the format of the race. When they tired, whether the race was for 24 hours or 1,000 miles, they would have a relief driver assume the driving.[4]

When an agreement was reached, the partners announced a 500-mile race, which was met with great enthusiasm. To increase the interest in the race, the owners decided to make the prizes far greater than what had previously been the practice at automobile races. For the premier Indianapolis 500-mile race, the partners provided $20,000 in cash prizes, of which

$10,000 would go to the winner of the race, thus making the Indianapolis 500 the highest paying sporting event in the world.[5]

The decision to hold the race on Memorial Day, May 30, 1911, was based on a couple of factors. The date was between the planting and harvesting of crops. By selecting a date in late May, the race would not normally face the hot, humid weather that often occurs in Indianapolis during the summer, which could depress attendance. Also entering into the decision was that the Memorial Day weekend races in 1910 had seen the highest attendance for any race during the two year history of the track.

The decision to have a huge purse for the race had the impact the owners desired by creating a lot of media attention. The first entry for the race arrived at Speedway headquarters on October 22 from J.I. Case Threshing Machine Company. By May 1, when all entries for the race were required to be submitted, there were 45 entrants. A new requirement was the paying of a substantial entry fee of $500. Although the Speedway had historically charged entry fees, the one set for the inaugural Indianapolis 500 was substantial in part to insure that only those truly interested in racing submitted entries.[6]

Although the Indianapolis race was one of the events which counted towards the AAA National Championship, the impact of the purse in short order caused the Indianapolis 500 race to take on a life of its own — to become THE RACE. There were many drivers and engineers who thought that the remainder of the AAA season was merely a warm-up to the event. Some even chose to skip the other races and concentrate solely on the Indianapolis 500. This resulted in many teams relocating to Indianapolis and the racetrack's importance in testing increased.[7] Even today, the racetrack is used by various auto racing teams to test their vehicles.

Changes were also made in the Speedway staff. Earnest Moross left to become the United States representative for Fiat. Theodore E. ("Pop") Myers, who was employed by the Globe Realty Company, the Speedway, Indiana, real estate company owned by Fisher and Allison, was hired to handle ticket sales and to run the office. Miss Eloise ("Dolly") Dallenbach was hired as Myers' assistant. Publicity was to be handled by C.E. ("Heinie") Shuart. Myers' nickname of "Pop" was given to him by Shuart, who had nicknames for many of the drivers.[8]

With the announcement of the first 500-mile race, Howard Marmon approached Harroun and asked him to reconsider his decision to retire from racing. As told in *Marmon Racing: Winning with the Wasp*, Marmon asked Harroun to drive the Wasp "just once more." Harroun responded, "No, I'm finished with racing. You won't need me anyway. Dawson could do just as well as I could." Marmon, who had been thinking about entering a second car in the race, broached the idea of Harroun's designing a four cylinder car, as it had the same type engine they were offering to the public. Harroun replied, "It probably would be just as fast if the piston displacement is comparable, but it wouldn't be as smooth, and I don't believe it would have as much chance of going the distance." Marmon, however, was insistent and asked Harroun to work out some of the bore and stroke combinations for a four.

Within a week Harroun had completed the preliminary designs and specifications for a large four with a displacement of just under five hundred cubic inches and an improved six cylinder for the Wasp as well. Yet Harroun remained noncommittal about driving the race, offering all sorts of reasons why he shouldn't, including the fact that "five hundred miles is too far for anyone to drive at high speeds." Marmon agreed, but was one step ahead of him on that point. Marmon had a relief driver available, Cyrus Patschke, who was prepared to give Harroun a break at 200 miles. Marmon tried to assuage Harroun's concerns: "He's had a lot of road racing experience in the East. I had a letter from him asking for an opening on the Marmon team. He helped Mulford win a twenty-four hour race at Long Island last year and shouldn't have any trouble getting acquainted with the car and track. How about it?" Harroun finally consented.[9]

In many ways, the financial success of the race hinged on the drivers who would be involved in the race. The lure for the manufacturers and the drivers was the prize money offered by the track. But the drawing card for many spectators was the drivers. Just as today, race teams had supporters and individual race car drivers were important to the success of a race. One of the best known racers of the time, Oldfield, was ineligible for the race as he had been placed on suspension by the AAA Contest Board for participating in unsanctioned events.[10] The disqualification of Oldfield was a disappointment to many racing enthusiasts.

Although there had been infractions before, the one leading to his suspension was the result of a long-simmering feud between Jack Johnson, the reigning heavyweight champion, and Oldfield's friend Jeff Jeffries. Jeffries was a boxing phenomenon at the turn of the century, having won the world heavyweight title. Jeffries retired from the sport in 1905. In 1908, Jack Johnson had defeated Tommy Burns to win the world heavyweight title. Johnson was not a popular title holder and a movement grew to encourage Jeffries to come out of retirement and regain the title. Although he was badly out of shape, Jeffries agreed to the fight, which took place on July 4, 1910. An out of shape Jeffries who had not fought in five years was no contest for Johnson and was soundly defeated.[11]

After the fight, Oldfield accompanied Jeffries on a Colorado fishing trip. At the conclusion of the expedition, Oldfield told the press that Johnson had won the fight because Jeffries was drugged. Upon hearing this, Johnson denied the accusation and challenged Oldfield to a road race, betting $5,000 that he could defeat Oldfield. Johnson had some previous race car experience, having driven in and won several of the previous winter's Southern California Racing Carnival. Oldfield accepted the challenge and his publicist, Will Pickens, was enthusiastic about the idea and began the publicity. The race was scheduled for Sheepshead Bay, a dirt track in New York, in October 1910. The AAA Contest Board did not agree to this unsanctioned race and sternly warned both Oldfield and Pickens that if they proceeded with the "unsanctioned farce" they would both be permanently suspended. Oldfield just wanted to settle the score with Johnson.[12] As it was believed that the AAA Contest Board was posturing and would never follow through on the sanctioned threat, preparations for the race continued.

Oldfield and Johnson met for the duel on October 25, 1910, with Johnson driving a Thomas Flyer and Oldfield piloting a 60 hp Knox. Oldfield easily won the first five mile race. Pickens encouraged Oldfield to make the second race more interesting. Oldfield complied with a slower speed; however, he stayed slightly ahead of Johnson throughout the second race. After the running of this contest, the AAA Contest Board immediately acted upon their word and suspended both Oldfield and Pickens. Stunned and hurt by this action, Oldfield fought this decision in court but was not successful. Without being able to participate in AAA sanctioned races, Oldfield continued to barnstorm throughout the United States. By 1911, he had earned enough money through barnstorming to retire. The former publicity man for the Indianapolis Motor Speedway, Earnest Moross, took over Oldfield's "Blitzen Benz" as well as two other racing cars.[13]

Although they had realized several years of racing success, the Marmon team did not start well in the 1911 season. They were disappointed with second and third place finishes in the Savannah Challenge held in early May. In the Vanderbilt Cup, Bob Burman, who had switched from the Buick team to Marmon, finished second, while teammate Bruce Brown finished a distant twelfth.[14]

Tire failure in the early years of auto racing was a regular occurrence. To see if they could uncover a solution for the tire failures, Nordyke & Marmon engineers had been running tests to determine the speed thresholds of the tire failures. The Marmon racing team felt a great deal of pressure, as the success of the race cars indirectly impacted the brand's reputation and thus its sales. If the team did well in the upcoming race, Marmon intended to continue the advertising of their superior engineering. The results of their tests at the Indianapolis Motor Speedway only heightened their concern about their chances for success in the quickly approaching race. In mid–May, Harroun and Patschke took the Wasp to the racetrack for practice runs. Other teams were also on the track practicing. The results of the tests were that the Wasp could complete a lap (2½ miles) with an average speed of 80 mph. Unfortunately, they also discovered that several rivals were considerably faster.[15]

But Harroun had an observation about the autos that were running faster. "Almost every time someone has passed me in practice, it is back in the pits a few laps to change tires. Anyone running flat out all the way will beat himself changing tires," Harroun told management.[16] Although his initial training was in dentistry, Harroun had become an engineer with Nordyke & Marmon. He suggested a higher gear ratio. Harroun and the Marmon racing team also worked out a strategy of running the race at an average 75 mph, which would save the wear on the tires and hopefully decrease the number of tire failures. Harroun assured Howard Marmon that if after 100 miles of racing this speed was too slow it could be increased.[17]

There were only two entry requirements for the inaugural 500 mile race: the vehicle's engine displacement could not exceed 500 cubic inches and the vehicle could run a quarter of a mile at better than 75 mph. Of the 46 entrants for the race, 40 vehicles qualified for the race. The starting position was determined by when the entry form was received. The intermingling of both fast and slow cars was a formula for multiple wrecks.

Always looking for promotional ideas to increase interest in the race, Speedway partners pursued the idea of breaking the speed record for one mile then held by Oldfield. Since Barney was disqualified, which driver would be selected for this attempt? On the day before the inaugural Indianapolis 500-mile race in front of 5,000 spectators, Bob Burman, in the "Blitzen" Benz, set a blistering pace, shattering the record with an average speed of 102.127 mph.[18]

That afternoon, Fisher led the entrants in a dress rehearsal of what was to become a tradition. The race was to be started in a rolling fashion rather than from the traditional standing start. The cars were arranged in eight rows, each containing five cars.[19]

Driving the white 1911 Stoddard-Dayton, Fisher, with Allison seated next to him, began rolling down the track. By the backstretch, he was traveling 60 mph. As the vehicles rounded the fourth turn of the track, rather than being in orderly rows, the cars were spread all over the track. A meeting was quickly convened and the drivers complained that they couldn't see the pace car at 60 mph with five cars in a row. An agreement was reached to have the pace lap be at 40 mph.[20]

Harroun's creativity was involved in a controversy that almost disqualified his car from the race. At the time of the inaugural 500, although it was not required, all racing vehicles had two occupants — the driver and the racing mechanic. In 1910, Harroun had designed a single seat vehicle which he had driven in various races, including those at the Indianapolis Motor Speedway. By 1911, the car had been streamlined. Suddenly, other drivers took notice and raised the concern that without a riding mechanic he would be unaware of someone attempting to pass, thus creating a hazard.[21]

When Harroun was a chauffeur to William Thorne, president of Montgomery Ward, he had seen an horse drawn taxicab with a crude mirror. The driver had attached a mirror to a pole, which he used to check for bicycles coming from behind.[22] Without room for a riding mechanic, Harroun faced expulsion from the race. Harroun reasoned that if he could fashion a mirror for the car, he would not need a riding mechanic. He experimented and created a steel frame mirror which was welded by four rods to the cowling of the car. Other drivers and racing teams cried foul, thinking that this gave him an unfair advantage. Despite the driver protest, Harroun was permitted to race on that May day in the Wasp without a riding mechanic.[23]

Speedway management was anticipating strong attendance at the race. Seat sales had started on April 4 and were quickly sold out. As a result, an additional grandstand was built at the Speedway to accommodate the anticipated crowd.[24] Another method employed by the Speedway to increase attendance was the use of "the world's biggest band," composed of volunteers carrying instruments marching down the straightaway. If you played in the band, there was no fee for admittance to the race.[25]

Allison, Fisher and Newby, who had been very focused on the inaugural running of the Indianapolis 500 as well as their other business interests, turned their attention to the Empire Motorcar Company. Robert Hassler had been running the company without direction from the other partners. When they reviewed the records of Empire Motorcar Company, they were confronted with results much worse than they had thought.

In an attempt to restructure Empire Motorcar Company, they hired Harry Stutz as the designer and factory manager of the company. At the time of the announcement, Stutz, the former chief engineer and designer for Marion Motorcar Company, was selling auto parts. In announcing the change, the partners announced that Stutz was "making radical and beneficial changes in the design of this car." What was unknown to the partners when they hired Stutz is that he was designing his own car. With five weeks before

Memorial Day, he developed a car which ran in the 1911 race. His focus was on his own design rather than on the Empire. It did not take long for Stutz's involvement in Empire Motorcar to end. By the end of 1911, the company was sold and the factory was retooled to manufacture Prest-O-Lite starters.[26]

On Memorial Day in 1911, the Speedway gates were opened around 8:00 A.M. By 9:00 A.M. between 75,000 and 80,000 people were in the stands waiting for the race to start. To acquaint the spectators with the cars and their drivers, each of the 40 cars in the field made a trip around the oval one at a time.

Shortly before 10 A.M., a bomb exploded at the south end of the pits signaling that the race was about to begin. The cars went to their positions on the racetrack.[27] At the next bomb explosion, Fisher, dressed in a white suit, drove the white Stoddard-Dayton car in the pace lap with Allison seated next to him. Behind the pace car were the forty racers. They went around the first and second turns and down the backstretch gaining speed. As they rounded the fourth turn and started down the straightaway, a final bomb rose and exploded into a huge starry flag as the pace car pulled off into the pits. The first Indianapolis 500-mile race was underway![28]

Indianapolis favorite Johnny Aitken, in a National, quickly took the lead but it was short lived. Amateur driver Spencer Wishart, in a Mercedes, took the lead on lap 5. By lap 10, Fred Belcher had gained control of the first place position. By the 50 mile point, Ralph DePalma had raced into the lead.[29]

Also participating in the race was Edd Rickenbacker driving a Firestone-Columbus, which had been developed by the Columbus Buggy Company of Columbus, Ohio. Rickenbacker drove his first race at Red Oak, Iowa, in June 1910 in the Firestone-Columbus car.[30] Although injured in the race when he lost control going through a curve and the car flipped, Rickenbacker was quickly bitten by the racing bug.[31] For the first Indianapolis 500, Rickenbacker was a relief driver for Lee Frayer, owner of the Columbus Buggy Company, in the four-cylinder Firestone-Columbus. Rickenbacker took over the driving duties early in the race. Frayer resumed driving at the four hundred mile mark, wanting to be part of the exciting end of the race. The car placed a respectable eleventh.[32]

Harroun, sticking to the strategy of an average 75 mph, was running respectably in fifth place at the 75 mile mark. At one hundred miles, Harroun had moved into second place.[33] At 175 miles, Harroun drove into the pits and was replaced by Cyrus Patschke according to the plan.[34]

By 250 miles (lap 100), new records had been set for 150, 200 and 250 miles.[35] On lap 100, Patschke returned to the pits and Harroun resumed the

Ray Harroun, winner of the inaugural Indianapolis 500 race in the Marmon Wasp, 1911 (courtesy Indianapolis Motor Speedway).

driving responsibilities of the Wasp. At that point, the Wasp was in second place. Around lap 100, the stress on tires caused them to begin to fail. Mulford had just passed DePalma and Aitken to move into second place when his right front tire exploded.

Driving intentionally, neither Brown nor Harroun had experienced tire failure. Brown, with an average speed of 78 mph, was leading the race and made a pit stop to change his tires. At the end of the 102nd lap, he was still in the lead. He lost a tire at the south end of the course and ran two miles on the rim to get back to the pits. It took nearly three minutes to get the tire changed. During this time, Harroun was able to take the lead.

Other cars were experiencing other difficulties. After reentering the race, Brown experienced ignition failure, which ended his racing day. Chevrolet and Aitken also dropped out of the race due to parts failures and Stang was a victim of failure in the steering.

Meanwhile, the track was becoming increasingly slick with oil that dropped from the vehicles. The Speedway crew were throwing shovels of sand on the track, particularly in the corners, to try to counterbalance the effects of the oil. Harroun, who was in first place, was finding it difficult to maintain an average 75 mph.[36]

By 300 miles, it had become a two car race — Harroun in the Marmon Wasp and Mulford in the Lozier.[37] On lap 137, Harroun's right rear tire exploded and Mulford took the lead. Within 10 minutes, Mulford made a pit stop to get new tires. His tire change was slow, as a rim had been damaged, and Harroun retook the lead. When Mulford returned to the track, he was chasing the Wasp. Averaging 80 mph, he was gaining on Harroun with every lap. With 24 laps remaining, Mulford pulled abreast of Harroun, regaining the lead on the backstretch. His lead did not last long. Within 5 laps, Mulford needed to make another pit stop and Harroun retook the lead. Harroun drove the final 19 laps and entered the record books as the winner of the inaugural Indianapolis 500 with an average speed of 74.59 mph. The race took 6 hours and 42 minutes. For his effort, Harroun received the first place prize of $10,000.[38]

During the summer of 1911, the AAA Contest Board imposed some new restrictions on auto racing. The first was the requirement that all vehicles have riding mechanics. This action prohibited a repeat of the win by Harroun without a riding mechanic. Whether or not this action influenced his decision is not known, but Harroun again announced his retirement from racing. Shortly thereafter, Ray Harroun left Nordyke & Marmon to start a carburetor manufacturing business.

15

Prest-O-Lite Building Collapses

In compliance with the city ordinance prohibiting filling operations inside the city limits, Prest-O-Lite transferred the operations of the charging plant to the new facility on River Road. The product line of Prest-O-Lite had been expanded to include the manufacture of electric starters at the South Street facility. This product was well received and the existing South Street facility was thus too small.

The partners decided to expand the plant by adding another story to the existing plant and to construct a new building adjacent to the South Street facility. Given the rapid growth of the business, the architect, Herbert Foltz, designed the new building to be two stories, with the structure being able to accommodate an additional story if needed. Allison explained the decision: "When we planned that building, we had not perfected the Presto automobile starter. Some weeks ago, however, the patent was obtained and we found that we would need more space in the building. We then consulted with Herbert Foltz, our architect. In the original plans, the building was designed as a two story structure built, however, to accommodate a third floor if we ever found it necessary to build one."[1]

Work began in early December and all three stories of the new building were framed, the concrete was poured and the roof was being installed. Up until then, Indianapolis had experienced a relatively mild winter, but a cold front blew through after the pouring of the concrete for the third floor.

The next day was bitterly cold. The workers arrived and built a fire on the third floor as a heat source. Although the third floor was sufficiently hardened to support the men, they were unaware that it was not properly cured. Throughout the morning hours, work progressed as anticipated. After a lunch break, the workmen heard the whistle calling them back to work. Some men were climbing up the ladders to their workplaces. Others had just picked up their tools and the clang of the first hammers echoed throughout the neighborhood. Suddenly, with a grinding shriek, the central part of the cement structure gave way. The workmen on the roof or near the windows hurled themselves from the structure and fell to the ground, while the workmen in the center of the building fell into the chasm along with tons of rubble. What had been an orderly workplace only moments earlier was transformed into chaos, the air punctuated by the screams of those men trapped in the rubble.

J.W. Skeel, a carpenter, was one of approximately twenty workers on the roof when the building collapsed: "There wasn't any warning. Frank Jessup was right near me and some of the other men were not far away. I yelled to him as the roof seemed to sink under us and we went down. I didn't seem to know anything until a minute after when I was strangling and in darkness. Then I realized what had happened and after the dust cleared a little, I could see above me through crevices in the wreckage. The sunshine looked mighty good."[2]

Frank Bowman, the foreman of the steam fitters, and Gus Krueger, a steam fitter, were entering the building at the moment the center began to collapse. Bowman later recalled shutting his eyes and putting his hands over his ears to shut out the crash of the falling pillars and cables, which was followed by a rain of smaller materials loosened on the upper floors. Not injured during the collapse of the interior of the building, Bowman and Krueger immediately began trying to free some of the trapped men. By clutching the arms and legs of the victims, they were able to drag several from the debris.[3]

Throughout the neighborhood, the men's cries could be heard. Across the alley from the building was St. Vincent's Hospital. Nurses and attendants from St. Vincent's as well as Prest-O-Lite workers rushed to the scene. Calls went out to the police headquarters and the nearby fire stations. As the responders arrived, they noticed a small fire which had broken out in the northwest corner of the building and immediately extinguished it.

As soon as the injured were rescued, they were rushed towards St. Vincent's Hospital where a line of nurses, doctors and stretchers awaited. The wounds were dressed at the hospital. Those people not seriously wounded immediately joined the search for those who were missing.

News of the accident spread rapidly by telephone to shops, factories and homes near the building. Mothers, wives and children of many of the workmen rushed to the scene to learn the fate of their loved ones. Curiosity seekers also thronged to the site of the disaster. The police quickly stretched ropes to restrain the spectators who were crowding the nearby streets, alleys and driveways. In order to control the crowd, reserve police were called from outlying districts.[4]

After all the victims who could be seen were cared for, a more thorough search was made of the collapsed site to determine if there were others still buried beneath the debris. Suddenly, a faint cry was heard at the northeast corner of the building. "Help me out, men! I'm here beneath a chuck of cement," called a trapped man. The workmen placed some heavy timbers beneath some of the wreckage and, using a fulcrum, lifted some of the debris, allowing some air in. Through the hole, they saw A.H. Dixon. They encouraged him to lie still until they could get him out. The workmen and firemen worked trying to raise the huge chunks of cement that surrounded Dixon. He helped in his own rescue, calling out to them to adjust a hoisting jack to the northeast corner of a cement block and also advising where, from his vantage point, a bar might be inserted which would help to relieve some of the pressure on his body.

Doctors who were on the scene inquired how he was feeling. He responded: "I'm all right, except that I'm getting a little weak in the legs. They are under a lot of dirt and cement. Have you got a drink of water handy? The dust is fierce." Since they were not yet able to reach Dixon, the rescuers inserted a long tube into the hole. When it got to Dixon, he put it to his lips and was able to quench his thirst. Later, to ease some of the pain and to lower Dixon's anxiety, the rescuers also provided some whiskey in the same manner.

After a considerable period of time, the hole was enlarged enough so that Dr. G.A. Petersdorf could examine Dixon, who remained trapped by the cement and cables. Dr. Petersdorf was able to relieve some pain by administering a pain reliever. Meanwhile, at the Prest-O-Lite plant, some of the workmen removed a brazing machine and carried it to the collapsed building. This machine was able to sever the girders which had entombed Dixon. Picks and shovels were then used to dig a ditch around him. At long last, the blocks of cement were hoisted away and around 4:30 P.M. Dixon was freed from the entrapment. He was rushed by gurney to St. Vincent's Hospital. Although he didn't have any internal injuries, his left foot was crushed and was later amputated.[5]

Dixon was one of the lucky ones. Throughout the night, using search lights, the rescuers continued to search for the victims of the accident. Found under tons of rubble on the first floor were the bodies of seven men. An additional 21 were injured, one of whom died later. All of the men who were killed were working on either the second or third floor when the collapse happened.

Otto Hoffmeister, a structural ironworker, gave his first person account of surviving the collapse of the building: "The crash came almost without warning. I heard the creaking of the cables. The building seemed to sway and I jumped. The next thing I knew, a pile of wreckage lay where the cement building had stood only a moment before."

Controversy immediately followed the accident. Harry Wilson, a night watchman at St. Vincent's Hospital, said that he had noticed the floor on the west side of the second story of the building sagging, which created a bulge in the west wall several days before the collapse. He told several workmen about his observations and they promised to bring it to the attention of the building superintendent. To the press, he said, "I have been expecting just such an accident as this. That building, more than two days ago, was in no condition to permit the employment of laborers there. Why that second floor, near the center, sagged fully two inches and the wall to the west bulged out so that you could notice it easily by looking across it on a straight line with the corners. Of course, I don't know much about building, but I do know that there was something wrong at that plant and that the awful accident could have been avoided if steps had been taken to brace that weakened part."[6]

Edward R. Wolfe, one of the owners of the contractor, Wolfe & Ewing, did not know why the building collapsed. "The supports beneath were as they should be. As to the bulging of the wall," Mr. Wolfe told the press, "there is nothing to that statement. If the wall bulged, I was not aware of it. But I believe there was no bulge there or it would have been noticed."[7]

The theories about why the building collapsed and which section collapsed first abounded. Some workers believed that the top floor fell and carried the lower floors down with it. Others were of the opinion that the first floor weakened and when it fell through into the basement the weakened supports of the upper structure caused the cave-in. Otto Hoffmeister speculated that the weight of the cement and other materials to be put on the roof that were stacked on the top floor might have caused the collapse.[8]

The third-floor pillars had been poured the previous Saturday and the cement in them might have been too green to handle the weight of the roof and other materials stored on the upper floor. Early in the investigation, this continued to be the best hypothesis, as the cause couldn't be established until all of the debris had been cleared out and the bases of the standing pillars could be examined.

Additionally, some rumors indicated that the owners had encouraged the contractors to rush the building. Allison, in speaking of the accident, said, "I know nothing of the cause of the accident. I walked through the building often while I was in the city and at no time saw anything or heard anything that would have given me cause for alarm. The whole affair was so unexpected and so terrible that I am really in no condition to discuss it." He also addressed the chatter about the building not having the proper permits: "We set to work on the plans for the third floor. They were submitted and accepted. The matter of constructing the addition as well as the building was left to Wolf & Ewing, the contractors and Foltz, the architect."[9]

Foltz indicated that he was in no position to attempt to place the blame for the accident or to discuss the responsibility. He also addressed the rumors about the third floor not having the proper permits:

> After the second story was under way and Messrs. Allison and Fisher found that they would need additional floor space, I was directed to proceed with the additional story. The drawings and specifications were prepared and the contract for the third story was awarded. According to the terms of the original contract, the firm of Wolf & Ewing, the contractors, obtained the building permit and the terms and conditions of the contract of the third story addition were the same as those of the original agreement. The question whether the building permit for the third story addition was necessary is a matter to be settled between the building inspector and the contractor.[10]

Very quickly, the building inspector, T.A. Winterrowd, determined that there was a building permit for the two story building and the additional story to the existing Prest-O-Lite building. But when the new building was expanded to include a third floor, the contractor failed to take out the necessary permit for the addition. As a result, the city filed charges against Edward Wolfe and Charles Ewing for this oversight.[11]

Calls for a thorough investigation of the collapse of the Prest-O-Lite building were quickly heard. The coroner announced that he was going to pursue an independent investigation. In talking about his approach to investigating the accident Coroner Durham said, "I want to make a clean, thorough and honest investigation of this case and I intend to receive the aid of all witnesses in the case as well. While at present it looks as if the case might be constituted of criminal negligence, I propose to determine the exact cause without fear or favor." He continued that "this cave-in which has cost so many lives, should be a great lesson to builders."[12]

A grand jury was assembled. The first witness was T.A. Winterrowd, who testified for about a half hour. It was believed that he was questioned about the plans for the building which collapsed and when and how it had been inspected. The foreman of the grand jury, George F. Kirkhoff, was a contractor and had some familiarity with reinforced concrete work. He quickly expressed his opposition to reinforcing concrete work in cold weather and favored a law prohibiting that class of work in winter. His opinions had an impact on the grand jury who ordered Mr. Winterrowd to immediately suspend all work on concrete buildings under construction in the city of Indianapolis pending a thorough inspection. Winterrowd was also ordered by the grand jury to refuse to issue a permit for the rebuilding on the site until the building plans were thoroughly scrutinized and approved by his department.

Meanwhile, engineers were busy trying to establish what caused the building to collapse. They studied remnants of the large pillars which supported the several floors in an effort to determine which part of the structure was the first to fall. In excavating, the men came across a pile of cinders lying on the ground beneath the wreckage. These cinders had been on the roof prior to the collapse. The third floor section of a pillar that supported the central part of the building was found buried beneath the crumbled flooring of the first and second stories, many feet to the northwest of the base of the column. The second-floor section lay higher up and nearer the remaining portion of the first-floor pillar, which was standing almost intact. Several of the pillars were found to lean towards the northwest, indicating the pressure caused by the fall of the upper floors was in that direction. Evaluating all of the evidence uncovered, the engineers thought that the roof and upper floor gave way first and fell with great force, crashing through the lower part of the structure.[13]

16

Prest-O-Lite Thrives

Despite the many explosions, not only in Indianapolis but also in other locations, Prest-O-Lite was a thriving company. The company advertised itself as the "World's Largest Makers of Dissolved Acetylene." They had charging plants not only in Indianapolis but also in seventeen other cities in the United States and in Winnipeg, Canada. In addition to the charging plants, there were branch stores and service stations located throughout the United States as well as relationships with various foreign agencies in locations including Vancouver, Calgary, Mexico City, Sydney, Tokyo and Yokohama, as well as Honolulu, Manila and San Juan.

The Prest-O-Lite lighting system had evolved from a simple canister with a tube to supply gas to headlights to a system best described by the company. (The company's system had three options — one for headlights only [cost of $13], one for headlights and tail lights [cost of $16], and one for headlights, sidelights and tail lights [cost of $19.50].) An advertising brochure described the Prest-O-Lite lighting system:

> Pushing the button gives a large electric spark at the burner tips, precisely as an electric door bell is rung by pushing a button. In fact, the Prest-O-Liter is about as simple and as reliable as an electric door bell. The gas is piped to the Controlling Valve within the driver's reach and from there to the lamps. The Prest-O-Lite valve is left open, and the gas is turned on and off at the Controlling Valve. Attached to the Prest-O-Lite is our Automatic Reducing Valve, which is a part of each Prest-O-Liter outfit. This automatically regulates the pressure so that when the gas is turned on, the flame in the lamps can never be too high, but is always correct and needs no adjusting. This valve keeps the pressure in the pipe lines uniform and correct, whether two three, or five lamps are burning, and whether the Prest-O-Lite is full, half full or nearly empty."[1]

As with Gillette and its razor blades and Hewlett-Packard and its inkjet cartridges, the lighting system was not the primary driver of profitability.

Prest-O-Lite factory in Speedway, Indiana, built in 1913. The building was unique due to the multiple large windows (courtesy Indiana Historical Society).

It was the supply of the gas canisters which was effectively an annuity. Prest-O-Lite had its charging plants located in areas where used canisters could be returned as late as 4:00 P.M. and returned the next day by train.

One of the challenges faced by Allison at Prest-O-Lite was the cost of calcium carbide, a key ingredient in the manufacture of acetylene. Union Carbide Company produced the vast majority of calcium carbide, which Allison believed caused the cost of this ingredient to be artificially high. If there was an alternative to calcium carbide, then the profits on the various Prest-O-Lite products could be increased.

With the majority of research in the 1910s centered in universities, Allison made inquiries and discovered that the Mellon Institute of Industrial Research might have the capabilities to pursue research into alternative sources of acetylene. Establishing a Prest-O-Lite Fellowship, George O. Curme, Jr., was hired by Mellon Institute to conduct the research.

Curme received his undergraduate degree in chemistry from Northwestern University. After completing a doctoral degree in chemical engineering from the University of Chicago in 1913, Curme traveled to Germany to continue his studies. Upon his return to the United States in 1915, he became the Prest-O-Lite Illumination Fellow at the Mellon Institute with a focus on finding a cheaper source of acetylene than calcium carbide. Within a year, Curme discovered that in an exothermic process organic liquids could produce not only acetylene but also a hydrocarbon gas rich in ethylene.[2]

The success of Prest-O-Lite led to the building of a new facility near the Indianapolis Motor Speedway. Allison commissioned the design of a three hundred thousand square foot building in 1910 to cost $500,000.[3] Expanding the product line, Prest-O-Lite introduced an acetylene gas starter in 1912 which was operated by a little pump. This starter eliminated the "tiresome, dangerous cranking as the acetylene gas keeps cylinders free from carbon."[4] For a four cylinder starter, the cost was $20 and a six cylinder starter was $25. At the time of the introduction on the starter, Prest-O-Lite had 15,000 exchange agencies throughout the world. It also expanded into batteries with the purchase of Pumpelly Battery Company in 1915.[5]

By the time Prest-O-Lite moved to its new facility in Speedway City on May 12, 1913, the company had expanded from 90,000 sq. ft. The plant's operations included Prest-O-Lite cylinders, Prest-O-Lite torch, Prest-O-Lite welder, Prest-O-Liter and the Prest-O-Lite automatic reducing valve. The company could produce 1,200 Prest-O-Liters a day.[6] Prest-O-Lite was sold by Allison and Fisher to Union Carbide in 1917. In the sale, the partners received one share of Union Carbide stock for two shares of Prest-O-Lite stock.[7] The sales price was $9,000,000.

17

Riverdale Springs

For the first year of her marriage to James Allison, Sara Allison continued to convalesce in Colorado Springs. When she was able to join Allison in Indianapolis, Jim and Sara established their home near the new Prest-O-Lite plant on the south side of Indianapolis on Three Notch Road. With increasing financial resources, Allison began to dream of an estate.

On the northwest side of Indianapolis, White River gently meanders through a wide flood plain. On the west side of White River was River Road, where Carl and Jane Fisher had built a home, "Blossom Heath." Frank Wheeler, another associate of Allison in the Indianapolis Motor Speedway, was also planning to build a home on River Road. Allison decided to purchase the property adjacent to Fisher's home on the north side. The area was still outside of the city limits and had historically been agricultural.

The property purchased was 62 acres of gently rolling land. On the River Road side, the southeast side of the property had a knoll overlooking the river. This small part of the property had been under cultivation for fifty years and included an apple orchard and cornfields. The larger part of the property consisting of 45 acres was a marshland, with Crooked Creek running through it. When the snow melted and spring rains came to Indianapolis, the land surrounding Crooked Creek frequently flooded and this part of the property was not under cultivation.[1]

As the United States transformed from an agrarian based economy to an industrial economy, there was a rapid growth in the number of very wealthy people. Beginning in the late 1800s, capitalists began building large country estates to reflect their position in society.[2] The building of Riverdale Springs was a statement of Allison's success. A perfectionist, Allison wanted the finest of craftsmen and materials in the home.

Allison hired the noted landscape architect Jens Jensen to design the landscape for the property. Jensen was born in 1860 near Dybbol, not far from Slesvig, Denmark, to a prosperous farming family. When his family disapproved of his marriage, Jensen immigrated to the United States.[3] Settling in Chicago, Illinois, in the mid–1880s, he and his family would travel on the weekends to the countryside, where he would observe natural landscapes. Working for the Chicago Parks Department, Jensen became the designer of Chicago's West Park Department. By 1895, he was the superintendent of Union Park and in 1896, he was appointed the superintendent of Humboldt Park.[4] The Chicago park system was run by political appointees and political corruption was rampant. Jensen lost his job in 1900 with the Parks Department as he chose not to participate in the political graft.[5]

Jensen who had developed friendships among Chicago's wealthy elite, began designing landscapes for individuals as a source of income after losing his job. His estate work ranged from designs for one acre to designs for hundreds of acres. Around 1910, Jensen designed the landscape for the estate of Sears & Roebuck's founder, Julius Rosenwald, in Highland Park, Illinois. The work for Rosenwald led to commissions by wealthy individuals building homes on Chicago's North Shore, which led to Jensen's work becoming a status symbol.[6]

By 1905, Jensen had returned to the Chicago Parks Department. He is best known for the consolidation of multiple greenhouses throughout the Chicago park system to Garfield Park, where he designed a conservatory that was the largest of its kind when it opened in 1907. The opening drew 25,000 visitors a day.[7]

Allison had met Jensen when Jensen did the landscape design for Fisher's home, Blossom Heath, in 1910.[8] Allison's selection of Jensen for the landscape design was a good fit for the topography of Riverdale Springs. Jensen's work was known for naturalistic settings with broad, flat water features — which Jensen called prairie rivers — areas of wildflowers and gently curving paths which would open up to a meadow and shady areas.[9] Another aspect of his landscaping was stonework that emulated limestone bluffs.[10] Jensen's prairie landscape design would complement the prairie style residence being designed by Herbert Bass, an Indianapolis architect. In the winter of 1911, Jensen surveyed the property and sited the home on the knoll overlooking the White River.

Herbert Bass designed the exterior of the home to be a blend of early Prairie School design combined with a Lombardy Villa. The two story house has a shallow-pitch hip roof with overhanging eaves. The exterior is constructed of deep red brick imported from Italy.[11] Many houses built in Indianapolis during the early 1900s were constructed either of dark red brick or wood painted dark colors. During the gray overcast winters, the houses blended into the sky. Although much larger than the typical Indianapolis house of the period, this home's exterior is plain.

Just down the road, Frank Wheeler was building his home, designed by the Philadelphia firm of McLanahan & Price. This house, called "Hawk-eye," is a Mediterranean looking villa with buff-colored brick walls and a green Spanish tile roof.[12] This house was a departure from the style of house built in Indianapolis and did not fade into the landscape during the long, dreary winter.

Jensen's landscape design for Riverdale used the natural topography of the property. The placement of the house allowed for views of both the formal and vegetable gardens and White River on the south side and Crooked Creek and the marshland to the north.[13] Jensen created a formal garden extending from the house that was delineated by two walkways, one to the west and one to the marshland. As the property had a significant slope down to the marshland, benches were placed to allow for enjoyment of the views. To the north side of the house, Jensen placed grape arbors. Just as on the south side of the house, viewing of the marshland was encouraged through the placement of limestone benches.[14]

One of the distinctive aspects of a Jensen design was the creation of a "player's green," a space for outdoor dramas, musical offerings or recitations. The stage was usually designed as a small clearing carved out of the edge of a wood, often with a background of red cedar. This design element was featured near the house and was anchored by red cedars. The placement of the player's green facing west allowed for views of the setting sun, as the performances generally started at dusk.

At the edge of the south side of the property was an existing apple orchard and a stable. Jensen utilized the apple orchard and incorporated a vegetable garden. The vegetable garden on one end had a greenhouse and a garage. At the other end was a tennis court. The greenhouse, which was divided into four sections covering over an acre, increased the cultivation area by 50 percent.

On the north side of the house, the property had a significant slope, in excess of 60 percent, to Crooked Creek and the marshland. The marshland and Crooked Creek were ideal design elements for Jensen. One of the most recognizable features of a Jensen landscape is a broad, flat body of water (the "prairie rivers"). The stonework with which Jensen backed many of these rivers was an attempt to capture the feeling of "the prairie bluff or stratified rock" of rivers and streams. Although typically the source of Jensen's water features was in a shady, rocky ledge, much as a natural spring emanates from a limestone aquifer, Crooked Creek provided a water supply. In some of Jensen's estate designs, these streams then emptied into small pools of water backed by a grove of arborvitae, cedar or hemlock with white birch and other light trunked trees as accents in the foreground. Some of these pools were intended for viewing in the moonlight.[15]

At the bottom of the slope, Jensen designed a large lake, which was created by the removal of four feet of soil from the area. Fed by a natural spring, the man-made lake was a quarter mile long for canoeing. At one end of this lake was a boathouse and further down the lake were viewing areas. A second man-made lake was constructed on the property. On the far north side was Crooked Creek.

Connecting the various water features to the house and formal garden was an interlinking system of trails and macadam roadways. In his landscape designs, Jensen carefully placed roads to permit visitors to experience a sequence of sun and shade, a design feature which is evident at Riverdale Springs. Paths were laid out in gentle curves rather than in straight lines. Jensen's gardens also had a hierarchy of trails leading to different parts of the garden.[16] The remainder of the property became a meadow. In the marshy areas, sycamore trees were planted.

Leading from the mansion to the meadow and water features were two winding staircases. This allowed for the meadow to be the focal point of the estate. It was visible from the mansion, the formal garden, and the ponds.[17] The meadow was planted in clover. Sara Allison would reminisce about how Allison would collect violets in the spring for her as a youngster. It is possible that the meadow area reminded Allison of those carefree childhood days.[18]

Crooked Creek was spanned by a pair of low bridges. To help maintain water in Crooked Creek, a dam was constructed to the west side of the first bridge. It allowed the creek to widen and also controlled the water flow during both the rainy season and the summer. Also incorporated on the property was a building which housed the servant's quarters, the garage and the heating system for the house. This building was connected to the house through an underground tunnel. Bass also designed a gardener's cottage and a pump house on the property.

Mrs. Allison was very afraid of fire and thunderstorms, which resulted in the house's being constructed of poured concrete two feet thick with reinforced steel. Sara recalled Allison's acknowledgment of her fear: "You're terrified of electrical storms, Sadie. In this house, you need never be afraid, no matter what."[19] The bones of the house were hidden by the exterior in the deep red brick and on the interior by wall coverings. In order to have construction continue throughout the winter, a large frame barn was built over the mansion. An additional benefit to the barn was that it sheltered the house from curiosity seekers.

Exterior view of Riverdale. The dining room is on the right side. On the far left, the one-story addition to the home is the aviary (courtesy Rolls-Royce Heritage Trust, Allison Branch).

Allison, liking the visual appearance of the exterior of Frank Wheeler's home, replaced Herbert Bass as the architect. The new architect, William Price, of the firm McLanahan and Price, was primarily responsible for the lavish interior of the home, which was in contrast to the plain exterior.

Price was born in 1861 in Philadelphia, Pennsylvania.[20] By 1881, having apprenticed as a carpenter and studied architecture with Frank Furness, Price and his brother, Frank, formed an architectural firm.[21] Most of this firm's early designs were homes built in Wayne, Pennsylvania, a suburb of Philadelphia.[22] Over the years, the scope of Price's residential work grew. By 1905, he was designing primarily mansions for the newly wealthy. In 1910 Price designed a large stone Gothic mansion for Frank Van Camp, an Indianapolis pork and beans manufacturer, and designed a stone mansion for Charles Fairbanks, vice president of the United States, who resided in Indianapolis.[23] Price also received a commission from Allison's associate, Frank Wheeler, for a real estate development, Wheeler Heights, and a downtown hotel, although neither design came to fruition.[24]

The interior of Riverdale Springs designed by William Price was in stark contrast to the plain exterior. The front doors give a glimpse into the grandeur of the interior. Made of bronze, the entry doors are flanked by alcoves of Grecian marble. Entering the house, a visitor steps into an imposing two

Aerial view of Riverdale circa mid–1930s. To the left are the garage, greenhouses and tennis courts. Two of the lakes are visible to the right of the house (courtesy Marian University, Indianapolis, Indiana).

story foyer which measures 40 feet by 40 feet. Across from the front door, there is a massive gas log fireplace hand-carved of Indiana limestone by Indianapolis sculptor William A. Kriner.[25] The fireplace is large enough for a person to stand upright in it. Flanking the fireplace on both sides are French doors with mirrored glass. A one ton silver chandelier hanging in the foyer was made in Germany. The inlaid oak floor was covered by an oriental rug.

A visitor's eye is drawn to the right side of the entrance where a grand staircase of solid walnut ascends to the second floor.[26] Carved phoenixes, symbolizing immortality, sit atop marble banisters.[27] The upper landing forms a balcony along the entire back wall and partway along the side walls. The walls of the foyer were hand-carved with a leaf and berry motif from Circassian walnut, a rare hardwood marbled with deep hues of brown and purple. On the balcony above the lower-level fireplace is a second fireplace also constructed of Indiana limestone. The interior of the home was in a was done in a high Renaissance style.[28]

To the left of the front hall was the music room. This room has French doors providing access to a screened porch and an open terrace. Directly

Shed built to protect the Allison home, Riverdale, from winter weather during construction. The picture might have been taken by James Allison, who was an amateur photographer.

across from the French doors is a hand-carved marble fireplace. The 42 foot by 25 foot room is decorated with hand-carved white mahogany panels. The furniture in this room was made to order of white mahogany covered with gold damask. The designs in the furniture matched the carvings in the panels.

The music room had an $18,000 Aelean organ[29] with hand-carved woodwork hiding the organ pipes. Sara, who had studied voice, recalled many happy evenings at Riverdale with Allison operating the player organ. The organ would play the dear favorites that both enjoyed, always ending with "Loves Old Sweet Song." Then Allison would say, "Lady, dear — the concert is over," and with their arms about each other, they would go upstairs.[30]

On June 14, 1919, the music room was also the scene of the wedding of Allison's stepdaughter, Cornelia Parker Allison. Set directly across from the music room, she came down the grand staircase on Allison's arm. The music for the wedding was played on the organ.[31]

Allison, who did not finish high school, treasured books and had an extensive collection, which was located in the library, a 20 foot by 20 foot

The Riverdale foyer (courtesy Indiana Historical Society, W.H. Bass Collection).

room located across from the music room. This room features English oak paneling and has large built-in bookcases with leaded glass doors. As in other rooms, the library has a massive fireplace surrounded by carved wood, the mantel featuring gargoyles and suspended lanterns. Above the mantel are carved panels depicting women and children in a garden setting looking at a globe. On either side of the fireplace were lanterns. The library was decorated in brown leather and a deep red velvet. Before the fireplace in the center of the room was a hand-carved table with a bronze lamp. This room was frequently used by the family, Allison sitting in a big brown leather chair on one side of the massive table and Sara in a smaller velvet chair on the other. Also located in the library was a smaller writing desk and in front of the windows was a couch covered in red velvet.[32]

Bringing the outdoors into the house was a marble aviary more than fifty feet long and located at one end of the house.[33] The stained glass ceiling is believed to have been crafted by Tiffany.[34] At the center of the aviary was a water feature imported from Europe which had a glass bulb into which goldfish could swim. The Allisons' collection of exotic birds were allowed to fly throughout the aviary.

Allison selected Charles Latham to construct the house. One of the tales of the building of Riverdale is that when the home was completed, Allison gave Latham a bottle of crème de menthe. This bottle wasn't opened until the late 1930s. When it was opened, the crème de menthe had crystallized.[35] A wives' tale of the early 1900s about tuberculosis was that an animal would "take" the germs of the disease from the human victim. Sara Allison would walk with a pet monkey throughout the grounds. When the monkey died, it was buried by the porch. Several years later, workmen were digging by the porch when they uncovered the monkey's skeleton.[36]

At the time Riverdale Springs was built, it was equipped with state of the art conveniences including a central vacuum system, a telephone intercom system, automatically lighted closets and indirect lighting. Also unique in this home was an elevator, which frequently broke. Allison solved the issue by installing a chair in the elevator. When it malfunctioned, he would sit on the chair and wait for the butler to come.[37]

The Allisons employed a large staff to care for the property. Taking care of the house were over 40 people; the gardens required an additional staff of 26.[38]

18

The Second Running of the Indianapolis 500

One of the ongoing challenges for the owners of the Indianapolis Motor Speedway was maintaining interest in the race. Although Indianapolis had the biggest purse, there were other racetracks located in the Midwest and other races, such as Savannah, which were also well known. Although automobile racing was very popular, all of the racetracks were in competition for the best drivers and cars.

In 1912, the partners increased the ante for the race to a total purse of $50,000. The purse included $20,000 for the first place finisher, $10,000 for second place and $5,000 for third place. Additionally, the fourth through twelfth place finishers were also awarded monetary prizes that decreased to $1,400 for the twelfth place finish. To offset the increase in prize money, the partners also increased the cost to see the race. Fans who were willing to stand in the infield or take less desirable seats could enter the track for $1. If they wanted to sit in a grandstand at the start/finish line, the cost was $10 per seat.[1]

Speedway management also faced challenges due to actions taken by the AAA Contest Board at its mid-summer meeting. The board limited the number of starting positions for any race over fifty miles to one for every 400 feet of track. This would limit the field on race day to thirty-three cars.[2]

With the number of vehicles in the race limited by the AAA Contest Board, management was concerned about the impact upon smaller manufacturers. Fisher felt that if the larger manufacturers had three or four vehicles in the race, the field would be dominated by well financed companies. This could have the impact of limiting interest in the race. Fisher proposed that the race field be limited to two cars from any manufacturer.

As president of National Motor, Newby believed that many manufacturers would limit the number of vehicles in the race due to the cost of sponsoring a racing team. He thought the days of a team such as Buick with fifteen cars and forty drivers and mechanics were over. He felt that manufacturers would focus on one good car. He also thought that some participating in the 1911 race wouldn't be back if they didn't think their car was competitive. Newby was concerned that if they limited the number of participants per manufacturer they might have only twenty-four or twenty-five cars in the race. Allison offered a compromise of initially limiting the number of vehicles per manufacturer to two. Then if they didn't have a full field, they could accept additional entries.[3]

One of the most popular racing teams in the Midwest was Indianapolis-based Marmon, which had won the inaugural 500 mile race. The owners felt that if they entered a vehicle in the 1912 race and it didn't win, their reputation would be damaged, which could impact the level of sales. Additionally, Marmon business was thriving, as the number of orders increased after the 1911 Indianapolis 500 victory.

After winning the 1911 Indianapolis 500, Nordyke & Marmon announced their decision to exit from track racing. Walter Marmon explained the withdrawal from racing in an interview by W.A.P. John of *Motor* magazine in November 1922:

> First, if we went on racing, we had everything to lose and nothing to gain from the sporting standpoint. We had won about everything in sight and to keep from going backward we had to keep on winning with clock-like regularity. And there were other reasons more important. There is a tremendous expense to maintaining a racing team ... and the benefits accruing from racing must be in keeping with the cost if it is to be regarded from a sound business angle. And in 1911 the name Marmon was as well known as winning races could possibly make a name. Also the grueling test of maintaining high speeds over race tracks and roads had enabled our engineers in three years to establish what they wanted to know ... the best and most efficient principals of design and construction such as oiling systems, bearings, spring suspension, character of steel alloys in certain parts and similar information that could be obtained most quickly and most accurately by designing cars for continuous high speed work.

The decision by Nordyke & Marmon not to participate in the 1912 race was a huge disappointment to Speedway management. In addition, Buick was very disappointed in the performance of its team and decided not to participate in the second 500-mile race.[4] Another Indianapolis-based manufacturer, National, had a popular hometown driver, Johnny Aitken. His participation in the race would create lots of interest. Unfortunately for National and for the Indianapolis Motor Speedway, Aitken had announced his retirement after the inaugural 500-mile race and had been named the director of the National racing teams by the company president, Arthur Newby.

By mid–April, there were 25 entries on file that included local manufacturers National and Stutz, as well as Mercedes, Case and Lozier with two vehicles each. Stutz and National both applied to have another vehicle in the field, which was granted.[5]

Oil dripping from the cars onto the track had been an ongoing issue for the drivers on the racetrack. The early race cars frequently had leaks and little incentive to stop them. There was no limit to the amount of oil which could be used and many cars used between fifty and sixty gallons of oil in the 500-mile race. So, when a car went to the pits for fuel and tires, it was not unusual for them also to take on several additional gallons of oil.[6] Speedway management attempted to control the slickness by throwing sand on the track. Despite this action slickness, particularly in the curves, continued to be dangerous for the drivers.[7] Confronting these issues, the drivers selected Ralph DePalma as their spokesman.

DePalma complained to C.A. Sedwick, who was part of the Speedway management, about the track conditions. DePalma also wrote a letter to Mr. Wagner, the veteran AAA Contest Board starter. In his complaint, DePalma said that it looked as if several barrels of oil had been dumped on the track at each turn. Sedwick immediately took action and had the track scrubbed with a strong lye solution. This was a satisfactory resolution for the drivers and they went on to practice on the track, some sustaining speeds of 90 mph.[8]

Wagner interpreted the letter as management's intentionally dumping oil on the track to hold down the dust which collected in the crevices of the bricks. He did not realize that Speedway management had already addressed the issue to the satisfaction of the drivers. In a heated conversation in Fisher's downtown office, Wagner threatened that if the oil wasn't removed from the track no race would be held on Memorial Day. Fisher angrily responded that Wagner didn't know what he was talking about and ordered him out of the office. He punctuated his displeasure by telling Wagner that this would be his last race at the Speedway.[9]

Wagner conducted the standard prerace meeting with the drivers, discussing the race and reviewing the flags to be utilized. At the conclusion of the meeting, he declared that the race would be started without the use of a pace car. Word of the revised start quickly got back to Fisher. Rather than confront Wagner, Fisher went to Wagner's superiors and the use of the pace car for the race was reinstated.

After the pace lap, which featured a Stutz Torpedo roadster[10] driven by Fisher accompanied by C.W. Stoddard of Dayton-Stoddard,[11] the 1912 race started at a furious pace. A three way duel between DePalma, Wishart and Tetzlaff ensued, for the first 20 miles. Members of pit crews began to wonder how long this fast pace could continue without creating tire problems. The answer came shortly thereafter, when after 35 miles Wishart was forced to make a pit stop for new tires. At the end of 250 miles, DePalma was comfortably leading by two full laps. His lead continued and with 100 miles to go it had increased to 5 laps.[12] As the miles continued and DePalma maintained a seemingly insurmountable lead, spectators began to leave. Those who left the track were disappointed not to see the unanticipated finish.

On lap 195, DePalma's car began to slow after a broken connecting rod damaged the crankcase, leaving only three of the car's cylinders functioning. As DePalma tried to nurse his car through the remainder of the race, Joe Dawson (who, although employed as an engineer by Marmon, was driving for the National team[13]) steadily made up ground. By lap 198, Dawson's car was within three laps of DePalma, whose car was then going only 40 mph. Less than a mile from the finish, DePalma's engine quit running. As DePalma and his riding mechanic, Rupert Jeffkins, were pushing the car through the remaining turns and down the home stretch, Dawson roared past to capture the victory. As DePalma crossed the finish line, the crowd roared, which was acknowledged by DePalma by a wave of his right hand.[14]

The race had not concluded before another dispute arose between Wagner and Fisher. With prizes to be awarded to the top twelve finishers, the tenth place car, a Knox driven by Mulford, remained on the track with more than one hundred miles to go. The car had serious clutch issues and Mulford was trying to nurse the car around the track in order to claim the prize. Wagner wanted to stop the race and award Mulford tenth place and the monetary prize. Fisher did not think this was fair as Mulford had not completed the race — and in fact DePalma had not been recorded as the second place finish because the car did not cross the finish line under its own power. Fisher asked Wagner how he was going to explain to DePalma that Mulford was going to be awarded the 10th place purse of $1,200 for completing four hundred miles of the race while DePalma was going to get nothing for completing four hundred ninety-eight miles. Wagner angrily replied that Fisher had no intention of giving away all of the prize money. Fisher retorted that they had offered $50,000 in prize money and that indeed $50,000 would be given away. He told Wagner if he wanted to stop the race, the remainder of the money would be pooled and given to the drivers on a proportional basis based on the number of laps completed.

When Mulford entered the pits for fuel, Fisher explained the situation to him. Mulford decided to go back on the track and continue to drive the remainder of the race. Shortly after 6:00 P.M., Mulford again entered the pits and told his crew that he couldn't drive any further. His crew responded by encouraging him to get out of the car, take a break — and then reconsider his decision. While he was taking a break, the pit crew changed the shock absorbers on the car. After a 20-minute break, Mulford got back into the Knox and drove the remainder of the race. To collect the $1,200 tenth place prize money, Mulford had driven for nine hours.[15]

True to his word, Fisher had the remainder of the prize money pooled and it was divided among the 14 remaining drivers based upon the number of laps they had completed. Each mile of the race was valued at $1.9213. DePalma's share of the pool was $380.42.[16]

Just as Marmon had done after winning the 1911 Indianapolis 500, National Motors decided to get out of the racing business. Newby communicated the decision not to participate in the 1913 race to his fellow owners prior to its being made public. He also indicated that he knew of a couple of other racing teams which were considering not participating. Fellow owner Frank Wheeler was particularly upset by this news. He felt that as an owner of the Indianapolis Motor Speedway, Newby should have the National team participate. Newby indicated that National's stockholders had decided the same as Marmon had; there was too much at risk in terms of their reputation by running in the race.[17]

Additionally, both Marmon and Buick announced that they would not participate in the 1913 race. This meant that three of the stronger racing teams would not be present at the race. The owners became concerned both about the size of the field and the quality of the participants.

With his involvement in the manufacture of cars Newby advised his fellow Indianapolis Motor Speedway owners that the industry trend for passenger cars was towards smaller engines. Thinking of a strategy to encourage some manufacturers of smaller cars to participate, Newby proposed that for the 1913 race, the size of the engines be reduced 25 percent, from a maximum six hundred cubic inches of displacement to four hundred fifty cubic inches. The partners agreed with this idea.[18]

Management also made modifications to the track. The press and judges stands near the starting line were torn down and a five story control center, resembling a Japanese pagoda, was erected. Allison enjoyed watching the races from the pagoda. The control center had a concession stand and telephone and telegraph facilities on the first floor.[19] The partners also constructed a second tunnel under the track.

With the smaller sized engines and three strong racing teams not participating, the partners thought if they attracted some European drivers and cars they could maintain interest in the race. Sedwick was sent to Europe to talk to manufacturers about having teams as part of the race. His trip was successful: he persuaded several drivers to cross the big pond.[20] Appearing in the 1913 contest were teams from Britain, France, Italy and Germany. America was also well represented with entries by Stutz, Case, Mason and Mercer, which all had three teams. Additionally, there were ten other American entries, each with a single car.[21]

Among the entries from France was Jules Goux driving a blue Peugeot. He had been part of the engineering team of Georges Boillot and Paul Zuccarelli which had designed the auto, an L.76. The vehicle had a 7.6 liter engine delivering 148 hp and it delivered strong results in competition. In the Grand Prix, sponsored by the Automobile Club of France, it won the race driven by Boillot. Boillot also set the record for the Mont Ventoux hill climb in 17 minutes, 46 seconds. Jules Goux won the Sartha-LeMans Cup in 1912 and set a record for a flying ½ mile speed run at the Brooklands racecourse at 110 mph.[22] The Peugeot had the reputation of being "the fastest car in Europe."[23]

During practice at the Speedway, the foreign cars had difficulty negotiating the racecourse. Although offers of help had been made by American racers, the Europeans were suspicious that the Americans might learn things about their cars which would benefit the competition. After several days of practice and experiencing tire failure, Jules Goux of the Peugeot team asked Fisher for a recommendation of someone who could serve as a technical advisor. Fisher recommended Johnny Aitken, the former National driver. Newby was agreeable for Aitken, who continued to work for National Motors, to be a technical advisor for Goux. After watching Goux practice, Aitken advised Goux that he was entering the corners too high and too fast. Additionally, Aitken recommended using different shocks and Firestone tires.[24]

To increase interest in the race, management decided to bring the Remy, Prest-O-Lite and Wheeler-Schebler trophies out of retirement. The Remy trophy would be awarded to the driver leading the race at 200 miles, the Prest-O-Lite trophy for the leader at 300 miles and the Wheeler Schebler trophy for the leader at 400 miles. The winner of the race would be awarded the L. Strauss & Company trophy. L. Strauss was an Indianapolis clothier of fine menswear. Prior to World War II, this trophy was a work of art imported from Europe.[25]

In late May 1913, Indianapolis was experiencing a heat wave. At race time on Memorial Day, the temperature was a very toasty 90 degrees. Saluting the international field, six bands started the festivities by playing the national anthems of France, Germany, Italy and England. Bringing a huge cheer from the crowd, the bands concluded with the familiar strains of "The Star-Spangled Banner."[26]

Before the start of the race, after viewing the various trophies, Goux declared that he would win all four of them. The initial pace at the beginning of the race was fast, with the leaders driving at 90 mph. As with previous races, the tires were not capable of handling the high speeds, and the heat only exacerbated the problem. The tire trouble started on the fourth lap when two cars experienced tire failure. Goux took the lead by the 20th mile. Leading in the 15th lap, Goux's car joined the list of those experiencing tire problems and Goux headed into the pits.

While his rear tires were being changed, Goux complained about the heat and said that he wouldn't be able to continue in the race without some wine during his next pit stop. The pit crew, which was led by Aitken,[27] responded that wine wasn't possible. But Goux reiterated that without the wine, he wouldn't be able to continue the race. With that, he roared back onto the track two laps down. The pit crew found out that there was an Alliance Francaise group from Pittsburgh and New York cheering for the French racing team. This group was glad to provide a bucket of ice and six half splits of champagne.[28]

The leader at lap 55, Bob Burman, made a pit stop for new tires. Although the tire change was done quickly, his engine stalled and the crew was unable to restart it. To get the car back on the racecourse, his team had to change the carburetor. This long pit stop handed the lead back to Goux. At lap 60 (150 miles into the race), Goux headed back into the pits. He was delighted to find that his team had some wine waiting for him. As the crew changed the two right tires, he drank two bottles of the bubbly. Back onto the track he went. At 200 miles, he was in the lead, capturing the Remy trophy.[29]

About 30 minutes later, Goux needed another tire change and headed back into the pits. In addition to the new tires, he added fuel to his car and drank another bottle of champagne. At 300 miles, he remained in the lead and won the Prest-O-Lite trophy. At 310 miles, he made another pit stop in order to have the front right tire changed — and drank his fourth bottle of wine. This pit stop cost him the lead. As he exited the pits, Anderson, driving a Stutz, had a 23-second lead. The Goux team thought that Anderson might not need another change of tires and gave Goux the signal to increase his speed in an effort to recapture first place. Increasing his speed to 90 mph, he retook the lead at lap 136. Shortly thereafter, Anderson's car suffered a broken crankshaft and there were no other challengers to the lead which had been built.

Crossing the finish line after completing the 500 miles in 6 hours, 35 minutes and 5 seconds, Goux became the first driver to complete the race without turning the wheel over to a relief driver.[30] On the way to winning the Indianapolis 500, Goux also captured the Wheeler Schebler trophy as well as the L. Strauss & Sons trophy. As he took his victory lap, Goux displayed both the American and French flags. In the picture of the winner, Goux, in the Peugeot, is holding a bottle of champagne. The caption read *"Sans le bon vin, je ne serais pas etat de faire la victorie"* (Without the good wine, I would not have been able to win).[31]

19

The Europeans Dominate the 1914 Race

Continuing the trend started with the 1913 race, Speedway management turned once again towards Europe to increase the interest in the race by increasing the competition. With the entry fee dropped to $200,[1] at the close of the entry period in April there were 45 applicants, of whom twelve were European.[2] Prize money for the race had increased to $39,750.

Returning to the Speedway was Jules Goux, the winner of the 1913 Indianapolis 500. Goux was very cocky, stating that he and his teammate, Georges Boillot, would be victorious in the contest. He commented, "We will have to go a little faster this year perhaps, but we will take your fine money. We only worry about each other," referring to the other French Delage team of Rene Thomas and Albert Goyot and Joseph Christiaens driving an Excelsior.[3]

American hopes were pinned on the three car Stutz team. Harry C. Stutz had designed a new car, the Bearcat. This car was the most popular of the season and by May 1914 the demand for the vehicle had outstripped the supply — you couldn't buy one.[4]

Creating additional interest in the race was Oldfield's reinstatement to racing by the AAA Contest Board in 1912 and his return to the Indianapolis 500 in 1914. Although he had been banned from racing after the James Johnson race and his subsequent "retirement," Oldfield missed the thrill of racing and the racing fraternity. His first move was to contact Harvey Firestone of Firestone Tires and ask for a job as a salesman. Although he had been banned from racing, he believed that they could not prohibit him from being at various racetracks as a representative of Firestone Tires.

In April 1911, "Wild" Bob Burman broke Oldfield's land speed record in the "Blitzen Benz," formerly owned by Oldfield, at 141 mph. This new record combined with another record falling to Burman and to Ralph

DePalma in 1911 increased Oldfield's desire to return to racing. Will Pickens, his publicity agent, thought that the time might be right to gain favor with the AAA Contest Board, particularly since there was a new chairman, Bill Schimph. At a special session of the AAA Contest Board, Schimph said, "This organization is still growing and we're still trying to establish ourselves as a governing power with the public. We must have their support. Now as you all well know, there is but one driver in the business whose tremendous popularity is unquestioned, who represents auto racing to the public mind. We need him as much, or more, than he needs us. Gentlemen, although many of you may not approve, we're going to bring Barney Oldfield back to the AAA."[5]

It took longer for Fisher to agree to allow Oldfield to participate in the Indianapolis 500. Although Oldfield had gained reinstatement to AAA sanctioned races in April 1912, Fisher did not relent until 1914.[6] Oldfield affiliated with the Stutz team for the 1914 Indianapolis 500. The addition of Oldfield to the Stutz team gave the Indianapolis crowd hope that Stutz would win the race and continue the dominance of an Indianapolis manufacturer claiming the trophy. Despite his reputation and the promise of the Stutz car, Oldfield had difficulty qualifying for the race. It took four attempts and he began the race with the 29th place out of 30 starters.[7]

Other American contestants included the Mercer team (Caleb Bragg and Spencer Wishart) and the Burman Specials (Bob Burman and Louis Disbrow). Joe Dawson returned to the race in a privately owned Marmon after missing the 1913 contest. Howdy Wilcox, a popular Indianapolis driver, was at the wheel of a Gray Fox. Fred and Augie Duesenberg had started their own company and had built two cars (one a Duesenberg and the other a Maxwell).[8] The Duesenbergs had hired Edd Rickenbacker in the winter of 1912-1913 as a mechanic. The Duesenbergs had entered three cars in the 1913 race under the Mason title, of which one placed seventh. Having been sanctioned by the AAA, Rickenbacker was part of the pit crew.[9] The Duesenbergs' 1914 entry into the 500-mile race was with Rickenbacker as the manager.

Harroun, the winner of the inaugural Indianapolis 500, had been engaged by the Maxwell team to design and build two cars capable of breaking the Speedway's one lap record speed of 93 mph. His payment was contingent upon the performance of the car in the time trials. He had patented a new type of carburetor designed for kerosene instead of gasoline. In the time trials, both of the cars drove faster than the required 93 mph.[10]

The strength of the field centered in the Europeans, who had all twelve entrants qualify for the race. The Peugeot team with Goux qualifying at 98.3 mph and Boillet qualifying at 99.85 mph was clearly the team to beat. The starting positions for this race were done by a drawing. On May 30, some 100,000 spectators arrived at the Speedway for the race. At 10:00 A.M. the pace car began the race with a rolling start.

Early in the race, a wreck ended the racing career of the 1912 winner, Joe Dawson. After qualifying for the race, Ralph DePalma withdrew, complaining of "excessive vibration." Taking DePalma's place was Ray Gilhooly. On the 42nd lap, Gilhooly lost control of his car and spun out of control. Trying to avoid Gilhooly's vehicle, Dawson crashed upside down, ending up in the hospital for several weeks to recover from his injuries.[11]

By 250 miles, it was clear that the French drivers were setting the pace. With 300 miles completed, the closest American competitor was 15 miles off the pace. Crossing the finish line first was Rene Thomas, who won with a ten mile advantage over the second place finisher, a Duray vehicle which was a modified Peugeot with a piston displacement of 183 cubic inches. Guyot was third and Goux was the fourth finisher. Oldfield was the first American to finish. As Thomas was crossing the finish line, Oldfield was some 30 miles off the pace. The Harroun-designed Maxwell was able to complete the full 500 miles on 30 gallons of kerosene in 9th place. With kerosene averaging 6 cents per gallon, this remains the most economical high-speed performance in automotive race history.[12]

20

The Lincoln Highway

Fisher's involvement in the automotive industry through his dealerships, Prest-O-Lite and the Indianapolis Motor Speedway, led to another creative idea which would change the face of America. The primary mode of travel from town to town at the beginning of the twentieth century was the train. What roads had been constructed generally radiated from the train station. Although trains were efficient at transporting goods from one point to another, the challenge was getting the goods from the manufacturer to the train station and from the train station to the stores.[1]

As adoption of the automobile began taking hold, automobile owners began wanting roads that were better than what then existed. Automobile manufacturers also saw a benefit to better roads in the form of increased sales. The development of the roads was generally a town or county function with minimal involvement by the states. Those rudimentary roads which connected the major towns were not well maintained. Remembering his frustration on multiple road trips, Fisher one day expressed his desire for good roads: "A road across the United States: Let's build it before we're too old to enjoy it."[2]

The germination of the idea led to action by Fisher. Using Allison as a sounding board, Fisher's vision started to crystallize into a highway that would stretch from the Atlantic Ocean to the Pacific Ocean. Crucial to the plan being formulated was financing of the vision. Through conversations with Allison, a plan was crafted to raise $10,000,000 or more in private funds, beginning with the automobile manufacturers and suppliers.[3]

On September 6, 1912, the plan was unveiled to the automobile manufacturers with contributions to be based upon a percentage of each firm's revenues. A three year pledge would have ⅓ percent of each year's revenues or for a five year pledge ⅕ percent of each year's revenues.[4] With fund-raising in progress, a committee was established that adopted the name of the Lincoln Highway Association. Through an aggressive campaign, $4,000,000 was raised in pledges for the construction of the road.

In the fall of 1912, four participants in the "Four State Tour," which was sponsored by the Hoosier Motor Club and the Indiana Automobile Manufacturers' Association, started talking about expanding the "Four State Tour" to travel across the road envisioned by Fisher.[5] With fear of affiliation with the Lincoln Highway by this group, Fisher had not supported the tour. But by being sponsored by the Hoosier Motor Club and the Indiana Automobile Manufacturers' Association, the participants gained Fisher's support and participation.[6]

Plans for the tour began, with multiple localities across the West wanting to be included on the tour. When the tour left Indianapolis on July 1, 1913, notable participants in addition to Fisher included former Indianapolis mayor Charles A. Bookwalter; Elwood Haynes, the auto manufacturer; Harroun, winner of the Indianapolis 500; and various newspapermen and industry representatives. Among the nineteen automobiles and trucks participating were Indianapolis-manufactured Empire and Marmon.[7] The tour took 35 days to reach the West Coast. Due to the publicity generated, the interest in a transcontinental highway grew.

Also on July 1, 1913, the first organizational meeting of the Lincoln Highway Association was held in Detroit, Michigan, where they completed the paperwork for filing as a nonprofit organization and elected officers and directors. The purpose of the organization was "to procure the establishment of a continuous improved highway from the Atlantic to the Pacific, open to lawful traffic of all description without toll charges: such highway to be known, in memory of Abraham Lincoln, as 'The Lincoln Highway.'"[8]

More important, the executive committee of the Lincoln Highway Association began work on determining a route for the highway. Time was short as a meeting was being planned with the governors of the western states for August 22.[9] The highway was to take the most direct route between New York City and San Francisco, taking into consideration points of historical or scenic interest and centers of population.[10]

The route selected started in Jersey City and traveled through Philadelphia, Pittsburgh, Ft. Wayne, Indiana, and Chicago. At that point, the route took the Overland Trail to cross the Mississippi River at Clinton, Iowa. It then went west to Cheyenne and crossed the Rocky Mountains at the Great South Pass, which was used by both the miners in the gold rush of 1849 and the Union Pacific Railroad. After reaching Salt Lake City, the Lincoln Highway picked up the old Pony Express trail to Reno, Carson City, Sacramento and San Francisco.[11]

On September 14, 1913, the Lincoln Highway Association made a formal proclamation of their purpose and their route that was distributed across the

United States. With the distribution of the proclamation, enthusiasm spread and fund-raising began.[12] Until the forming of The Lincoln Highway Association was formed, Allison and Fisher had funded all of the preliminary expenses.[13]

The association, with a goal of raising $10,000,000 for the construction of the Lincoln Highway, additionally needed funds to support the operations of the association. The association started a membership drive, but this faltered as most contributors wanted their monies used for the development of the road and not for administrative overhead. The administrative funds were obtained from a small group, primarily the directors. With fund-raising slower than desired, the association decided to fund small sections of the road in each state through which it passed rather than waiting to obtain the full funding.[14]

By the end of 1913, the Lincoln Association was $21,700 in debt. As the association desired to clean up the debt, six individuals with close connection to the association were approached to donate funds, generally $1,000 or $2,000. This led to an underwriting system which began in 1915 with pledges lasting for three years. Among those contributing were Allison, Fisher, Newby and Prest-O-Lite.[15] In 1916, Allison joined the association's board of directors.[16]

One of the activities of the association was to encourage motoring. In conjunction with this, in 1919 the Lincoln Highway Association was behind the trip by the First Army Transcontinental Motor Convoy from Gettysburg, Pennsylvania, to the Pacific Coast. This trip focused attention on the need for highways for military travel as well as economic development. The trip resulted in the United States Congress passing the Federal Highway Act in 1923[17]. With this passage, the funding and maintenance of the Lincoln Highway was assured.

21

The War Years

Tensions in Europe spilled over with the assassination of the Archduke Franz Ferdinand, the heir to the Austro-Hungarian throne. In the fall of 1914, Europe was embroiled in a war which would last until 1918. This conflict had implications for the Indianapolis 500 before the United States joined the fray in 1917, since the majority of European race cars and drivers wouldn't be participating in the race. Although the first four years of racing at the Indianapolis Motor Speedway had been dominated by the American cars, it was not because they were the best in the world but rather that there was a lack of competition from the European manufacturers. With the sweep by the French autos in the 1914 race, the strength in auto racing clearly was in European designed and built cars. Without their participation, management of the Speedway would once again be challenged on how to maintain the interest in the race.

As the 1915 racing season began, auto racing had become a national pastime rivaling baseball. With road courses losing favor, eight board tracks had been constructed at a total cost in excess of ten million dollars.[1] Due to the success of the Indianapolis Motor Speedway, specially constructed racing tracks had been constructed in Chicago, Sioux City, Tacoma, Omaha, Twin Cities (St. Paul and Minneapolis), Providence, Detroit and Sheepshead Bay.[2] The Twin Cities course's president was Frank Wheeler, one of the founders of the Indianapolis Motor Speedway. Although the Indianapolis Speedway had plenty of competition, it still was the premier track in America. The race held at Indianapolis was the first in the multiple contests for the year. Aggregate prize money for all racetracks was approximately $250,000.[3]

In 1915, following the trend on the Continent, the displacement for engines was lowered to three hundred cubic inches.[4] Additionally, drivers had to achieve a speed of at least eighty mph for a one-lap timed run. For the first time, the starting position was determined based upon the qualifying speed, with the pole position going to the fastest qualifier.

Fifteen of the twenty-four entries had overhead valves, marking a new engine design. This design proved its worthiness, as both DePalma's and Resta's cars had this design. The three car Stutz team also featured this design, a new design for them.[5]

Towards the end of qualifying, which was held on May 20, 21 and 22,[6] the apparent pole position was going to DePalma, who had an average speed of 98.6 mph on his qualifying run. DePalma, who had lost the 1912 Indianapolis 500 with a broken tie rod late in the race, had purchased a Mercedes from Paul Daimler in France in July 1914 for $6,000. Daimler arranged for the car to be shipped back to the United States from Antwerp.

Howdy Wilcox, nicknamed Cocky, had joined the Stutz team in 1915 and prior to the beginning of qualifying for the 500 had set a speed record of 95 mph.[7] Wilcox saw Harry Stutz with a $200 diamond-studded tie pin. He asked Stutz if having one of his cars as the pole sitter was worth the tie pin. When Stutz agreed, Wilcox roared around the racetrack with an average speed of 98.9 mph, thus winning the pole position. Upon his return to the garage, Stutz not only gave Wilcox his tie pin but also a dinner at the best steakhouse in Indianapolis.[8]

Since Memorial Day was on a Sunday, the partners decided that in order to increase the spectator turnout the race would be run on Saturday, May 29. After qualifying, Indianapolis was drenched with rain and the racetrack experienced some flooding in the southwest corner. Based upon the weather reports of rain expected to continue on the 29th and the flooding of some major thoroughfares leading to the track, management decided to postpone the race until Monday the 31st. Unfortunately, some race fans were already en route to Indianapolis on Friday and were not aware that the race had been postponed. As the crowds descended upon Indianapolis, the available hotel rooms were quickly taken. Many people were knocking on the doors of private homes asking for a place to sleep. The crowds also had an impact on the food supply. With no deliveries on Sunday, many restaurants ran out of food and simply closed their doors for the day.

The 1915 race became a duel between DePalma and Dario Resta. Resta was driving a Peugeot that had been previously driven by Rickenbacker at a November 1914 three-hundred-mile race in Corona, California, and a March 1915 race at San Diego. Believing that the car needed more work than he could afford, Rickenbacker quit the Peugeot racing team. The car was purchased by Harry Miller, who overhauled it. The driver selected by Miller was Dario Resta.[9]

With about 165 miles remaining in the race, Resta experienced trouble steering his car. With these two cars substantially ahead of the remainder of the field, Resta's strategy focused on maintaining his second place position. As luck would have it, DePalma once again experienced car trouble near the end of the race. With three laps to go, the connecting rod of his Mercedes punctured the crankcase, draining oil from the engine. The lead over Resta was large enough that DePalma took the checkered flag. This was the first Indianapolis 500 race won by a privately owned vehicle.

Following the 1915 race, Johnny Aitken suggested to Allison that the Indianapolis Motor Speedway should develop its own racing team. During this period in automotive racing history, many racetracks maintained their own fleet of vehicles. Faced with the reality of Europeans not participating in races during World War I, Allison and Fisher decided to implement Aitken's idea.

They negotiated the purchase of two Peugeots from Europe, which arrived in Indianapolis on September 3, 1915. Fisher also commissioned the Premier Company, which was majority-owned by Fisher and Allison,[10] to build three almost identical to the Peugeot race cars. These five autos formed the nucleus of the Speedway Team Company, which was incorporated on September 14, 1915, with an initial capitalization of $20,000. The initial owners were Allison, Fisher, Newby, Wheeler and Theodore E. Myers.[11] Johnny Aitken was hired as the manager, chief engineer and ranking driver. Aitken hired Gil Anderson and Tom Rooney to drive for the Speedway Team Company.[12]

Eddie Rickenbacker, who would gain notoriety as a flying ace after the United States entered World War I, had participated in the Indianapolis 500 on two previous occasions. When Maxwell announced that their racing team would be withdrawing from competition, Rickenbacker, a member of the racing team, approached Allison and Fisher to start a second racing team. They purchased the two Maxwells and Rickenbacker was hired to head the Prest-O-Lite Team, which was also incorporated on September 14, 1915, with an initial capitalization of $20,000.

Rickenbacker was given a choice of two compensation packages. The first was that he would earn 50 percent of all winnings and would pay all expenses if the other driver, Henderson, was paid from Rickenbacker's cut. In this scenario, Prest-O-Lite would assume all maintenance expenses. The other option was that Rickenbacker would earn 75 percent of the earnings if he assumed all expenses. He chose the latter. The Prest-O-Lite Team won the first race it entered, which was at Narragansett Park in Providence, Rhode Island, in September 1915.[13]

Initially, the two teams were located in downtown Indianapolis. Allison soon realized that the location was detrimental to the success of the vehicles as, for any testing, they had to be driven from downtown to the racetrack. In late 1916, Allison said to Fisher, "Let's quit fooling around. This thing of running the cars out on the track for testing and then running them back to the shop three miles away is a nuisance and inefficient. Let me take over the company and I'll build a real shop out near the Speedway where it will be convenient."

Fisher, who had by this time become heavily involved in the development of Miami Beach, agreed. Allison bought Fisher's interest in Speedway Team Company and relocated the business to a one story building on Main Street in Speedway, Indiana, very close to the racetrack. Meanwhile, Fisher retained his interest in the Prest-O-Lite team.

The foresight of Allison and Fisher to purchase these cars was very beneficial. Of the twenty-six cars entered in the 1916 race, seven were from the Speedway Team and Prest-O-Lite Team companies. If Allison and Fisher had not purchased these vehicles, with only nineteen cars registering for the 1916 race, it might have been necessary to cancel the contest.

With the war raging in Europe, Speedway management faced other challenges brought on in part by the growing popularity of the sport. There were many racetracks in America and scheduling had become an issue. For the 1916 season, tracks at Chicago, Omaha, Sioux City, Tacoma, Twin Cities (Minneapolis) and Indianapolis formed the Speedway Association of America. The drivers also decided to form an association for the purpose of obtaining adequate insurance and instituting additional safety measures.[14]

Seeing the success of the Indianapolis 500, both Chicago and Twin Cities instituted the running of 500-mile races in 1915. The race at Minneapolis quickly failed due to poor attendance. Watching what happened at Minneapolis, Allison and Fisher became concerned that attendance for the 1916 race would be lower. Their anxiety increased when several automotive publications expressed the opinion that the races should be of shorter distances. Finally, they were also concerned that the cars might not be able to go the full distance of 500 miles. Allison and Fisher decided to shorten the race to 300 miles. This had the added benefit of lessening the purse by $20,000 as the AAA Contest Board had instituted a minimum purse of $100 per mile for all championship events on tracks which were greater than one mile in length.

Another impact of the failure of the Twin Cities 500 mile race was that Frank Wheeler, who had experienced financial reversals related to his investment in the Minneapolis racetrack, decided to sell his interest in the Indianapolis Motor Speedway. Wheeler had not only invested in but was also president of the Twin Cities racetrack starting in 1914. With the disappointing attendance at the 1915 Twin Cities 500, Wheeler increased his financial support of the Minneapolis track until April 1916. With mounting bills, Wheeler continued to support this competing racetrack until April 1916, when his liquidity had been depleted. Within months, the Minneapolis racetrack was bankrupt.

When the Indianapolis Motor Speedway required additional capital infusions in 1916, Wheeler decided to sell his shares of the Speedway. Allison initially approached Fisher to purchase 50 percent of the shares with Allison to acquire the other 50 percent. Fisher declined to purchase the shares due to his continuing cash needs to support his Miami Beach developments. The result was that Allison became the majority owner of the Indianapolis Motor Speedway on May 10, 1917,[15] by buying Wheeler's 25 percent interest and increased his ownership to 56.75 percent.[16]

As the majority owner of the Indianapolis Motor Speedway, Allison was confronted with the fact that two very popular race drivers were not participating in the 1916 race. The popular veteran driver of the Chevrolet team, Bob Burman, had been killed in April 1916 in an auto crash at the Corona Speedway.[17] Creating a lot of consternation among the Speedway owners was Ralph DePalma, who was then the most sought after driver in the United States. Since there was not a points determination of the driver of the year until 1916, DePalma was named the driver of the year by *Motor Age* magazine for both 1912 and 1914.[18]

DePalma, believing he was a strong drawing card, decided to negotiate $5,000 to enter the race plus any earnings.[19] Wheeler, having experienced the failure of the Twin Cities track, was sensitive to ticket sales being down. He was in favor of acquiescing to DePalma's demands, believing that he was worth what he was asking. Fisher believed this would set a precedent and wanted to turn DePalma down. He believed that if they paid DePalma to race then they and every other track owner would face demands by the top drivers for monies as a prerequisite to be a part of the field. Newby and Allison felt that they should not respond to DePalma's demands. Without receiving compensation for entering the race, DePalma eventually sent in an entry but it arrived after the stated deadline for racing applications.

To drive in the race, all of the drivers had to agree to the acceptance of the entry. Oldfield, who had heard of DePalma's demands, had approached Fisher for appearance money if others got it. With Fisher responding that no one was going to get any appearance money, Oldfield submitted his application for the race.[20] Oldfield refused to agree to the acceptance of the late application, pointing out that "the rules are the rules." The action by Oldfield began a long feud with DePalma.[21]

Fearing poor attendance at the 500-mile race, a publicity event was planned, with Barney Oldfield attempting to break the track record set by Georges Boillot in 1914 at 99.7 miles per hour. Prior to attempting to set a new record, Oldfield was driving an old Christie around the racetrack when the gas tank vibrated loose on the uneven brick surface. He had to drive with one hand while the other hand was extended backward trying to steady the gas tank. After watching this, Fisher attempted to buy the Christie from Oldfield, claiming that it was a death trap on wheels. Believing the Christie was the fastest sprinter in the United States, Oldfield challenged Fisher to a bet: if Oldfield was successful in breaking the record, Fisher would give him his white Stetson hat. If Oldfield was not successful, then he would buy Fisher five Stetsons. On the following day, Oldfield cranked up the old Christie and broke the 100 mph barrier with an average speed of 102.6 mph.[22]

With the race shortened to 300 miles, management decided to change the start time to 1:00 P.M. This only exacerbated the problem of late qualifying. On the day of the race, there were still entrants trying to qualify for a starting position at 10:00 A.M. In trying to encourage entrants to qualify early, management lined up participants according not only to the speed with which they qualified but also to the day.[23]

The purchase of the Peugeots and the establishment of two racing teams had a positive impact upon the race. Although there were 30 entrants for the race, on race day only 21 cars were qualified. Management-owned cars represented one third of the vehicles in the race.[24] Allison had the thrill of watching Johnny Aitken winning the pole position for the 1916 race while qualifying for the Speedway Team Company.[25] Qualifying in the second position was Eddie Rickenbacker driving a Prest-O-Lite team car, while

Allison Engineering, the one-story building built in Speedway, Indiana, to which Team Speedway was relocated in 1916 (courtesy Rolls-Royce Heritage Trust, Allison Branch).

starting third was Gil Anderson in a Speedway Team Company–owned Premier Special car.[26]

After all of the challenges Speedway management had faced in putting this race together, it wasn't much of a contest. The Memorial Day Classic was easily won by Dario Resta driving a Peugeot with an average speed of 94.4 mph.

With disappointment at the Memorial Day race and concern that World War I would eventually involve the United States, Fisher wanted to hold a day of races in the fall which would give them additional funds to carry them over should the war interrupt auto racing. Although his partners were concerned that the racing schedule was already full, Fisher eventually got their reluctant agreement. The Speedway announced a day of races in September called the "Harvest Auto Racing Classic." The races returned to the format of the first two years of the track, consisting of a 20-mile contest with $1,000 in prize money, a 50-mile race with $2,000 in prize money and a 100-mile race with $9,000 in prize money.[27] A week before the races were to be held, there was a competition in Cincinnati where many of the autos expected to be part of the Harvest Classic experienced engine difficulties. These cars were unable to participate in the Harvest Classic.[28]

The Harvest Auto Racing Classic had a disappointing 16 vehicles participating in the events held on September 9. Speedway Team had four teams participating in the races, including Aitken and Merz driving the Peugeots and Howdy Wilcox and Dave Lewis driving Premier Specials.[29] Hometown favorite Johnny Aitken, driving a Peugeot for Speedway Team Company, easily won the first two races of 20 and 50 miles. The final race of 100 miles had both Aitken for Speedway Team and Rickenbacker for Prest-O-Lite Team participating. This race also counted towards the AAA championship points.

The race was very close for the first 75 miles. At the 90 mile mark, Aitken's car had a steering arm break, which resulted in a lower speed for the vehicle. It appeared that Rickenbacker, driving for the Prest-O-Lite Team Company, would win. But at the 95 mile mark, Rickenbacker's left rear wheel's wooden spokes began to break. On the last lap of the race, Rickenbacker's tire burst and he lost control of the car. Aitken won the race driving for Speedway Team. Rickenbacker, disappointed that he wasn't going to win the AAA championship, decided to quit, which led to the disbanding of the Prest-O-Lite team.[30] Although the turnout for the Harvest Special was a very low 10,000, the races provided a small profit to the Speedway. Of the $12,000 in prize money, $5,900 was won by Speedway-affiliated cars.[31]

The Harvest Special races were Aitken's last appearance as a driver at the Indianapolis Motor Speedway. Johnny Aitken retired from racing with a remarkable record. In a career which started in 1905, he won 15 races at the Indianapolis Motor Speedway and remains the all-time leader of career wins there.

Team Speedway Company, which began as a high end machine shop developing automobile parts for the race cars owned by Team Speedway, had by 1916 developed a reputation as a center for automobile invention. The twenty man shop pioneered designs and models not only for Speedway Team Company but also for other racing teams. With a passion for quality, Allison insured that this company had the finest tools available.

In December 1916, the Team Speedway Company shop superintendent resigned. Aitken recommended his friend Norman Gilman, who had just resigned from National Motors, for the job. Prior to Christmas, Allison interviewed Gilman at Riverdale and Gilman became the shop superintendent on January 1, 1917.

Despite the low number of vehicles participating in the 1916 event, a 1917 race was planned. Its announcement was delayed due to a dispute between Fisher and Indianapolis hoteliers over the cost of rooms. Historically, the cost of a room in Indianapolis would double or, in some instances, triple for the race. Fisher believed that this was unfair and threatened to move the event to Cincinnati, which had just opened a two mile track. At long last, a compromise with the Indianapolis hoteliers was reached and the running of the 1917 race was announced in mid–March.

On February 23, 1917, the successor corporation to Team Speedway Company was incorporated as Allison Experimental Company. On April 16, 1917, the United States entered World War I. The next day, unable to reach either Fisher or Newby, Allison made the decision to cancel all races at the track and phoned the newspapers to tell them of the cancellation of the races until the conclusion of the war.[32] The fuel administration for the War Department did not request a cessation of racing activities until September 1917.[33] Allison then went to his new shop superintendent, Norm Gilman, and said, "Go find out how we can get war orders rolling. Take any jobs you like, especially the ones other fellows can't do, anything that will help us get started. Don't figure costs or wait to quote prices. We'll take care of that later."

The entry into World War I was a life changing event for Allison Experimental Company. Nordyke & Marmon, the Indianapolis firm which produced the Marmon automobile, landed government contracts to build both the Hall-Scott and Liberty aircraft engines. From the Production Board drawings, Allison Experimental constructed two master model Liberty engines which were used to build a variety of tools, jigs and gauges for the Liberty aircraft engines manufactured by Nordyke & Marmon. The shop also built a variety of items including high speed crawler type tractors for hauling battlefield equipment, Whippet tanks, and production superchargers. The company quickly grew from a 20 man shop to one with a staff of 50 to 100. Production workers routinely worked 50 to 100 hours per week. Additionally, up to 150 temporary draftsmen were hired to make production drawings to insure that the parts would work together.

Like many of their compatriots, Fisher and Allison became involved in the war effort. A training route for aviators was developed between McCook Field in Dayton, Ohio, and Chanute Field, which later became an air force base in Rantoul, Illinois. Being located approximately midway between these two points, the Indianapolis Motor Speedway, with a landing strip in the middle of the racetrack, was turned into an aviation repair depot and landing field for planes.[34] To upgrade the track for aviation training, two hangars were built and an aviation tower and floodlights for night landings were constructed. Additionally, experimental aircraft were tested at the track.[35]

The Indianapolis Motor Speedway was able to generate some cash flow from two sources in addition to its military contracts. Indianapolis manufacturers continued to use the track to conduct their final predelivery tests on their passenger cars. During the war years they tested 2,998 passenger cars, paying the Speedway $1.25 per car. Additionally, unused acreage was put into crop production (48 acres each for oats and wheat and 28 acres for timothy).[36]

Fisher and Allison received $9,000,000 from the sale of the majority of shares of Prest-O-Lite to Union Carbide in 1917. Freed of the management responsibilities at Prest-O-Lite and with the Speedway not running any races, Allison declared that he would retire. He was then 45 years old. The Allisons decided to visit Miami Beach in the fall of 1917. Like Fisher before him, Allison had succumbed to the charms of Florida. It was, after all, warm and sunny during those winter days when at home in Indiana the skies were frequently gray and cold.

Although he continued with some business interests in Indianapolis, he became more and more involved with various activities in Miami Beach. Among his first interests was deep sea fishing. For 1918, the Allisons spent a longer time in Florida, with Allison spending much of his time in his sport boat fishing. One day, there was a picture of Allison in the *Miami Herald* with a group who had been on the boat. One of the people was a very pretty young lady, Lucille Mussett, who was Allison's secretary. Nineteen eighteen was also the year of the great influenza epidemic, which claimed the life of Johnny Aitken in Indianapolis on October 15, 1918.

With the signing of the armistice on November 11, 1918, Allison, Fisher and Newby decided to return to their original mission for the Indianapolis Motor Speedway. They immediately began to make preparations for a renewal of the 500-mile race. And Allison Experimental Company returned to machining parts for race cars, including those owned by Allison.

Allison Experimental, the small high-end machine shop, had established a national reputation for quality machine parts and had entered the aircraft engine business. By Armistice Day, November 11, 1918, over 20,000 Liberty engines had been manufactured by numerous U.S. engine makers. Of these, approximately 10,000 engines were stored at Wright Field in Dayton, Ohio. Although not known at the time of the Armistice, these engines would be central in the growth of Allison Experimental over the next several years.

22

Racing Resumes

As soon as the Armistice was announced, Speedway management began making plans to reinstate the Indianapolis 500. In early 1919, at the small machine shop on Main Street in Speedway, Indiana, the Peugeot owned by Allison and driven by Johnny Aitken in the 1916 races was brought out of retirement.[1] This particular car could have been one of the Peugeot cars which won the 1913 Grand Prix.[2] Allison Engineering was again focused on auto racing.

With the return of racing to the United States, European entries helped to swell the field to 42. This was the first time since 1914 that there was a full complement of 33 cars for the Indianapolis 500.[3] Missing from the 1919 race was popular driver Barney Oldfield. He had once again retired from racing after another suspension by the AAA for racing in unsanctioned events. Although the AAA was willing to reinstate Oldfield with the payment of a $1,000 fine, he chose not to return. Instead, Firestone Tire & Rubber established a new company, Oldfield Tire and Rubber Company with headquarters in Akron, Ohio, and Oldfield as the president. This enabled Firestone Tire to capitalize on the Oldfield name with the introduction of a new line of tires.[4]

Patriotism was at a fever pitch following the return of soldiers from the conflict. In the days leading up to Memorial Day, several Indiana politicians criticized the race as being "unpatriotic" and "a desecration of the one day in the year which should be devoted exclusively to the memory of our war dead." Since Memorial Day fell on a Friday, Allison decided to hold the race on Saturday, May 31, and to change the name of the race to the "Liberty Sweepstakes."[5]

By the end of May, the Speedway Team Company had three vehicles ready to run in the Classic.[6] The Peugeot owned by Allison would be driven by Howdy Wilcox, a native Hoosier and a favorite of the crowd.[7] In this car, Wilcox was the first driver to break 100 mph, in a qualifying run during the

1919 time trials.[8] Driving the other two Speedway Team Company Premiers were Jules Goux and George Buzane.

During the qualifying trials, Rene Thomas, the winner of the 1914 Indianapolis 500, won the pole position driving a Ballot at 104.70 mph[9] and breaking Wilcox's short-lived speed record. Although the qualifying races promised a fast-paced contest, the 1919 Indianapolis 500 became a test of endurance. For the first time since 1911, the race had fatalities — three in total.[10]

There was also a bizarre accident which nearly claimed a fourth life. Amazingly, the accident happened on the main straightaway in front of thousands of people, most of whom were unaware of the unfolding drama. The right rear hub broke on Louis Chevrolet's car, causing the vehicle to lose one of its wire wheels. Dragging across the track, the broken hub snapped the thin electric timing wire stretched across the bricks at the start/finish line. Elmer Shannon was driving closely behind Louis Chevrolet and swerved his car to avoid hitting Chevrolet's. As he did so, the thin electric timing wire which was waiving in the air, caught Shannon under the chin and severed an artery. Losing strength from the loss of blood, he managed with the help of his riding mechanic to complete the next lap and brought his car into the pits before passing out. Quick action by his pit crew saved his life.[11]

Wilcox, driving Allison's Peugeot, was the first to take the checkered flag, winning the race with an average speed of 88.05 mph.[12] His riding mechanic was Russell Wright, an engineer at Allison Engineering.[13] With Wilcox the apparent winner of the race, the band started playing the familiar jazz tune "Back Home Again in Indiana," which was very popular among Hoosiers serving in World War I.[14] Written in 1917 by lyricist Ballard MacDonald with the melody composed by James F. Hanley, the tune was popularized when it was released by Columbia Records[15]:

> Back home again in Indiana,
> and I think that I can see.
> The gleaming candlelight,
> still burning bright,
> through the sycamores for me.
> The new mown hay sends out its fragrance,
> through the fields I used to roam.
> As I dream about the moonlight on the Wabash,
> then I long for my Indiana home."

(The playing of this tune became an annual tradition associated with the Indianapolis 500 beginning in 1946.[16] Although closely aligned with the state of Indiana, it is not the state song. "On the Banks of the Wabash, Far Away," written by Paul Dresser in 1898 and adapted by the Indiana legislature in

1913, holds that honor.[17]) Second place in the 1919 race was taken by Hearne driving a Stutz some four minutes later, followed by Jules Goux in a second Speedway Team Company Car.

After winning the 1919 Classic, Allison sold the race cars and the focus of Allison Experimental turned towards the development of aircraft engines. By 1920, the partners were considering other ways to use the Motor Speedway property besides the automobile races. In the development of Miami Beach, Fisher had promoted polo matches as one of the things to do while at the beach.

The first polo match in Florida was at Fisher's Miami Beach polo fields in 1919. By 1920, the popularity of the sport had grown in Miami Beach, with matches being played three times a week, generally Tuesday, Thursday, and Saturday.[18] By the end of 1920, polo had become well established in Miami Beach. Fisher, along with J.C. Andrew, owned twenty polo ponies including some of the best in the country, which at the end of the season were shipped to Indianapolis.[19]

Fisher and Allison discussed the possibility of bringing polo matches to the Indianapolis Motor Speedway. Fisher proposed to Allison that they establish a polo club at the Indianapolis Motor Speedway. The membership cost would be $50 per person. Fisher's belief was "everybody in town who has fifty dollars would want to belong to the Polo Club — and have the games only for members and their friends." He believed that 1,000 people in Indianapolis would join the polo club, which would provide a guaranteed revenue of $50,000 per year.[20]

One of the issues facing Fisher and Allison was the boarding of the polo ponies in Indianapolis. Allison proposed that rather than build horse barns, which had been discussed, they convert garage space after the running of the 1920 Indianapolis Classic: "Immediately after the races are over, we are going to have a lot of garage space that can be used very nicely for stalls by hauling in several inches of earth, so that the horses would not have to stand on the concrete floor. Think that this would be much better than building new barns until we find just how the polo business goes."[21]

Fisher made a deal with George Miller to bring fifteen ponies from Texas to Indianapolis for schooling. If Miller was able to sell the ponies after schooling, he could keep the profit from the sale of the ponies. Those ponies which weren't sold would be shipped to Miami Beach in November for the winter polo matches.[22]

Fisher was optimistic about the demand for polo matches in Indianapolis: "I believe we can work the thing up to the point where we will have about four big games during the Fall season — and I wouldn't be surprised if we could have a ten to fifteen thousand dollar gate to see a match game between the Cubans and the Dayton team."[23] Unfortunately, there is no evidence that polo caught on in Indianapolis.

Believing that the 300 cubic inch displacement resulted in cars which were too speedy for the Speedway,[24] management lowered the maximum engine displacement to 183 cubic inches (3 liters) for the 1920 running of the 500-mile Classic. The 3 liter engine was also the engine displacement for all European made cars,[25] establishing the International Formula standards. Without adopting the International Formula standards, the Indianapolis 500 would not have the participation of European entries.[26] Since auto racing did not resume in Europe until 1921, the Indianapolis 500 was the first race under the International Formula standards.[27] The lowering of the engine size also had the benefit of making the previous race cars ineligible for competition. Management believed that this would not only improve the competition on the racecourse but would also ultimately have a positive impact upon the automobile industry.[28]

The qualifying trials were changed for the 1920 race, requiring four laps to be run, the same format used today. The entrants had three opportunities to qualify; however, only one of the attempts could be completed.[29] Creating additional interest at qualifying was the entry of a twin engine Duesenberg in which Tommy Milton had set a new world's record of 156.046 miles per hour at Daytona Beach, Florida.[30] Continuing the tradition of offering large purses for the race, prize money increased to $93,500.

The 183 cubic inch engine performed well during the 1920 Indianapolis 500 and established the smaller car as an equal to the older, heavier models.[31] The race also featured a number of firsts. It was the first race in which passenger car manufacturers didn't compete, since they couldn't compete with cars custom designed for racing. It was also the first time that there were prizes awarded by "accessory" companies, tire and ignition manufacturers being particularly active.[32]

Firestone introduced the "Oldfield" line of tires named after Barney Oldfield. The cars driven by Oldfield in the race had painted on the tires "My only life insurance is Firestone tires."[33] Other tire companies participating in the Indianapolis 500 included Goodyear and Goodrich.[34] Champion and AC challenged KLC for spark plug supremacy. Delco Company offered a total of $25,000 in prize money for each driver finishing.[35]

For the first time, lap prizes were awarded. Miss Dolly Dallenbach, Pop Myers' assistant, came up with the idea of the Citizens of Indianapolis Lap Prize fund with a goal of $20,000, which would be paid out at the rate of $100 for each lap a driver led the race.[36]

Howard Wilcox, winner of the 1919 Indianapolis 500, in the Peugeot owned by James Allison (courtesy Indianapolis Motor Speedway).

The 1920 race, which had 23 participants on race day,[37] was won by Gaston Chevrolet in a Monroe. The Monroe was designed by Gaston's brother, Louis Chevrolet. Additionally, an identical car raced under the Frontenac trade-style.[38] The Chevrolet-designed Monroe/Frontenac cars had seven entries in the race and two were in the top ten (first and eighth).[39] The "Oldfield" tires on Gaston Chevrolet's car performed well; this was the first race in which there wasn't a need for a tire change.[40]

Just prior to the running of the 1921 Indianapolis 500, one of the founders, Frank Wheeler, took his life on May 27. Suffering from diabetes, he was distraught over the loss of a close friend to the disease.[41] Also missing from the track was the 1920 winner of the race, Gaston Chevrolet, who had died the previous Thanksgiving racing in a 250-mile event in Beverly Hills, California. It was the first death of a winner of the 500-mile Classic.[42]

The 1921 race had a paltry 25 entrants. By race day, twenty-three cars had qualified, with the pole having been won by Ralph DePalma in a year-old French Ballot. The race field was dominated by two teams: Frontenac had six drivers (Tommy Milton, Mulford, Tom Alley, Jules Ellingboe, Percy Ford and Van Ranst) and the Duesenbergs also had six drivers (Sarles, Boyer, Hill, Jimmy Murphy, Eddie Miller and Albert Guyot).[43] For this race, the three car abreast format was adopted.[44] The early pace was set by DePalma, who was running at an average of 92 miles per hour. When DePalma experienced a bearing failure, Milton took the lead. Milton had been steadily running at 90 miles per hour as he didn't want to risk engine trouble. Running closely behind Milton was Sarles in a Duesenberg, setting up the match for the remainder of the race. At the finish, Milton, in a Frontenac vehicle owned by Louis and Arthur Chevrolet, received the checkered flag.[45] Frontenacs had a big day at the races with three vehicles placing first, third and ninth.[46]

In September 1921, the Indianapolis Motor Speedway held a fifty-mile invitational as part of the American Society for Steel Treating convention. Approximately 10,000 people watched an exhibition of airplane stunts prior to the running of the fifty mile race. Leading throughout this race was Jimmy Murphy in a Duesenberg, until his vehicle failed on the last lap. Wilcox won the race in a Peugeot and Murphy's Duesenberg coasted across the finish line in second place.[47]

The 1922 Indianapolis Classic was dominated by the Duesenberg automobile, with seven Duesenbergs scoring in the top ten finishers.[48] Duesenberg, which had relocated in 1921 from Elizabeth, New Jersey, to Indianapolis, had seven cars qualify for the race.

Another milestone of the 1922 race was the dominance of the eight cylinder engine. The race was won by Jimmy Murphy in a Murphy Special that was a modified Duesenberg. Murphy had driven this car to victory in the French Grand Prix in 1921. After purchasing the Duesenberg, he replaced the Duesenberg engine with a straight-eight Miller engine upon his return to the United States.[49]

The winning of the race by Murphy and the strong showing by Duesenberg was the beginning of the dominance of the race by these two groups for the next several years. The Miller engine in the Murphy special began a dynasty which lasted for decades.[50]

23

Miami Beach

The peninsula that would become Miami Beach was inhabited by the Tequesta tribe of Native Americans when the first Spanish explorers arrived in the Biscayne Bay area. The Tequesta, a seminomadic people, spent their summers on the peninsula and their winters further south. The area was inhospitable, with mangroves, crocodiles, coral snakes, rattlesnakes and millions of mosquitoes and sand flies.[1]

The early settlers along the Atlantic Ocean coast in the territory which was to become Florida were primarily engaged in the salvaging of shipwrecks. When Florida became a territory in 1821, the United States required licenses for those participating in the salvage business in order to cut down on the intentional removal of markers along the coast.[2] In 1876, the United States government began building a series of stations to aid those sailors who had been shipwrecked. Prior to that, the sailors were left to their own survival skills. The Biscayne House of Refuge was the station for the Biscayne Bay area. It was managed by a keeper who would transport the stranded sailors to Miami or to Biscayne, now known as Miami Shores.[3]

The development of Miami Beach can be traced back to the 1870s when Henry Lum and his son, Charles, visited.[4] Henry Lum was a nurseryman in Ohio prior to joining the California gold rush in 1849. Although he was not successful in gold mining, he began baking breads for the miners. With $2,000 in earnings from the baking business, he returned to Ohio and later went to New Jersey to work in the nursery business.[5] In Florida he saw several coconut trees growing on the beach and decided to grow coconuts on the small strip of land between the ocean and Biscayne Bay. By 1882, Lum was ready to start his coconut plantation.

After obtaining some land at the south end of the peninsula, he joined forces with Elnathan Field and Ezra Osborn, who were also from New Jersey, to import and plant coconuts from Trinidad.[6] The coconut plantation soon failed when wild rabbits ate the coconut shoots. Various friends of Lum,

Osborn and Field invested in these ventures, including John Collins, a New Jersey farmer. Upon the failure of the coconut plantation, John Collins, who had invested $5,000 in the coconut operation, visited the property and decided to grow avocados on the land.[7]

Accelerating the growth of south Florida was the extension of the Florida Coast Railroad from West Palm Beach to Miami in 1896.[8] Once the railroad reached Miami, the town's population exploded. By the late 1890s, residents of Miami would travel by boat to the small barrier peninsula which was to become Miami Beach to enjoy the ocean.[9] In 1904 Richard Smith built a two story building that included bathing facilities as well as a dance hall known as Smith's Casino. He also started a ferry service between Miami and Smith's Casino which brought residents and visitors to Miami Beach.[10]

Collins began his avocado and potato farming operation in 1907. One of the issues he faced was transportation of the produce to market. He had to transport it over land and then by boat to Miami for further transportation by rail to northern markets. In 1911, Collins decided to dig a canal from Indian Creek to Biscayne Bay. Running out of money, he turned to his children. The children decided to visit the operation prior to make an investment. What they saw was the potential of the peninsula for development. The children and Collins reached an agreement. They would provide Collins money to complete the canal. In return, he would build a bridge across Biscayne Bay, thus making the peninsula accessible by auto. The Collins family, including John Collins' son-in-law Thomas Pancoast, formed the Miami Beach Improvement Corporation.[11]

Also seeing the potential of development of Miami Beach were a pair of Miami bankers, brothers John N. Lummus and James E. Lummus, who formed the Ocean Beach Realty Company. Collins and Pancoast, aided by some financial investment by the Lummus brothers, began the construction of a wooden bridge across Biscayne Bay in 1912.[12] With the announcement permits for the bridge being obtained from the War Department, the momentum for development at the beach exploded.[13] The Lummus brothers were the first to file a development plan, on July 9, 1912.[14]

Construction of the two and one half mile Collins Bridge began on July 22, 1912, at an estimated cost of $75,000. The construction costs soon exceeded the estimates and the construction period grew from an estimated four months to ten months. Part of the delay was caused by the need to place concrete around the submerged pilings to prevent damage from marine worms.[15]

With the bridge partially completed in 1913, Collins and Pancoast were out of funds. Fisher had first visited Miami in 1910 at the suggestion of John

Levi, the captain of Fisher's yacht. Having been involved along with Allison in the development of the city of Speedway, Fisher quickly saw the possibilities presented by the sun, the sand and the warm weather. With plenty of money earned from Prest-O-Lite and the automobile dealerships, Fisher loaned Collins and Pancoast $50,000 to complete the bridge. In return, Fisher received 200 acres of land.[16] At the opening ceremonies of the Collins Bridge, which was completed in June 1913, Miami's Mayor Watson predicted the future, saying, "I see the beach becoming so popular that within two years another bridge will become necessary."[17]

Likewise, the Lummus brothers' development, Ocean Beach Realty Company, had been slowed by a lack of funds. Fisher loaned the Lummus brothers $150,000 and in return received 150 acres of land. Having accumulated land, Fisher formed Alton Beach Realty Company and started development work. Over the next ten years, the face of Miami Beach would change from a small barrier peninsula with mangrove swamps on the Biscayne Bay side to an island for wealthy tourists and winter residents.[18]

24

The Miami Aquarium

Fisher, who was always enthusiastic about any project he undertook and needing more capital for development, tried to encourage his fellow owners in the Indianapolis Motor Speedway to join him in the development activity. Newby and Wheeler both declined to participate. Allison also chose not to join, telling Fisher that there were too many responsibilities in Indianapolis. Prest-O-Lite had grown rapidly and needed a new building to meet the ever increasing demand for its products. Allison thought that the building needed to be at least 150,000 square feet. Recognizing that Fisher's focus was on Miami Beach, he knew that he would bear the responsibility for the new Prest-O-Lite facility.[1]

During the winter, Indianapolis is drab, gray skies dominating the landscape from November through March. Adding to the misery, the temperatures are frequently very cold. After beginning his development activities at Miami Beach, Fisher frequently urged Allison to come for a visit. Always the salesman, Fisher would tout the benefits of Miami Beach in the winter months — the sun, the warm temperatures, and the increasing number of activities Allison could enjoy.

With Prest-O-Lite's expansion and several acquisition inquiries from Union Carbide, Allison had begun thinking about retirement, even though he was only in his mid–40s. Undoubtedly in the back of his mind were the untimely deaths of his father (at age 43), and his brothers, Dellmore (at age 44) and Wallace (at age 35) as well as his own heart attack at age 41. One day, he brought up the idea to Sara Allison of possibly becoming involved in Fisher's activities. "I may retire from active business before many years. Wouldn't it be nice for us to go down to Florida, to Miami Beach and maybe, invest there? I want to look it over."[2]

One of the challenges during the early development of Miami Beach as the "World's Winter Playground" was creating things for wealthy tourists to do during their visits. Always a promoter, Fisher had multiple ideas for how to entice wealthy tourists to Miami Beach, including polo matches, golf, and speedboat races.[3] Miami Beach also had several casinos, including Smith's, Hardie's, and the Miami Beach Casino. One of the ideas Fisher floated by Allison was the development of a botanical garden, which Allison declined.[4] As with his activities in Indianapolis, Allison would invest his time and money in something that had personal appeal.

The casinos of early Miami Beach were not for gambling but rather provided social centers for dancing, eating and swimming. Frequently they held dances several times a week. The Miami Beach Casino had one of the largest ballrooms in the South, the music supplied by well-known orchestras, including the Ray Manderson Orchestra. Smith's and Hardie's casinos would run boats to the casinos from Miami.[5]

The Allisons traveled to Miami in February expecting to stay for a month. The Miami Beach which Allison first saw wasn't far removed from its inception. Although Fisher had been involved with developing Miami Beach for several years, the development was still largely a vision in Fisher's mind. Fisher's vision was to make Miami Beach a resort that would appeal to the wealthy. It did not take much urging by Fisher for Allison to see the development potential.

On the first day of their time in Miami, Allison went with Fisher to see what he was doing. By lunchtime, Allison was enthusiastic about Fisher's vision for Miami Beach. Later that day, Allison returned with a telegram that one of his brothers, Wallace, was critically ill. The Allisons returned immediately to Indianapolis.[6] Despite the short stay of less than 24 hours, Allison had been charmed by this seaside village with the balmy temperatures, the blue skies and the tropical breezes.

After Allison's retirement from Prest-O-Lite, he had other business interests in Indianapolis, including Allison Engineering and serving on the board of directors of the Fletcher American National Bank. But without the pressure and stress of managing Prest-O-Lite, Allison had the time and finances for enjoying the winter in Miami Beach. He had the ability to hire qualified managers for his various business interests while he provided both the oversight and the financing.

As early as 1916, Allison became involved in the development of Miami Beach primarily as a financier. Fisher, Allison, John Levi, the Lummus brothers and others formed the Miami Ocean View Company to develop and market Miami Beach real estate. Just as in the Prest-O-Lite investment, timing in Miami Beach real estate was perfect.

After the conclusion of World War I, Miami Beach joined a number of locations in Florida experiencing a building boom. This boom was in part due to the rapid expansion of the automobile industry, which had adapted mass production methods. By lowering the cost of the automobile, it became affordable for a large number of Americans. Also contributing to the boom in Florida tourism was the Dixie Highway, which provided a network of paved roads from the Midwest to Florida. When Miami Beach incorporated in 1915, it had $244,815 in property assessments. Just four years later, assessments had increased to $2,251,000.[7]

One of the challenges of getting to Miami Beach was that of traveling by automobile from Miami. In 1913, the Collins Bridge — the wooden bridge partially funded by Fisher in exchange for land which formed the beginning of the Alton Real Estate Company — was completed.[8] Recognizing that the Collins Bridge wasn't adequate to provide for the anticipated influx of cars to Miami Beach, Fisher, J.E. Lummus and J.N. Lummus spearheaded an effort to build another bridge and contributed $2,000 in support of the effort to build a county causeway. The funding and the plans for the bridge were secured in 1917. Due to the delays during World War I, the opening of the bridge did not occur until February 17, 1920. The new County Causeway connected 13th Street in Miami with 5th Street in Miami Beach. In anticipation of increased traffic, Miami Beach made improvements to 5th Street from the bay to the ocean by adding curbing and sidewalks.[9]

Additionally providing access to Miami Beach was a trolley, which took the County Causeway from Miami to Miami Beach and then made a circular route in the southern part of Miami Beach. The trolley system opened in December 1920.[10]

In 1919, Fisher added polo as a draw for the wealthy. This sport, which had been introduced to the United States in the late 1800s, was very appealing to the wealthy and soon caught on in Miami Beach.[11] Another sport appealing to the rich, which swept across the country in the early 1900s, was golf. The Miami Beach Golf and Country Club was developed directly across from the Lincoln Hotel and sponsored a golf tournament every other week.[12] Although Allison was not actively involved in either polo or golf, there were social events tied to these activities which he could enjoy.

Miami Beach in 1920 was quickly changing and had plenty to appeal to Allison. He had his large yacht, *L'Apache*, on which he spent much of his time in Florida sport fishing. He also enjoyed the speedboat regattas that were begun in 1922. He had the *Aye-Aye-Sir II* built for participation in the 1924 regatta. However, the boat sank in Biscayne Bay after the propeller shaft broke and punctured the hull. Both Fisher and Newby were also active participants in the regattas and this added to his interest.[13]

With the number of tourists increasing annually, Miami Beach had few hotel rooms available and many people stayed in private homes or in camp-grounds. In fact, the 1920 census reflects Allison as a guest in the home of John Levi. Fisher had built the Lincoln Hotel in 1916 and it had been expanded for the opening of the 1920 tourist season. Rooms were also available at Brown's Hotel and the Breakers as well as at small apartment buildings.[14] It was obvious that Miami Beach needed additional hotels for the anticipated influx of visitors for the 1921 tourist season. Without additional hotel rooms, the sale of resort real estate would be negatively impacted.

Responding to the need for additional hotel rooms, Allison and Fisher began planning to build a grand hotel, the Flamingo, to appeal to the wealthy. It was an eleven story concrete structure with 200 guest rooms, each with a bath, and 20 guest cottages. The public rooms would be for socializing and dining. Although the Flamingo Hotel was on the bay, all guest rooms faced either the bay or the ocean. Included in the amenities were several tennis courts and a golf putting course.[15] The Flamingo Hotel was close to golf courses, the casinos, polo fields and the beach. When the plans for the building were initially made, the cost for the Flamingo Hotel had an estimated price of $750,000.

As is so often the case with building booms, there were sharp increases in building materials costs and a shortage of labor. When the contractor bids on the hotel were received, the cost had escalated to the $2,000,000 range. Analyzing the additional costs required for the hotel, Allison decided not to be a part of the venture.

As a youngster in Indianapolis, Allison had pictured himself sponsoring the finest collection of fish in the world. Throughout the years, he clung to that dream. Having developed a passion for sport fishing, he began to dream in 1919 about creating a world-class aquarium that would have as its focus tropical sea life. Not only would this aquarium be for the exhibition of the tropical fish but there also would be a laboratory to expand knowledge about sea life. Allison decided to concentrate on the building of an aquarium.[16]

When Allison told Fisher about his desire to build an aquarium, Fisher was enthusiastic about the potential appeal to tourists. Likewise, the Dade County commissioners were amendable to Allison's proposal to build it. In conversations with the county commissioners, the possibility of locating the aquarium on the south end of the causeway from Miami was raised.[17] There was also a parcel of land available on the north side of the causeway. Allison was much more enthusiastic about this property, as "the principal traffic of people who would be interested in our Aquarium would turn north at this point and not south, and I believe we would have a better opportunity of getting them on the way to the Casino or Hotel or wherever they might be going, than on their return."[18] Once the decision was made to build an aquarium, Allison forged ahead with plans with the goal to open the aquarium for the 1920 tourist season. This was a very aggressive goal because a location for the aquarium needed to be determined, the building needed to be designed and built and a director for the aquarium needed to be hired. Ultimately, the parcel of land located on the north side of the County Causeway was selected for the site of the aquarium. Allison believed that locating the aquarium on the causeway would be the first sight visible to visitors as they crossed Biscayne Bay.

Allison selected M. Hawley McLanahan, a partner in the firm of Price & McLanahan in Philadelphia, to design the building. He was familiar with the firm's work as Price had designed the interior of Riverdale Springs and the home for Frank Wheeler. As the firm's business expanded from homes for the wealthy to commercial buildings, it developed a reputation for designing hotels and other commercial buildings, including the Grove Park Inn in Asheville, North Carolina. With Sara Allison spending time in Asheville, Allison was familiar with their expanding design expertise.

The design of the aquarium was in the shape of a Maltese cross with a rotunda at the center of the building. The building design also included a two story section which allowed for the laboratories, offices and an apartment on the second floor. The plans for the aquarium included a 60,000 gallon saltwater tank. The pumps to bring the water from the bay into the tank could handle 400 gallons per minute and were provided by the American Steam Pump Company.

Allison turned to John (Jack) LaGorce, associate editor of the National Geographic Society and a winter resident of Miami Beach, for advice on the director of the aquarium. Over the previous three winters, the two men had become friends. LaGorce had knowledge of many leaders in the natural world through his association with the National Geographic Society. One of the individuals known by LaGorce was Louis L. Mowbray, an assistant director of the New York Aquarium. Based upon LaGorce's praise for Mowbray, Allison hired him as the director of the Miami Aquarium.

When Mowbray was a sickly child growing up in Bermuda, his physician suggested that he spend time outside to improve his health. Mowbray developed a love for the sea and a fascination with birds and fish. After working as a photographer's apprentice in New York, he returned to Bermuda and started a photography studio. In the room next to the studio, he maintained an extensive collection of fish and bird specimens. A group of scientists visiting Bermuda saw the collection and were so impressed they gave him a four volume book of fishes. With a growing reputation, Mowbray was asked to join the staff of the Bermuda Biological Station. He was later hired by the Bermuda Natural History Society to convert a gunpowder magazine on Agar's Island into an aquarium and marine research center. During the time he was on Agar's Island, he sent several shipments of fish to the New York and Detroit aquariums.

Having developed a reputation in the United States, Mowbray was selected in 1911 to develop an aquarium in Boston, which he ran until 1914. From the Boston Aquarium, he was hired as the superintendent of the New York Aquarium.[19] Having established a reputation for building and running aquariums, he had the attributes Allison considered important for the Miami Aquarium. In May 1919, Allison hired Mowbray to be the director of the Miami Aquarium.

The agreement for employment of Mowbray indicated a salary of $2,500 per year plus a bonus dependent upon the profitability of the aquarium. Additionally, Mowbray was given a month of vacation. He was responsible for the operations of the aquarium as well as the equipping of it. The contract also specified that the aquarium would provide a boat between 28 and 30 feet equipped with a live well.[20]

Allison also enticed a number of notable people to serve on the aquarium's advisory committee, including Alexander Graham Bell, Gilbert Grosvenor (president, National Geographic Society), Dr. Charles D. Walcott, (secretary, Smithsonian Institution), Dr. Hugh M. Smith (U.S. commissioner of Fisheries), Dr. Charles H. Townsend (director, New York Aquarium), Henry Fairfield Osborn (president, New York Zoological Society), and Dr. Barton W. Evermann (president, California Museum of Science). These individuals were not only of assistance in advising on the aquarium but also on advertising it.[21]

By January 1920, the construction work on the aquarium was progressing nicely. It was under roof with the exception of the skylights that were to provide lighting for each of the interior tanks. The exterior concrete water tank was almost completed and work was beginning on the interior display tanks. The expectation was that the aquarium would be completed by the middle of February.

Complicating the rapid construction of the aquarium, as well as the Flamingo Hotel, was a logjam of ships with building materials waiting to be off-loaded in Miami. As a potential solution to this problem, Allison started a ship repair yard where the first piece of business would be building three large barges to hold construction materials.[22] With the delay in receiving building materials, construction of the aquarium was not as quick as had been hoped. In late April 1920 the interior tanks had been installed but the tourist season for 1920 had been missed. The grand opening of the aquarium was planned for January 1, 1921, to complement the grand opening of the Flamingo Hotel at a gala event on New Year's Eve.

During the spring of 1920, plans were made to begin collecting various specimens for the aquarium. The first expedition of aquarium staff, including Allison, Mowbray and Charlie Thompson, a local fishing captain, was not to find fish for the collection but rather to Andros, the largest of the Bahama Islands, in search of a large colony of flamingos. Although the flamingo was indigenous to Florida, it no longer inhabited the state by the early 1900s.

The aquarium party, which consisted of naturalists, ornithologists and artists, traveled to Andros aboard several vessels, including *L'Apache*, *Sea Horse*, and several flat bottomed boats which could traverse the shallow waters. During the days, the party would board the flat bottom boats and go in search of the flamingos. At dusk, they would return to *L'Apache* and *Sea Horse*, which were anchored off the coast, in order to avoid swarms of mosquitoes.

Upon locating the flamingos, the Bahama colonial government gave permission for the aquarium staff to bring back a number of the birds to reintroduce them to Florida. The flamingos were relocated to a giant aviary on the shores of Flamingo Bay some three miles from the aquarium. Although it was hoped that the flamingos would reproduce, this colony did not thrive.

On July 3, 1920, one of the aquarium workers spotted some water on the concrete floor. Upon investigation, the worker noticed that this water was from a small leak in a large water tank. As the worker called another aquarium employee to come investigate, the water tank, which contained approximately 15,000 gallons of water, collapsed. The force of the water caused the lower two thirds of one side of the holding tank to give way. The collapse of the tank sent the water careening through the aquarium, resulting in the destruction of one of the large display tanks at the west side of the building. Some of the concrete blocks from this tank tore through the building and destroyed the pipe railing. The force of the water also caused some of the columns under the dome to collapse. Remarkably, only one of the employees suffered injuries and they were minor.[23]

The fish in the holding tank at the time of the collapse were strewn throughout the aquarium building. The aquarium workers on the grounds, along with a some plumbers and electricians, were able to rescue the struggling fish and return them to a second large holding tank. An investigation of the tank collapse revealed that it was caused by the design's not being followed. The tie bars between the beams that failed did not have the strength to support the structure, placing all of the stress on the concrete.[24]

In the fall of 1920, Louis Mowbray and Captain Charlie Thompson began gathering specimens for the Miami Aquarium. The technique employed by Mowbray and Thompson to capture specimens was novel in the 1920s. Instead of gathering the fish by rod and reel, they used traps along the sea floor with crawfish as bait. The traps with tropical sea life would be loaded into holding tanks on the aquarium's large fishing boat, the *Allisoni*. Upon the *Allisoni*'s arrival at the aquarium docks, the fish would be transferred to one of two large holding tanks located outside of the aquarium.

Allison returned to Florida in November 1920 on his yacht *L'Apache*, and stayed at the recently reopened Lincoln Hotel.[25] The winter season of 1920-1921 promised to be full of activities for Allison. In many ways, this winter season was reminiscent of the early days of Prest-O-Lite when Allison was focused on the growth of a new business venture as a businessman and his social life included the Zig Zag Bicycle Club's activities. Allison happily anticipated the 1920-1921 social season, as well as the opening of the long dreamed about aquarium.

As part of his dream of turning Miami Beach into a grand resort, Fisher

Miami Aquarium and Laboratory, which opened in January 1921. The picture was taken from Biscayne Bay (courtesy of Historical Museum of South Florida).

purchased the Miami Beach Casino and turned it into the private Miami Beach Club. Memberships were purchased to the club and it quickly became a focus of Miami Beach social life. On the eve of the Miami Beach Club opening, Allison attended a small party for close friends of Fisher and Fisher's wife, Jane. The next day, there was a gala opening of the Miami Beach Club with an evening of dinner and dancing.

The final touches were being made to the Flamingo Hotel, and the Miami Aquarium was ready to receive visitors. The grand opening of the aquarium was planned as part of a gala occasion for the celebration of New Year's Eve 1921. Prior to the opening festivities, Allison participated in a stag cruise to Havana on the passenger steamship *City of Miami*, an outing planned by Fisher for a group of 200 businessmen, officials and residents of Miami and Miami Beach.[26]

The *City of Miami*, owned by the Cuban-American Steamship Company, was the largest passenger ship to enter the port of Miami, with a draft of 16 feet. With accommodations for two hundred and four passengers, the *City of Miami* was to provide travel between Miami and Havana. A challenge for the Port of Miami was the shallow waters of Biscayne Bay, which averaged twenty feet and at least on one shoal was 16.5 feet. To accommodate the *City of Miami* as well as freighters, the channel was being dredged.[27]

The *City of Miami* left Miami on Wednesday, December 29, at low tide. As part of the after dinner entertainment, Fisher had arranged for the Ray Manderson Orchestra, which frequently played at Fisher's Miami Beach Club, to be onboard. Also planned were boxing matches which were to take place in a makeshift ring on the boat. Early the next afternoon, the party arrived in Havana, where they were met by Colonel Eugenio Silva of the Cuban Army and M. Salmon, a businessman who had been in Miami earlier in 1920 for polo matches.

The cruise was to leave later that afternoon for the return trip to Miami but was delayed due to engine trouble. While in Havana, the ship took on 25 schoolteachers who had traveled to Havana on an earlier trip of the ship. The steamship company arranged for a dance for the teachers and the Fisher group was invited. The *City of Miami* arrived back in Miami around 4:00 P.M., several hours later than planned, but still in time for the opening festivities for the Flamingo Hotel that evening.[28]

On January 1, 1921, the Flamingo Hotel opened to the public. On New Year's Eve, there was an "invitation only" formal dinner and reception at the hotel. Allison had to hurry from the *City of Miami* to the Flamingo Hotel for the evening's activities. The next morning, the Miami Aquarium opened for visitors, with Allison greeting the first visitors.

As visitors entered the aquarium, which had a soft gray exterior appearance, they were greeted by brightly colored Moravian Pottery tile. The window trim and doors were painted to pick up the bright colors of Moravian tiles lining the buttresses. On the walls, there were fourteen reproductions of water colors done by H. Murayama, a Japanese painter who had worked at the aquarium the previous summer. On either side of the entrance were two mounted fish — a marlin and a tuna.[29]

The tuna was the first of its kind taken from the South Atlantic waters. John T. Nichols talked about the discovery of this tuna in an article, "The Modern Aquarium," published in *Natural History*: "Mr. Mowbray had not been on the ground long when several great tuna were taken in nearby waters which he immediately recognized as representing a species never before examined and described by naturalists. The tips of their back and anal fins were greatly prolonged in narrow, band-shaped points."[30] It was named *Thunnus allisoni* (Allison's tuna) by Mowbray for Allison.

Along the corridors extending from the Maltese cross entryway were fifty exhibition tanks. Skylights located over each of the exhibition tanks enabled the visitor to see the multihued fish from the tropics without the optical illusions which arise from artificial lighting. One of the glass fronted tanks was possibly the largest in the world with measurements of 36 feet long, 15 feet wide and 10 feet deep. It could hold a fish up to twelve feet long.

The aquarium featured tropical fish caught within 50 miles of Miami Beach. To facilitate the capture of fish, the aquarium had three power cruisers equipped with special live wells. At the opening of the aquarium, the collection had 2,500 specimens ranging in size from the great tarpon to the tiny angel fish. Outside the aquarium building were two open tanks which contained a 15 foot long manatee weighing half a ton and otter and alligators. Also popular was the display of octopuses.[31]

For many visitors, this was the first exposure they had to the wonders of tropical fish. Although there were other significant aquariums in the United States, particularly New York and Boston, the focus on tropical fish was something that the other aquariums could not offer without great expense. The Miami Aquarium utilized water from the Gulf Stream that stayed between 63 and 85 degrees depending upon the season. Other aquariums further north had to heat the water.

Part of the aquarium facilities was a laboratory used to study tropical fish. Allison hoped that through understanding the food value of various fish, the food supply could be expanded. One focus of the aquarium was on the propagation of spiny lobsters and large stone crabs. Spiny lobsters are comparable in size and flavor to North Atlantic lobsters but they were not widely known.[32] Stone crabs were widely available in the seas surrounding Miami Beach. Unfortunately, although the claws were edible, they had too much iodine, making them unappealing to the majority of people. A small restaurant in the South Beach area of Miami Beach, Joe's, had developed a reputation among the locals as having wonderful, fresh fish. A Harvard researcher from the aquarium told the proprietor, Joe Weiss, that the poor taste of the stone crab claws was caused by too much iodine. As an experiment, Weiss boiled the stone crab claws before chilling them. By boiling the crab claws, the iodine was removed and the result was a very popular dish at Joe's Restaurant, today known as Joe's House of Crabs.[33] The aquarium also planned to popularize the study of fish life by making motion pictures of the fish. The movies would record their habits, including the hatching of eggs and the ability to take on protective coloration when frightened.

On January 29, 1921, President-elect Warren Harding planned a visit to Miami. Knowing a visit by Harding would have immense advertising value, Fisher invited him to the newly opened Flamingo Hotel, which invitation Harding initially declined. Although the visit was planned to be to Miami, Harding's time there was ultimately limited to a greeting and a dinner as he ultimately accepted Fisher's invitation. Rather than staying in Miami, Harding stayed at the Flamingo Hotel and played a round of golf. He also visited Allison's recently opened Miami Aquarium.

After two days on Miami Beach, Harding, Fisher, Allison and Charlie Thompson, the fishing guide, went to the Cocobolo Cay Club for two days of fishing.[34] Cocobolo Cay Club was a private fishing retreat located on 70 acres on Adams Key, about thirty miles south of Miami Beach. The clubhouse had eight bedrooms on the second floor with three shower baths. On the first floor was the main lobby, dining room and dancing hall. For the comfort of the members, the property had its own electrical plant and ice plant. Membership in the Cocobolo Cay Club was limited to 100 individuals.[35]

In the first year of the aquarium, the advertising was very subtle; a plain boxed announcement in the newspaper that it was open, the location, and the cost (50 cents for adults and 25 cents for children). By the second year, the advertisements had evolved to include caricatures of folks arriving at the aquarium by automobile and a description of the fun inside:

> We pass through the turnstile. Excited groups of men, women and children stand in front of the glass front tanks in the corridors. We step up to the railing. In front of us cruising about in the water we see the Silvery Moon fish. Passing on we see the Queen Trigger,—the Snook Robolo,—the Black Trigger. At the end of the corridor we perceive the largest exhibition tank in

the world. A Green Turtle weighting 500 pounds swims about. Monster grouper here and there. Sting Rays undulate their cephalic fins as they "shoot" swiftly by. We turn, opposite us there are excited exclamations "The octopus are performing, etc.[37]

Along with his ownership of the aquarium and his real estate investments, Allison was also involved with the establishment of the First National Bank of Miami Beach in 1922,[37] the first bank in Miami Beach. Allison served as a director of the bank until his death.

In 1923, the *Miami Herald* ran a series, "Fish in Miami Waters," which promoted the aquarium. Number sixty-nine featured the gray parrot:

> This demurely tinted relative of the vividly hued rainbow, blue and plum-colored parrot fish frequents the rocky shores of the Keys, especially those with abundant kelp growth, for the gray parrot is strictly herbivorous in its feeding habits. Although not as abundant as the other members of the family, the gray parrot may be caught in traps or with nelmes. Slightly broader through the head region than the other parrot fish, the gray parrot retains the family characteristics in the peculiar fusion of the teeth to form a bony beak resembling that of a parrot. A slight roseate that differs in quantity in various specimens and from time to time relieves the somberness of the gray hue. It reaches a length of twelve inches or more. On exhibition at the Miami Aquarium.[38]

On March 20, 1923, the aquarium announced the birth of hundreds of sea horses. The parents had been captured a week before and Mowbray began making preparations for the upcoming birth. The aquarium staff removed the sand flounder, pipe fish and slippery dicks that shared their tank. Mowbray also made a special trip to the Gulf Stream to acquire seaweed, which not only was food for the sea horses but also provided shelter.[39]

The aquarium closed after the 1922-1923 winter season. Allison stated that during the three years of its existence, approximately 110,000 persons paid admission to the aquarium. Of these, less than 10 percent were children. Many thousands of children were admitted free, including school children, Boy Scouts and YMCA members.[40] Allison had shared his decision to close the aquarium with Fisher prior to making the announcement to the public.

Fisher urged Allison not to close it. In a March 30, 1923, letter, Fisher wrote, "The Aquarium has been a good thing for the Beach. It is like a lot of other investments at the Beach; while it may not return enough to be self supporting, it is one of the necessary attractions of the Beach, in fact, it is a very good thing for the entire State, and I think we should make quite an effort to see that the Aquarium is kept open during the winter season, just the same as you did this year."[41]

Allison's decision to close the aquarium came after a review of the financial results. Although attendance had increased in each of the three years the aquarium was opened, losses had continued and in the 1922-1923 season had increased by approximately 10 percent. Allison explained his strategy for the aquarium: "It was not my intention to take out any profits or dividends but to use any excess over the year's operating expense in extension and development of the work. I had firmly hoped and believed that the aquarium by this time would have become self-sustaining, but each year seems to show a larger loss than the year before."[42]

Allison also explained the "hidden costs" of the aquarium operation: "It is a big expense, but the general public doesn't realize it. The public is admitted to the aquarium only between 10 o'clock in the morning and 6 o'clock at night. During the remaining 16 hours, our force of attendants is hard at work. Fish must have a constantly changing diet and none of us as yet know just what they best like and it is a big job, a man's job, to see that they are properly fed and kept alive and well."[43]

He continued on the decision to close the aquarium: "I am firmly convinced that the aquarium cannot function as a self sustaining unit. February in each season, has been the only month during the three years during which we operated at a profit. During the summer months we wouldn't take in 25 per cent of the operating expenses. It costs just as much to operate the aquarium when 5 persons a day visit it as when 1,000 persons do. There seems but no other avenue, but to abandon it."[44]

Allison arranged for the fish to be distributed to the Detroit Aquarium as well as back to the warm waters of the Caribbean. John Timmons, the director of the Detroit Aquarium, understood the value of the aquarium to the community:

> It would certainly be a catastrophe for the Aquarium here not to re-open next year. It seems as if the county should provide the necessary amount of funds to insure its continuation. The exhibit should be made free — as it is in the municipal institution in Detroit. Free admittance could be granted for a season or so until the people started to come in large numbers and then a small admission could be charged to meet the expenses. At that time the people would be accustomed to come and look over the collection and would, no doubt, do as they do in Detroit, return time and again to go through the building and to look at the collection. Mr. Allison has done a real service by starting the Aquarium and the public should see that it does not close. In few places are there buildings so admirably equipped to maintain a wonderful collection as here.[46]

Jack LaGorce of the National Geographic Society also expressed his opinion on the loss of the Aquarium to Miami Beach:

Curator of the Miami Aquarium and Laboratory, Louis Mowbray, with the Allison Tuna (courtesy Louis Mowbray).

Only five great cities in the United States have aquariums worthy of the name: New York, Boston, Detroit, Philadelphia and Miami. Many of our larger inland cities gladly would supply $100,000 yearly to perpetuate such an educational and fascinating exhibit for their citizens, young and old yet the people of Miami generally, as it seems to me, have not realized the importance to the city, state and country of this great exhibition. The aquarium has been of potential value to Miami and the community from an advertising standpoint, not only by stories carried back by thousands of visitors, but by articles which have appeared in 500 dailies in the United States having a circulation of 14,000,000 copies and in hundreds of smaller dailies and weeklies and the larger magazines."[46]

Community leaders began to understand the value of the aquarium to the cities of Miami and Miami Beach and to formulate strategies for keeping it open. The Kiwanis Club put forth the idea of raising the millage rate one-half percent for publicity purposes, which they believed would raise approximately $13,000. Additionally, there was discussion of establishing an aquarium association to raise additional funds. The Rotary Club made a proposal to finance the deficit for a period of three years. Estimating the annual deficit at $20,000, Allison promised that if outside funds were raised to take care of the deficit, he would forget about his investment in the buildings and would donate his services in managing and maintaining the aquarium.[47]

Various civic clubs, including Rotary, Kiwanis, Civitan, Exchange, and Women's, as well as the realty board, banded together and met with the county commissioners with the proposal developed by the Kiwanis Club. The county commissioners did not approve the increase in the millage tax.[48]

When the aquarium was dismantled for the construction of a hotel, Allison had the special glass and the pumps donated to the City of Miami to be used in the event they decided to build another aquarium.[49] The property was sold and became the location for the hotel.

25

Prohibition

Having grown up in the Midwest, Allison had been exposed to the prohibition movement throughout his life. Although there had been temperance movements throughout the history of the United States, the movement which was to lead to the 18th Amendment to the United States Constitution had its roots at Oberlin College in Ohio.

The temperance movement was closely aligned with the Methodist church. As early as October 1828, the Temperance Society of Marion County was organized at the Methodist meetinghouse in Indianapolis.[1] The purpose of the Temperance Society was to "discontinue the use of ardent spirits, except as a medicine, both by precept and example." When the Temperance Society of Marion County was formed, ardent spirits did not include items such as beer, wine or hard cider.

During the 1880s and 1890s, there was a surge of concern for society's ills, which included poor working conditions, poverty, and the use of liquor. One group of reformers, the National Temperance Society, focused on alcohol. Its strategy was on education through churches and church Sunday schools rather than through political engagement.[2]

One effective tactic pursued by the ladies of the church was to pray outside the saloons for the souls of the people who frequented them. As Allison's family was actively involved in Roberts Park Methodist Church, he undoubtedly heard rhetoric of the temperance movement.

In 1887, the Oberlin College–based temperance movement persuaded Howard Hyde Russell to lead an option for a local option in Ohio. Russell, a graduate of Oberlin, was a Congregational minister.[3] At the time, those favoring temperance were in the minority (approximately 40 percent). But, there was a big divide. The people in the cities, particularly Cincinnati and Columbus, were opposed to the temperance movement while those in rural communities were in favor. The local option strategy allowed communities to decide whether they wanted to be "wet" or "dry." By appealing to the local citizens, the anti-liquor forces were able to gain a foothold during a time when the general population of the United States was against prohibition.[4]

In May 1893, the Oberlin College temperance group reorganized as the Ohio Anti-Saloon League with a goal to eradicate all saloons, beer and other liquor outlets.[5] By 1895, the temperance movement had gained traction when they held a national meeting in Washington, D.C., with a focus on establishing a nationwide network of Anti-Saloon Leagues. This was the first special interest movement in America.

The prohibition movement did not have organized opposition.[6] It was not that Americans were in favor of being "dry." As an example, of the 1,250,000 voters in Ohio, only 400,000 favored prohibition.[7] Yet the "drys" were able to control the legislative agenda, as the rural areas had greater representation per voter in the legislature than did the urban areas.

Also contributing to the growth of the prohibition movement was the fact that the manufacturers of beer and liquor did not effectively mobilize. During the late 1800s, the liquor industry, which included beer, contributed between 20 percent and 40 percent of the national tax revenues.[8] The distillers and brewers erroneously believed that the politicians would never allow prohibition to gain control of the national agenda and threaten the tax base.

But the Anti-Saloon League's Howard Hyde Russell had hired Wayne Wheeler as an organizer. His focus was to preach on Sundays to spread the word and during the other six days of the week to organize legislative districts. Wheeler was very effective in the organizational duties and became the force behind the prohibition movement.

The Anti-Saloon League got a boost from anti–German sentiments prevalent during World War I. There had been significant immigration of Germans in the 1880s and 1890s and they had brought with them their culture, which included beer and beer gardens.[9] When World War I broke out, Wheeler was able to increase the hostility against the German Americans and their beer gardens. Although the vast majority of German Americans were supportive of the United States once it entered the conflict, Wheeler was able to take advantage of the anti–German sentiment.[10]

The 18th Amendment, which prohibited alcohol, came before the United States Senate in 1917. After a mere thirteen hours of debate, it passed with a lopsided vote. A few months later, the amendment came before the United States House of Representatives and was debated for a day before passing. As an amendment to the Constitution, the legislation required ratification by three fourths of the state legislatures. By January 1919, the requisite ratifications had been gained and Prohibition was passed into law.[11]

The Volstead Act prohibited the manufacture of liquor, although there were certain exemptions, including medicinal use. The act did not prohibit people from drinking from their own supply in their own homes.[12] This led to Americans stocking up on liquor supplies during the closing months of 1919 until the implementation of the act on January 17, 1920. Those who could afford to stocked up on liquor and stored it in their homes, in warehouses and even in safe deposit boxes. On January 15, 1920, John C. Knox, a New York judge, decreed that all liquor stored outside of the home was illegal and therefore subject to seizure. With a mere two days before implementation of the Volstead Act, there was panic among those who had stored the liquor outside of their homes to bring as much as possible to their homes.[13]

Florida, like many states, had become a mixture of dry and wet localities. By 1913, Miami Beach had voted itself "dry." As long as Prohibition was a local issue, few who wanted a drink went without one. That changed when liquor was outlawed by the passage of the 18th Amendment. With prohibition enforced by federal authorities, a drink became more difficult to obtain.[14] Allison had planned ahead and had a significant cache of liquor stored in his private apartment at the Miami Aquarium.

The Federal Prohibition Bureau, which was part of the Department of the Treasury, was responsible for the enforcement of the Volstead Act. When the Volstead Act was passed, nobody envisioned that enforcement would be difficult. John F. Kramer, the first Prohibition commissioner, proclaimed, "This law will be obeyed in cities, large and small, and in villages, and where it is not obeyed it will be enforced.... The law says that liquor to be used as a beverage must not be manufactured. We shall see that it is not manufactured. Nor sold, nor given away, nor hauled in anything on the surface of the earth or under the earth or in the air."[15]

Congress voted slightly more than $5,000,000 for the enforcement of the act. The allocation allowed for the hiring of 1,520 men, which was insufficient for the enforcement along the roughly 18,700 miles of coastlines and borders. Additionally, the Prohibition agents were poorly paid, with annual salaries ranging between $1,200 and $2,000.[16]

Despite enforcement efforts, liquor continued to be easily available. In 1924, the Department of Commerce estimated that $40,000,000 in liquor flowed into the United States. Assistant secretary of the Treasury, General Lincoln C. Andrews, estimated that in 1925 Prohibition agents intercepted a scant 5 percent of the liquor smuggled into the county. Ships brought in rum from Bimini or Belize, either entering United States ports or off-loading the cargo to motorboats. Rail cars from Canada had whiskey interspersed among other cargo. Additionally contributing to the supply of liquor was illicit distilling. By 1930, illegal distilleries were supplying an estimated seven to eight times the level of liquor being smuggled into the United States.[17]

Enforcement in the southeast corner of Florida was particularly difficult due to two factors. First was the population, with a significant number of both residents and visitors to Miami and Miami Beach being well-heeled. These people were not as likely to be pursued by the Prohibition Agents as were those less well connected. The second was that many liquor distillers had taken their stocks to the Bahama Islands in anticipation of implementation of the Volstead Act. Those islands are a quick boat ride away from the Miami Beach area, which fact gave rise to the southeastern coast of Florida becoming an off-loading point for bootleggers.

As enforcement of the Volstead Act began, the *Miami Herald* regularly had a story of a large supply of liquor being confiscated. A frequently used method for importing liquor was in the hulls of boats arriving from Cuba or the Bahamas. People would off-load the supply onto smaller vessels for the last three miles of the trip. Other methods of importing liquor was in private railcars as well as in touring vehicles.

Prohibition did not deter Allison and his crowd from enjoying their favorite alcoholic beverages. They also kept one another abreast of enforcement happenings. On April 5, 1920, Allison sent Fisher a letter issuing a warning about a potential raid: "By the way, when I was in Washington, I got a tip from Jack [LaGorce] that there are about a half dozen Secret Service men in Miami looking around and trying to get a line on any information as to the location of any wet goods. So it might be a pretty good idea to have anything that your friends may own placed in a safe place. I think that Peterson is putting everything I am interested in in the new storage place, where I think that it will be all right."[18]

It had long been rumored in Miami Beach that Allison had a cache of liquor. In April 1921, Dade County sheriff Louis A. Allen had been told that liquor was stored in the tower of the Miami Aquarium. He secured a search warrant from county judge W. Frank Blanton. Deputies Flood and Rolfe went to the aquarium to search for the cache of liquor. They searched the tower, the water tanks and Allison's private yacht, *L'Apache*. Despite the information that they had received and a search of the premises, they were unable to locate the liquor.

As Deputies Flood and Rolfe were leaving the premises, five federal agents arrived, also with the mission of searching for the supply of illegal liquor. The federal agents inquired of Deputies Flood and Rolfe if they had been searching for the liquor. Flood and Rolfe confirmed that they had been but they were unsuccessful. One of the federal Prohibition officers replied, "Come with us and we will show you where it is." With that the men followed the diagram of the building provided by a former employee of Allison. Without searching anywhere else, they followed the diagram to the location of a vault inside of Allison's second floor apartment in the aquarium building. At the location where the liquor was allegedly stored, they discovered a plastered wall. Without delay, they took a hatchet to tear away the plaster. Very quickly, they uncovered an iron door measuring two and a half feet by three feet. Upon opening the door, they uncovered the supply of liquor. Inside the vault were two hundred cases of liquor containing 2,400 bottles. Among the supply were bottles of champagne, other fine wines, vermouth, martini cocktails, gin, and Scotch and Irish whiskeys. After they listed the cache, all of it was destroyed by the federal agents with the exception of enough for evidence.[19]

Allison was in Indianapolis at the time of the raid. Fisher reported to him that the *Miami Herald* had been very discreet in its coverage of the raid.

> The Revenue Officers came over yesterday afternoon with a diagram of the entire lay-out of where you had placed "your" liquor. You will note I say "your" liquor. They were very nice, very polite and completely thorough. It seems as tho' your former chauffeur (and this is confidential) had stolen 35 cases from the place before you had it sealed up: he went back to steal all of it and found it sealed. He became frightened and left, not attempting to break into this sealed part. However, they caught him for bootlegging, probably gave him the Third Degree, and he told just where he got the liquor. The first information came from this chauffeur telling a hired stool pigeon. This dope we got from people friendly to us.[20]

It does not appear that Allison suffered any significant financial consequences from the seizure of the liquor other than the loss of his supply and a $500 fine. During Prohibition, the wealthy were virtually immune from prosecution. Prosecution was targeted for those who were unable to defend themselves — the poor, the illiterate and immigrants. Although the liquor was seized from the aquarium, Allison continued to have a supply through the remainder of Prohibition.

26

Allison Assumes Indianapolis Motor Speedway Presidency

The winter of 1922 was a period of angst for the owners of the Indianapolis Motor Speedway. The 1922 race by all accounts was the most successful of all of the contests up to that point. But management faced issues in that automobile manufacturers' interest in the race continued to decline. This trend started with the 1920 race when passenger cars were no longer competitive in motor races. Another issue facing Allison and Fisher was the condition of the track. The track needed approximately $200,000 worth of repairs and upgrades.[1]

But a larger issue was looming. Perry Faulkner, the American Legion's state commander, had started a campaign to make all "commercialized sports" illegal in the state of Indiana on Memorial Day. This action would prohibit the running of the Indianapolis 500 on Memorial Day. Even though the membership of the American Legion didn't support the action, Faulkner continued to pursue this legislation. The Robert L. Moorhead Memorial Day Bill was pushed through the Indiana legislature. After having passed both houses of the legislature, it was vetoed by Governor Warren McCray after Indiana attorney general U.S. Lesh issued an opinion that the law was unconstitutional based on the grounds of "class legislation." The Indiana senate upheld the veto by a vote of thirty-three to five.[2] With the veto by Governor McCray, the 12th running of the Indianapolis 500 occurred on May 30.

The underlying goal for Fisher and Allison of improvement in the automobile was displayed in the continued reduction in the size of the engine. A mere twelve years before, Harroun's car had an engine of 477 cubic inches. By 1923, the engine size was reduced to two liters (122 cubic inches).[3] The ability of a smaller engine to mimic the output of a larger engine has to do with the revolutions per minute of the engine. The smaller engine does more revolutions per minute to mimic the performance by fewer revolutions per minute of the larger vehicles.[4] This race also eliminated the requirement for a riding mechanic, a rule that had been in place since the 1911 win by Ray Harroun. Every car entered in the race was a single seater.[5]

The pace car for 1923 was an Indianapolis-built Duesenberg, which several weeks prior to the race had set a 3,100 mile nonstop record on the speedway. Upon leaving the track after the pace lap, the car driven by Fred Duesenberg was reaching 70 mph.[6]

On May 31, 1923, Fisher stunned the Indianapolis 500 crowd with his consideration of selling his shares. His focus was on maintaining the track for testing of automobiles. The growth of the 500-mile race was of secondary importance to Fisher. If he wasn't able to find a buyer for his shares, he indicated, he would recommend selling the property for other purposes.[7]

Fisher approached Allison with the idea of buying his shares in the Indianapolis Motor Speedway. Fisher was in need of funds to support his Miami Beach development and he also had begun a similar development in Montauk, New York. Allison was amenable to buying Fisher's shares; however, the valuation was problematic. Allison wrote Fisher: "Regarding the fair price for your stock in the Speedway, it looks that you are looking at it from slightly the wrong angle. If you have your way about it, the track should be valued at simply a real estate proposition." Allison estimated the maximum value of the real estate at $326,400 and believed that could be 10 percent high. In 1922, Allison had attempted to find a buyer for the racetrack as an operating entity at $648,000 but was not successful. Since that point, it appeared that the troubles with the legislature could further decrease the marketability of the Speedway.[8]

On June 11, 1923, Fisher stepped down from the presidency of the Indianapolis Motor Speedway and Allison became the president in addition to being the primary stockholder.[9] He and Fisher would continue to travel to Indianapolis for the races but the daily decision making had been turned over to others.

With the Florida market soaring and their interest in the Indianapolis Motor Speedway waning, Fisher and Allison began exploring purchasers for the track. One prospective owner envisioned the track as a real estate development. Despite their declining interest, Fisher and Allison remained committed to maintaining the track for the testing of automobiles.

In July 1921, Allison was also deeply involved in the purchase of the controlling interest in Fletcher American Bank from Stoughton Fletcher. The bank was having liquidity issues resulting from the economic downturn following the conclusion of World War I. As a board member and a large stockholder, Allison was intimately involved in the raising of additional capital for the bank in April 1923. The bank's capital was increased from $2,000,000 to $3,000,000, which enabled the bank to write off $2,000,000 in delinquent loans incurred under the previous management.[10] Within a year, operations of the bank had improved to the point that it acquired National City Bank.[11]

The 1924 race was run in front of the largest crowd in the history of automobile racing. Joe Boyer, driving a Duesenberg, set a record pace of 98.24 mph.[12] The car, designed by Fred Duesenberg, was the first American-built car to be designed with a supercharger. The impact of the supercharger demolished the average speed record of 94.48 mph.[13] When the lineup for the 1925 race was determined, every car was equipped with a supercharger.[14]

After the 1924 race, *Motor Age* magazine extolled the fact that the Indianapolis Motor Speedway had achieved the impact on the development of automobiles envisioned by its founders. The cars in the 1924 race were, according to *Motor Age* magazine, not only the fastest but also the most reliable cars ever to race on the Speedway. Development of a new design for a car required only one year to "bring a new design to a very high state of perfection." Lastly, the development of the supercharger ushered in a new era of race cars that allowed for greater speeds with less piston displacement. *Motor Age* magazine predicted that cars would become more efficient and obtain higher speeds.[15]

By 1926, the maximum engine displacement had been reduced to 91.5 cubic inches. The slower average speed of this race for the winning car of 94.63 mph was caused by the weather. A rain-soaked track required a break early in the race. A second downpour around 3:00 P.M. caused the race to be called at 400 miles.[16] The winner of the race, Frank Lockhart, was a rookie. He previously had been a dirt-track racer and arrived in Indianapolis as a relief driver for Peter Kreis. A good showing during qualifying and the illness of Kreis gave Lockhart the driving responsibilities.[17]

When Tommy Milton retired from race car driving in 1926, Fisher believed he would be a logical purchaser of the Speedway. He approached Milton with the proposition that they would sell the Speedway to him for $100,000 less than the offer from the real estate developer. Milton expressed no interest in the Speedway. If it wasn't fun for Allison and Fisher, he was sure it wouldn't be fun for him. Instead, Milton expressed an interest in investing in the Montauk, New York, development.[18]

The winner of the 1927 race was George Souders driving a Duesenberg. Like Lockhart the year before, Souders was an unlikely winner as his previous experience had been on dirt tracks. His victory was aided by twenty-one of the thirty-three entries into the race because they did not finish.[19] The race was marked by spectacular incidents. One of them occurred early in the race when Norman Batten's Miller Special caught on fire. With flames coming from the rear of the car, Batten drove the vehicle in front of the grandstand. As the car slowed at the end of the pits, Batten was able to leap from the burning car.[20]

Eighteen months after Fisher approached Milton to purchase the Indianapolis Motor Speedway, another potential buyer appeared. Former race car driver and World War I ace Eddie Rickenbacker shared the long-term vision for the now historic track that it should remain as a place for testing cars and for running the 500-mile Classic.

Rickenbacker had difficulty finding financing for the purchase of the track. After receiving an extension from Allison, he was able to obtain funds from Frank Blair, a Detroit banker who provided a $700,000 bond issue with interest at 6.5 percent. Rickenbacker purchased the track. He owned 51 percent of the common stock when the deal closed on November 1, 1927.[21] Fisher and Allison remained on the board and Allison relinquished the presidency of the Indianapolis Motor Speedway to Rickenbacker.[22] There still remained the need for approximately $200,000 in repairs.[23]

27

Allison Engineering

Jim Allison, a perfectionist, took great pride in the work of Allison Engineering. He once told an employee, "I want you to remember that this is not just another machine shop. Whatever leaves this shop over my name must be the finest work possible."[1] This set the high standard at the shop for the quality craftsmanship of the engines and transmissions produced.

Allison Engineering's roots trace back to the Speedway Team Company founded by Allison and Fisher to own and fix racing cars. When Allison became the sole owner of Speedway Team Company in 1916, it was relocated to a one-story building on Main Street in Speedway, Indiana. This was a precision machine shop which Allison equipped with the most modern equipment. Work was done by twenty highly skilled mechanics and engineers. During the early years of Allison Engineering, the skilled machinists employed there had learned their craft at various automobile companies in Indianapolis, particularly National Motorcar.[2]

John Goldthwaite, in his oral history of Allison Engineering, described the machine shop as a "rich man's plaything." Allison loved the shop and was proud of the work it produced.[3] Allison's considerable wealth afforded the engineers and mechanics at Allison Engineering to develop solutions to complex problems at their own pace.[4]

In January 1917, Allison hired Norman Gilman as the chief engineer and superintendent for Allison Experimental. It wasn't long before the United States entered the fray of World War I. The entrance of the United States on April 17 was to have a significant impact on the company. The next day, Allison told Gilman, "Can't have any more races. Quit work on the cars, but hold the men and keep on paying them." Allison continued: "Go out and find how we can get the war orders rolling. Take any jobs you like, especially the ones the other fellow can't do."[5]

Gilman responded positively to this charge. Allison Engineering gained a variety of jobs, including the development of production models of trucks, superchargers, Whippet tanks and high speed tractors.[6] The largest contract gained by Allison Engineering was to improve a Caterpillar-type tractor. The United States Army was trying to find a vehicle to carry artillery.[7]

When the United States entered World War I, the War Department had only fifty-five planes, the majority of which were training craft. With the need for more planes for the war effort, the War Department focused on increased production. Over the next nineteen months, over twelve thousand planes would be manufactured.[8]

Even more significant to the future of Allison Engineering was the development of the tools, gages, models and fixtures for the Liberty Engines for Nordyke & Marmon.[9] Allison Experimental made the original Liberty engine cut out of solid billets of steel. This model served as the tooling model for Nordyke & Marmon. It was then copied in the manufacturing of the engines.[10] Allison Experimental staffing quickly increased to 100 mechanics and engineers and 150 temporary draftsmen.[11] To provide space for them, Allison constructed a two-story building on Main Street in Speedway.

The United States Navy needed an aircraft capable of making transatlantic flights. The solution was a modification of the Liberty engine to include reduction gears that allowed both the engine and the propellers to operate at peak efficiency. The epicyclic reduction geared Liberty engine was designed by Packard Motors with the assistance of Mauric Olley, a Rolls-Royce engineer loaned to Packard for this project. In January 1918, Allison Engineering won a contract for the production of 250 epicyclic reduction geared Liberty engines.[12]

Throughout most of the 1920s, Allison Engineering was the only company with the knowledge and skill to build aircraft reduction gears. They supplied reduction gear to Wright Aeronautical and Curtiss Engine as well as for the United States Army.[13]

With the death of Johnny Aitken in October 1918 from the influenza epidemic, Allison promoted Gilman to vice president, general manager and chief engineer of Allison Experimental. Gilman, like Allison, was a self-educated man. Having learned his engineering skills through a mail order course, Gilman had a talent for mechanical proportions and an ability to figure out ways to make things work.[14] As World War I drew to a close, the company returned to the development of parts for auto racing machines.

With the sale of the racing vehicles after the 1919 Indianapolis 500, Allison directed Gilman to pursue contracts such as the company had performed during World War I. Just as he had in 1917, Gilman responded positively to Allison's directives. With Allison's primary focus being on his Florida investments, the daily management of the company was turned over to

Gilman. To reflect the change in focus, the company's name was changed to Allison Engineering.

One of the projects undertaken by Allison Engineering around 1920 was the development of a marine engine. Allison and Fisher had been involved in yacht racing on the Great Lakes. They were looking for a better marine engine. The company, using its expertise in the development of the Liberty engine, designed a marine engine with a horsepower between 400 and 450. Using cast-iron cylinders and a heavy bronze crankcase, the engine was lighter than the conventional marine engine made of welded steel. It was effectively a waterproof aircraft engine which had been modified for use in a yacht.

Allison, Fisher and Newby each bought engines for $25,000 per engine. The "Allison 12" engines had the desired impact. Allison's boat, the *Sea Horse*, was equipped with two Allison 12 engines and achieved a speed of 26.5 mph. The *Sea Horse* won the express cruiser race in the 1921 Buffalo regatta and placed third in the Detroit regatta. Another Allison yacht, the *Aye-Aye-Sir* also raced in the 1921 Buffalo Regatta and placed second in the free for all and third in the 1921 Detroit Regatta. Impressively, this boat ran the 260 miles from Detroit to Buffalo without having any engine maintenance.[15] Allison also had an Allison 12 installed in the *Aye-Aye-Sir II*, which was built for the Miami Regatta in 1922. The boat had a speed of 43 mph. It didn't participate in the races, as the propeller shaft snapped and broke a hole in the hull of the boat, which sank in the shallow waters of Biscayne Bay.[16]

Several of Fisher's yachts were equipped with the Allison 12.[17] Fisher sang the praises of the Allison 12 after the boat traveled from Miami Beach to New York City: "The *Shadow F* arrived day before yesterday, in perfect condition, after a 1,000, mile run; nothing was necessary to do to the engines except to tighten one governor spring, which required about five minutes to do so. The job of building is perfectly beautiful — I haven't seen any boat job to equal it, and the engine installation is marvelous. Yesterday we took the boat at full speed for about twenty miles without anybody being in the engine room."[18] Arthur Newby's yacht, *Altonia II*, was equipped with an Allison 12 engine.[19] Due to the expense of the marine engine, it was never brought to market.[20]

The Liberty engines, which had been manufactured for use in World War I airplanes, had one significant flaw. After about 50 hours of operation, they would suffer a failure of the connecting rod. Gilman and the Allison Engineering engineers diagnosed the problem as the distortion of the rod bearing shell at high speeds. At that time the rod bearing had a heavy bronze shell lined with babbitt.[21] The bearing had been clamped onto the rod. As the bronze rod worked back and forth, it would begin to deteriorate. Gilman proposed the solution of making the rod with steel rather than bronze. Although this improved the strength of the rod, the steel did not function well. After running various tests, Allison engineers were able to heat the steel shell until it was red hot and then they cast a molten lead bronze mixture around it. This solution provided the strength of steel but the properties of bronze. The rod was then milled to the proper specifications.[22] This extended the life of the Liberty engine from about 50 hours to hundreds of hours. The creative solution led to Allison Engineering's gaining army contracts after the war to retrofit new bearings into surplus Liberty engines.[23]

In 1921, Allison Engineering began to manufacture steel bearings with a bronze liner for the Wright Aeronautical Whirlwind engines. They were of such high quality that Charles Lindbergh insisted that the engine in the *Spirit of St. Louis* manufactured by Wright Aeronautical utilize Allison bearings prior to his famed flight to Paris. John Goldthwaite believed that one of the things that made long flights such as Lindbergh's possible were the Allison bearings.[24]

By 1927, the bronze backed engine bearings developed at Allison Engineering became used in all U.S and most foreign made piston type aircraft engines. Allison soon became a major supplier to aircraft engine manufacturers throughout the world.[25] The use of the Allison bearings for both automobile and airplane production resulted in orders not only from the United States Army, Navy and Coast Guard but also Curtiss Aeroplane and Motor Company, Armstrong-Siddley Motors of England, the Italian Air Ministry, Rickenbacker Motor Company, Marmon Motorcar Company and Mitsubishi of Japan. The bearings were the primary product for Allison Engineering. Sales more than doubled in 1927 and 1928.[26]

At the conclusion of World War I, one desired improvement was an aircraft engine which would run at high speed while the propeller would run at a lower speed. The solution was in gear reduction. The then prevailing thought was that high speed would destroy any gearing through vibration. Additionally, the loads were too high to permit a safe design within acceptable weight limits.[27] Although there were some primitive reduction gears in Europe, the United States had not yet developed this technology.[28]

In 1923, Allison Engineering designed and built reduction gears for the United States Navy's *Shenandoah*, a zeppelin-type aircraft (blimp). The *Shenandoah* required reduction and reverse gearing with clutches, brakes, extension shafts and vibration dampers.[29] Based upon the success of the reduction gears for the *Shenandoah*, Allison Engineering was the successful bidder on a prototype extension shaft gear for Goodyear. This extension shaft gear was the longest shafting used in aircraft at that time.[30]

World War I vehicle used to carry artillery, the engine manufactured by Allison Engineering (courtesy Rolls-Royce Heritage Trust, Allison Branch).

In 1924, Allison Engineering designed its first engine for the military market, a 4,520 cubic inch air-cooled engine which generated 1,200 hp. The engine, the X-4520, was designed for a large biplane and was the largest engine known at the time of development. When Ford developed a trimotor transport, the monoplane with multiple power sources was established as a viable option for powering large aircraft.[31] Although the X-4520 engine was not utilized by the Army Air Corp, it was displayed at the Century of Progress Exposition in Chicago in the mid 1930s.[32] (This engine, which was discovered in an airplane junkyard in New England, is now on display as a part of the collection of Rolls-Royce Heritage Trust — Allison Branch in Indianapolis, Indiana.)

In the mid–1920s, the company also manufactured high speed blowers for aircraft engine supercharging.[33] These were sold to foreign governments as well as to Pratt & Whitney.[34] The Pratt & Whitney R1340 Wasp engines using Allison Engineering reduction gears set altitude records for several years during the late 1920s.[35]

Another Allison Engineering development in the mid–1920s was that of gears for a helicopter. A Russian named DeBothezat convinced the United States Army that he could build an aircraft which could rise from the ground by a huge propeller on a vertical shaft. His problem was that, although he could design the aircraft, he didn't have the technical expertise to design the

Allison Engineering, two-story building built during World War I. The original one-story building is on the right side of photo (courtesy Rolls-Royce Heritage Trust, Allison Branch).

gears and shafts. Allison Engineering was able to design the parts which would turn the large propeller including the gearing, the shaft and the bearings. Unfortunately for DeBothezat, his design when built could only rise about five feet from the ground.[36]

Allison Engineering was also involved in the development of a diesel powered engine to be used in the zeppelin-type airships at the request of the United States Navy. The original power source for the airships was gasoline based.[37] By 1927, Allison Engineering had developed an air-cooled engine for the Army Air Force which had 1200 horsepower and weighed 2700 pounds.[38]

In the 1920s, futurists started talking about the development of a "flivver," a small plane conceived for everyday family use.[39] The engineers at Allison Engineering were designing a small aircraft engine to be used in this personal aircraft when it was developed. This engine was not brought to commercial use.[40]

One of the issues for Allison Engineering was the lack of a product line which would generate sustainable profits. Allison understood this was an issue but didn't have any interest in pursuing contracts. He wrote to Carl Fisher:

Top: "Allison 12" engines (also known as "Miami 12" engines) on the shop floor of Allison Engineering. These are the engines built by Allison Engineering that were used in the yachts owned by Allison, Fisher and Newby. *Bottom:* Three engines made by Allison Engineering. On the left-hand side is a Liberty engine. In the middle is an "Allison 12" (marine) engine. On the right is the Allison Lite, which was used for auxiliary power on the yachts when the Allison 12 engine wasn't running (both photographs courtesy Rolls-Royce Heritage Trust, Allison Branch).

Going into a regular manufacturing business would mean that I would have to pitch in and build up a selling organization, and as long as I am comfortably located on Biscayne Bay, listening to the rattle of the trucks over the Causeway and enjoying the cool breeze at the Fish house, my mind does not hanker to tackle another job. What's the use? I have sufficient to eat to satisfy my tummy, more to drink that the aforesaid tummy can properly take care of, and plenty of leisure to do anything else my strength will allow me to, so I can't see where I could gain anything by adding another bunch of dividends and I can see a whole lot to be lost by going to work again.[41]

Throughout the history of Allison Engineering, the emphasis was on the develop of superior products and solving engineering problems. Allison himself did not have a mandate for the firm to be profitable and was content to break even. His only charge to the management of Allison Engineering was that "I want that Allison name something to be proud of." He encouraged risk taking in terms of developing something which had seemed impossible.[42]

Although the company that bore his name was becoming very successful, Allison was losing interest in it as his health deteriorated. Although he would eventually visit the plant only once a year, he remained proud of the innovation and the products which occurred at Allison Engineering.

28

Allison Hospital

As with his other business ventures, the founding of Allison Hospital was driven by Allison's passion.

After a long day of pursuing his business interests, Allison was often found relaxing in the Riverdale basement, which stretched the full length and width of the house. Unlike most homes, the basement did not contain the furnace and coal room. Rather it was a place to relax and entertain. The primary entrance of the basement was through the aviary. As with the upstairs rooms of Riverdale, the basement rooms were well appointed. Among the unique features of Riverdale was an indoor swimming pool which measured 70 feet by 22 feet. In addition to the swimming pool, the basement featured a Bavarian style rathskeller which was used as a billiard parlor. Next door was a card room with a Gothic arch ceiling and medieval hunting scenes painted on the ceiling.[1] Allison would have his friends downstairs to play pool or for a game of cards. Frequently joining the card games was his pet monkey, Jackie. The basement also included a photography lab, a laundry room and a fruit cellar.

Prior to dinner, Allison would frequently take a swim in the indoor pool. When he was 41 years old, he came home to Riverdale Springs in March 1914 after a long day at work. Accompanied by his wife, he went to the swimming pool. As Sadie Allison sat in the pool area, Allison dove into the pool. The shock of the cool water brought on chest pains. Leaving the pool, Allison took the elevator to the second floor and changed for dinner.

After dressing for dinner, he joined his wife in the well appointed dining room. The room was masculine, with three quarter length paneling of hand-carved old English walnut. The carvings were in a bacchanalian design of grape and grapevines. At the west end of the room was a Gothic-style fireplace with lion heads supporting the mantle. Throughout the meal, Allison continue to suffer chest pains. Later in the evening, his personal physician was summoned. The chest pains were an indicator that Allison had suffered a heart attack.

Upon his retirement upon the sale of Prest-O-Lite, Allison still had business interests in Indianapolis, including Allison Engineering and the Indianapolis Motor Speedway. During the winter months in Miami Beach he became deeply involved in real estate development. And in 1920, his Florida interests expanded to include the Miami Aquarium and Laboratory. His retirement was still filled with business activities and social events.

Although the Miami Aquarium was well received at its opening in January 1921, his friends were aware that his health was continuing to deteriorate. In April 1921, Jack LaGorce, the National Geographic Society executive, expressed concern about Allison's health to Fisher in a letter: "I have been very much worried over Allison's condition. I have never seen him so depressed and thoroughly unhappy as he was this winter or yet with so little strength."[2]

Upon returning to Indianapolis in April 1921, Allison found himself again hospitalized. He had left Florida in early April with a cold. Arriving in Indianapolis, his condition had deteriorated and he was admitted to St. Vincent's Hospital with a diagnosis of bronchial pneumonia, which he attributed to "not having the sense to go to bed."[3]

After closing the Miami Aquarium in April 1923, Allison traveled to Indianapolis for the festivities associated with the running of the Indianapolis 500. While in Indianapolis, Allison, who was on the board of directors and a major stockholder of Fletcher American National Bank, was instrumental with its financial restructuring.

In early August, 1923, Allison's health deteriorated further. He had what appeared to be a severe case of bronchitis. By mid–August, he was hospitalized in Indianapolis with a sinus infection. Undergoing sinus surgery aggravated the bronchitis. Following the surgery, an additional complication arose when he also developed digestive issues. These medical issues caused additional stress upon his already weakened heart.

Throughout this hospitalization, Allison was anxious to return to Florida. By mid–September, plans were being made to travel to Ft. Lauderdale, where he would regain his strength at Dr. Scott Edward's hospital. When he was stronger, he would return to Miami Beach.[4] In late October, Allison traveled by his private rail coach to Ft. Lauderdale.

In Ft. Lauderdale, his health continued to be precarious and it is believed that he suffered another heart attack. In a late October letter to Sadie Allison, who had remained in Indianapolis, Fisher wrote, "Jim had a very close call, and he is not out of the woods yet, but he is gaining. He has gained four pounds in weight recently, but his pulse now is not quite normal and the doctors do not want him disturbed." The stay at the Ft. Lauderdale

Hospital was depressing for Allison. The man who loved the outdoors was confined to a sterile white room and found the food poor.

Allison's frequent hospitalizations left him with a very poor opinion of hospitals. After recovering his strength, he told Sara Allison that he was going to build a fine hospital in Miami Beach: "This hospital I've in mind will be for rich people" he said. "All hospitals are alike — white walls, white beds, bare floors, bare windows. Take a sick person away from a luxurious home and put them in one of these rooms — and they often die. I want rooms that will be in keeping with what they have been accustomed to, to make them comfortable and satisfied."[5]

He talked with Fisher of his ideas for a hospital, which was a cross between the Mayo Clinic and Maxim's.[6] It would cater to the wealthy and provide them with the accouterments to which they were accustomed. Fisher was equally enthusiastic and believed that the hospital would be another drawing card to the wealthy individuals who had built winter homes, or were visiting, in Miami Beach. By the start of construction in 1925, J.C. Penney, James Snowden (a wealthy oilman), Clarence Busch (a brewing magnate), Harvey Firestone and Arthur Newby had homes on Miami Beach.[7] Fisher donated eight and one half acres on the southern tip of a man-made island he named Allison Island being created on Indian Creek.[8]

When Allison made the decision to build the hospital, south Florida was experiencing a real estate boom. It started in 1923 when the economic recession which had begun in 1921 was lifting. As business prospects improved, Americans began to feel more comfortable with the future. With the freedom gained by the automobile and better roads, many began to travel to warmer climates in the winter.

The tourist season in 1923 witnessed a significant growth in the number of visitors to Miami Beach and the purchase of lots and completed homes. The hotels were filled to capacity as were the three golf courses. The Miami bathing casinos had at times more than 10,000 people. On the real estate front, in January 1923, building permits were more than eight times larger than in January 1922.[9]

In preparation for the 1924 season, additional hotels were built, including the Nautilus by Carl Fisher, the Pancoast by J. Arthur Pancoast and smaller hotels in South Beach, providing enough rooms to accommodate 4,000 people. Anticipating a strong tourist season, many of the hotels opened earlier than the traditional January 1.[10] The real estate boom was in full force throughout south Florida and peaked in 1925. Between March and August 1925, there were "binder boys" who purchased options for real estate for a small payment, frequently 10 percent. The binder boys then flipped the property, thus escalating the price. For example, in 1925, a property purchased by N.B.T. Roney and James M. Cox for $3,000,000 was sold to the binder boys for $7,600,000. Within a week, the binder boys had sold the property for $12 million.[11]

Allison hired August Geiger to design the hospital, which was sited at the south end of Allison Island. Geiger, who grew up in New Haven, Connecticut, had located to the Miami area in 1905. His father was a manufacturer of moldings and fine woodwork for interiors.[12] Throughout his career, Geiger was a well recognized Florida architect. Allison was familiar with Geiger, as he had designed Fisher's oceanfront home and the Lincoln Hotel.[13] Allison also hired Geiger to design his residence on Star Island.

The three story Spanish style building contained forty patient rooms, all with views of the water, and a solarium and a boat dock. In accordance with Allison's vision, a special effort was made to keep the building from having the white, sterilized atmosphere of the average hospital. The walls of the first floor, which contained offices, X-ray rooms, dental parlors, an emergency ward and a dining room and kitchen, were a pale cream color. The operating rooms, located on the second floor, were painted a pale green. The patients' rooms, situated to overlook the water, were painted a pale cream color. Elevators went to the roof where convalescents could enjoy the view of the ocean and Indian Creek.[14]

Also part of the Allison Hospital facilities was a separate laundry and a nurses' residence. Allison's humor was expressed in a letter to Fisher describing the arrangements for the nurses: "blonds on one side, brunettes on the other, no red heads."[15] As plans for the hospital developed, Allison's vision expanded: "I have in mind the possibility of a wonderful world wide health resort taking the whole island."[16] Fisher was less enthusiastic when he conveyed that, although he thought the health resort was a good idea, it would need to be self-sufficient.[17]

As the hospital was being constructed in 1925, south Florida was experiencing a railroad and shipping crisis. Building in south Florida was outstripping the ability of the laborers to unload the building materials arriving on freight cars and steamers. Unable to unload the freight cars, the Florida East Coast Railway declared an embargo on additional freight traveling to south Florida. With the labor force stretched beyond capacity and an inability of raw materials to keep up with the demand, prices soared.[18]

Allison's Hospital opened January 1, 1926. He had hired a French chef from the Waldorf-Astoria in New York. The food was served on fine china and the flatware was sterling silver. The cost of the hospital was $3,652,000. When it opened, it had fifteen patients and nine staff doctors. Upon its open-

Allison Hospital, which opened in January 1926. The hospital was located at the southern end of Allison Island in North Miami Beach. To the right is the Atlantic Ocean. The nurses' home is to the left of the hospital. Biscayne Bay would be to the left (courtesy Historical Museum of South Florida).

ing, the hospital developed a reputation as one of the finest in the world. Just like the Miami Aquarium, the timing for the opening of the hospital was terrible. The real estate boom in Florida peaked in 1925. Many visitors after the 1925 season returned to the north with tales of inadequate housing and crowded conditions. They also told tales of the rapidly escalating prices of real estate. Adding to the tales from south Florida were newspaper articles in northern newspapers reporting milk and bread shortages and that much of the Florida real estate being sold was underwater.[19]

On January 11, 1926, the *Prinz Valdemar*, a large sailing ship, overturned in Biscayne Bay, effectively blocking the small port of Miami for forty-two days.[20] This caused a further backlog of building materials, which was widely reported on a nationwide basis. Fewer people visited Miami Beach in 1926 and the real estate boom busted. Properties which had been escalating in price weren't selling. Those who had bought on speculation stopped paying.

Throughout the growth period of Miami Beach, south Florida hadn't been hit by a hurricane, the last occurring in 1910. In July 1926, a small hurricane hit north of Miami, causing minor damage. In mid–September, the United States Weather Bureau advised of three tropical depressions. One of the storms passed to the east of Miami Beach and brought large rains to the area. The second storm passed over the Virginia Capes area. On September 18, a hurricane with wind gusts up to 132 miles per hour hit Miami Beach and did significant damage to the resort.[21]

The hurricane caused floodwaters to cover Allison Island to a depth of two to three feet. The dock and Allison's $25,000 speedboat floated away. The dock was discovered at the rear of the hospital and was used for firewood. Allison's boat was not recovered. During the hurricane, the hospital provided refuge for 125 people in addition to treating 150 people with injuries; it did not sustain significant damage other than broken windows. The nurses' residence, however, was severely damaged. Like the blockage of Miami Harbor, the news of the hurricane quickly swept across the country. A second, smaller hurricane struck Miami Beach on October 20, 1926, which impeded progress on repairs to Miami Beach caused by the September hurricane.[22] When the winter season of 1926-1927 began, tourism was down significantly.

It did not take Allison long to realize that the economics for the hospital did not make sense and he approached a sanitarium to take over the hospital. When the negotiations failed, his Florida bookkeeper, Joe Lazry, suggested that he talk to Msgr. William Barry, the priest of St. Patrick's. Father Barry suggested the Sisters of St. Francis in Allegany, New York. The sisters had experience running hospitals in the north. Allison talked with the sisters but continued to hold out hope of continuing to run the luxury hospital. His health had deteriorated to the point that he was in a wheelchair and according to Sadie Allison was using narcotics for pain relief. With reluctance, in October 1927 Allison agreed to let the Sisters of St. Francis run the hospital for a year.

He immediately regretted the decision. The sisters put cost controls in place, including the use of paper napkins, the firing of five landscape gardeners and the usage of the resident manager's Dodge by the sisters. There was continuing conflict between Allison and the sisters and Allison quickly decided not to renew the sisters' contract.[23] Prior to termination of the contract, Allison died.

The sisters continued to run the hospital, renaming it St. Francis upon its purchase for $250,000 in 1929.[24] The hospital was closed and the land sold to a developer for $12,000,000 in the early years of the 21st century. The very low sales price to the sisters for the purchase of the 8-and-a-half-acre waterfront site was driven by the necessity to change the zoning from solely medical use to high density housing.

29

The Divorce

Jim and Sara first went to Florida around 1914. Allison was quickly enamored with the warm weather and the ability to sports fish to his heart's content. His marriage was starting to unravel, quickly, after the first trip to Miami Beach. Sara's tuberculosis had resulted in her being a semi-invalid, which limited her activities. Although Allison's health was deteriorating, he enjoyed the active life on his fishing vessel and socializing with friends and colleagues.

When the Allisons first began going to Florida for the winter, Allison had built a large oceanfront house, which was sold to Harvey Firestone. By 1920, the marriage had deteriorated to the point that Sadie Allison stayed at the Lincoln Hotel, which was more of an extended-stay apartment house. When the Miami Aquarium was built, Allison occupied an apartment on the second floor.

Although they were married, they apparently had little interaction. Sara became aware of Allison's social secretary, Lucille Mussett, who was a contemporary of her daughter, Cornelia. Sara suspected that Allison had an attraction to Miss Mussett after seeing a picture of her as part of a fishing party on Allison's vessel *L'Apache*. Cornelia, Sara Allison's daughter, confirmed that Miss Mussett was very attentive to Allison and was rather pretty.

After the aquarium closed, Allison started making plans for a new home. During the next year's visit to Miami Beach, Allison told Sara, "I'm going to build a house, a home for myself. A bachelor's home on Star Island."[1]

Star Island is the first man-made island in Biscayne Bay. A group consisting of various friends and associates of Allison and Fisher formed the Miami Ocean View Company. In 1916, they purchased bottomlands in Biscayne Bay from the State of Florida. Designed by the architectural firm of Price & McLanahan, a bulkhead was poured and filled in to create Star Island.[2] Originally built as the site for the Miami Beach County Club,[3] Star Island is an oblong a quarter mile wide by a half mile long[4] consisting of 55 acres.[5] The plans for the club were scaled back, with the clubhouse and docks becoming the Star Island Yacht Club, where Allison was the first commodore. The remainder of the island, which had originally been envisioned as a golf course, became a wealthy enclave with a drawbridge and a gatekeeper. It was one of the original "gated communities" and was divided into 44 lots, each of which were 400 feet by 100 feet. The lots on the western side of Star Island, which faced Miami, cost $150/linear foot. The east side of Star Island was considered more valuable since there was a deeper channel of water. Lots on the east side of Star Island ran $175 per linear foot.[6]

Allison proudly spread the blueprints of the Star Island home designed by August Geiger out for Sara to see. "I've all my plans.... It's not made for any woman to live in, as you can see," he proclaimed. The downstairs was taken up with offices and a kitchen and one bedroom with a bath. Upstairs, his living room was 80 feet long by 40 feet wide with a great fireplace at one end. Near the pantries and kitchen, a bar was planned. Bookcases filled with books were to line all the other walls.[7] (Tom Pancoast, a Miami Beach acquaintance, once commented that Allison "was an inveterate reader and possessed a remarkable library."[8]) Just as with Riverdale, the interior would be well appointed. The beamed ceiling was to be constructed of colored inlaid woods, while the floor would be "just like they use on yachts," with a cost of $16,000. The house was constructed during the summer of 1925 and Allison moved in upon returning to Florida in the fall.[9]

Many of the furnishings for the Star Island house were brought from Riverdale. Another prized possession in the home was a Remington painting of two cowpunchers trying to sell a sorrel white footed cow pony to an Englishman. This picture had hung on the walls of the Detroit Athletic Club for years before Allison took possession of it. The painting had the title *Judging a Horse*.[10]

Around 1924, Allison also told Sara that he was creating a new will. Sara recalls Allison saying:

> I am going to arrange for you to have half of the income from my estate as long as you live. I want you to have Riverdale as long as you live. You can sell it if you want to or divide it and sell part of the grounds and invest the money. The income will be a great deal more than you can use. Of course, I know you will take care of Cornelia as long as you live and you'll save a hell of a lot besides. If you outlive me a few years, Cornelia will be a rich girl. Besides, I'm going to set aside $50,000 in your trust for her. She can have it when you are through with it.

According to Sara, the will also stated that she was to have the furnishings of Riverdale for her lifetime.[11]

On April 17, 1928, Sara received a letter from Allison which said that Riverdale was closed to her forever. She could not go to Riverdale, the home she loved, for a month, a week or a day: "It is barred to you, by law." Encouraged by Cornelia to protect whatever assets she could, Sara filed for divorce on the grounds of mental cruelty. On June 27, a judge in Miami heard the case and granted the divorce. According to published reports, the monetary agreement, which was not disclosed, was agreeable to both parties.

Sara Allison left Miami for Indianapolis that Saturday night. Cornelia and her new husband, Jack Frazur, took Sara to the train station and made sure that she and Rosetta, a personal servant, were comfortably settled in the drawing room. In Jacksonville, Sara Allison was sitting at the window, gazing out. Suddenly, across several railroad tracks as the train shifted cars and engine, she thought she saw Allison sitting at a window in a luxurious private car.

Sara Allison spoke to Rosetta: "I believe I saw Mr. Allison sitting by the window over there. It looked exactly like him. Could it be?" Rosetta replied, "He was to leave last night. It couldn't be him." For the remainder of the trip to Indianapolis, Sara Allison couldn't forget what she saw. She believed that Allison's private car was attached to their long train.[12]

Upon arriving in Indianapolis, Sara was met by a party which included her sister, Jessie. After exiting the train, Sara thought that she saw the young chauffeur of Myra Allison, Allison's mother. She gazed at him and he looked at her. Her first thought was that he might be there to watch her. Jessie told Sara, "Sadie, Jim is on your train and his mother is here to meet him and his party." Jessie continued to tell Sara of Allison's traveling companions: "There is a prominent doctor and his wife from Miami and his girl secretary and one or two others."

Sara Allison left the train station and went to her residence at the recently constructed Marott Hotel. Like the Lincoln Hotel in Miami Beach, the Marott was designed for long-term residency. Also maintaining a residence there was Myra Allison. Allison and his party went to Riverdale.

30

The End

In late July, Jim Allison and Lucille Mussett again boarded the private railcar and traveled eastward to Fisher's home on Montauk Point, New York. On July 31, 1928, at a very small ceremony at Fisher's home, Jim Allison and Lucille Mussett were married by Edwin Dunlevy, the pastor of Roberts Park United Methodist Church. The next day, Allison developed a cold. The Allisons began their honeymoon, traveling to Asheville, North Carolina, by his private railcar, *Advance*. At that point, his cold had become much worse and the decision was made to travel back to Indianapolis rather than going on to Florida.

After arriving at Riverdale Springs, Allison settled into the large master bedroom. Just as in the first floor rooms, it was well appointed. With large windows, it was flooded by light. The drapes were made of a blue and gray fabric. It had a fireplace of carved mahogany. The furniture was custom made of carved mahogany and included a four poster bed. The canopy for the bed was made of the same fabric which was used for the window treatments.[1] With Allison's history of heart and respiratory diseases, his private physicians were summoned. Upon arriving at the home, Dr. E.H. Adkins of Miami Beach and Dr. John Cunningham of Indianapolis immediately understood the gravity of his condition. Dr. Adkins sent a wire to Fisher: "In critical condition. End seems only a matter of a few hours."[2] Fisher and his second wife, Margaret, immediately made plans to travel to Indianapolis.

Various people came to Riverdale as word of the severity of the illness spread to the family and close friends. Allison's brother, Cornelius, his mother and Lucille were at his bedside.[3] Long-time family servant Lucien drove to the Marott Hotel to advise Sara that Allison was severely ill. Sara Allison went to the home and was able to spend some time with her former husband. By the time the Fishers arrived in Indianapolis, Allison had succumbed to bronchial pneumonia a mere five days after his marriage. Indianapolis learned the next day of the loss of a favorite son, as the headline of the *Indianapolis Star* read, "Allison, Speedway Promoter, Dies Here."[4]

The visitation and funeral for Allison was held in the opulent foyer of Riverdale. When the mourners arrived at the house, they walked through the large bronze doors flanked by Grecian marble into rooms where many of them had been entertained by Allison.

During the visitation period preceding the service, unexpected visitors arrived at the home. Although Sara Allison had initiated the divorce proceedings and had agreed to the financial settlement, she blamed Lucille Allison for the dissolution of her marriage. She had been in consultation with her Indianapolis attorneys and filed legal suit against the widow for "alienation of affection." In the suit, Sara Allison charged that the present Mrs. Allison "systematically and deliberately" sought over a period of eight years to win the capitalist's affections and destroy his love for his former wife, beginning with Lucille's employment as Mr. Allison's secretary in 1919 or 1920.[5] During the visitation, process servers provided Lucille Allison with notice of a legal suit having been filed by Sara Cornelius Allison seeking $2,000,000 in compensation.

For those at Allison Engineering, the death of Allison was received with a sense of personal loss. It also meant a time of not knowing the future of the organization, which had been dependent upon its founder. In times when the company needed funds for payroll or other purposes because a government check had been delayed, all that had been needed was for Luther Langston, Allison's secretary, to go to the downtown banks and money would be deposited in the Allison Engineering account. This was done not on the basis of the financial strength of Allison Engineering but on the personal reputation of Allison.[6]

As Allison's wealth had grown, more people were wanting a piece of the pie. He would complain that everybody had their hand out for his money. The depth of the frenzy over his money soon became apparent. His estate was sought by his bride, Lucille Mussett Allison, his ex-wife, Sara Cornelius Allison, and his mother, Myra Allison. Long-time friend and business associate John Levi wrote that "when Mr. Allison died they all started a dog fight over his estate. They say his will was destroyed and he died without a will, therefore the heirs are all beginning to fight."[7]

The executor appointed for the estate was Tom Pancoast, which was very upsetting to Allison's Florida friends and business associates. Fisher believed that John Levi should have been appointed as the executor because Levi, secretary of the Allison Realty Company, was very familiar with Allison's various business interests in Miami Beach. Fisher expressed his opinions to Frank Shutts and Elmer Stout over the appointment of Tom Pancoast:

> Don't understand your action in appointing any other man than John Levi as one of the executors of Jim Allison's estate unless it is that the law interferes with such appointment. Levi is better qualified than any other man in the United States to act as Allison's executor for the reason he has been in constant touch with all the investments and moves Allison has made and is a co-partner in some of these investments. If the law decides he cannot be the executor then there is no further comment otherwise your appointments are entirely wrong for the interests of Allison.[8]

Elmer Stout, president of the Fletcher American National Bank in Indianapolis, explained the decision to Fisher:

> Like you, I naturally assumed that John Levi would be selected. However, several angles to the situation developed here which apparently made his appointment impossible. The problem as to who should be appointed was discussed by those interested in the estate for a period of over two weeks and there was no hasty action taken. I happen to have been in the Allison home when the lawyers fully explained those interested in the estate their rights as to appointment and designating other persons to be appointed. An agreement was finally reached in favor of Mr. Pancoast.[9]

Pancoast did not have an easy task as executor of the estate. The estate was complicated by the ownership of various properties and businesses in both Indianapolis and Miami Beach. Included in the Indianapolis interests were ownership of Allison Engineering and partial ownership of Globe Realty, Speedway Realty and the Wayne Sewer and Drain Company. Besides Riverdale Springs, Allison had owned a farm outside of Indianapolis. Additionally, there were several Indianapolis properties jointly owned with Fisher.

The Florida assets were estimated at $1,250,000.[10] At the time of his death, Allison owned 1,000 shares of Union Carbide, which was from the sale of Prest-O-Lite. The stock was in the name of Allison Realty, one of his Florida real estate interests. Additional Miami Beach interests included the Allison Hospital and his Star Island home, which had an appraised value of $175,000. Prior to his death, Allison had sold his yacht *L'Apache* to James H. Snowden and had taken a waterfront lot on Indian Beach valued at $300,000 in trade. Another complicating factor was that Allison jointly owned with John Levi two oceanfront lots. They had been purchased for $85,000 and $78,000 and Mr. Levi's interest approximated $67,000.[11]

A will was not discovered. Rumors also circulated throughout Indianapolis that Lem Trotter, Allison's business partner in Globe Realty, knew where the real will was as well as there being a fake codicil to the will. Allison had talked with Elmer Stout, the president of Fletcher American National Bank, shortly before his marriage to Lucille Mussett and had indicated that he would have a new will drafted when he returned to Florida.[12]

Prior to his death, Allison had discussed with Fisher the possibility of selling Allison Engineering. He believed the value of the company approximated $650,000 and had thought about issuing two classes of stock, preferred ($350,000) and common ($300,000). He would continue to hold the preferred stock and would share the common stock with the employees of the company. He had also considered selling the company directly to the employees.[13] By January 1929, an agreement had been reached by Allison's estate for the sale of Allison Engineering, as well as a lot across the street for $90,000, to Eddie Rickenbacker. The sale of Allison Engineering four months later to Fisher Brothers for $500,000 and shortly thereafter to General Motors led many to speculate that Rickenbacker was a front for General Motors, which wanted the company.[14] At the time of the sale to Fisher Brothers, Allison Engineering's net worth was $492,866.88.[15]

Allison's 50 percent ownership in Speedway Realty Company was sold for $112,000. His stock in this entity had been placed in trust for Sara Cornelius Allison.[16] Allison had also told both Fisher and Lucille Mussett Allison that he wished to provide for Mr. Bingham, who had been in his employ for several years, as well as Dr. Adkins.

Paul Y. Davis and M.E. Foley, attorneys for Lucille Mussett Allison, by the middle of October 1928, proposed a settlement for the estate. Mrs. Allison had signed a prenuptial agreement and the settlement proposed was in addition to this agreement. The proposal included that Lucille's share should not be less than that of Allison's surviving brother, Cornelius Allison, and sister, Lena Adkinson, which would be approximately 20 percent of the net estate after providing for his first wife (Sara) and estate expenses.[17] The Allison family did not agree with the settlement proposed by Lucille Allison.

As a settlement had not been reached, a probate hearing was scheduled for December 1928 in Indianapolis. If the probate had been successful, a substantial amount of the estate would probably have gone to Sara Allison. Under Indiana law, Lucille Allison would have received nothing due to the prenuptial agreement.

In April 1929, the estate of James Ashbury Allison was settled after the lengthy court battle waged by Sara Allison, Lucille Allison and Myra Allison. Judge Mahlon E. Bash of Indianapolis set aside the alleged will signed by Allison in which he left the bulk of the estate to Sara Allison. This will would have provided her with $50,000, the use of the Indianapolis estate for life and 50 percent of the income for life. Myra Allison would have received income from 25 percent of the estate. The remainder of the estate would have been distributed among the other heirs and their descendants. In making the decision to throw out this will, Judge Bash heard testimony from Elmer Stout, president of Fletcher American National Bank and George Forrey, vice president of Fletcher American National Bank that they had witnessed Allison tear his signature from the codicil of the will and announce "I revoke it."[18]

Judge Bash ruled that Allison died without leaving a will, as the tearing of his signature from the codicil made it invalid. This ruling was affirmed by the Florida court. After this ruling, Sara Allison did not receive anything from the estate. The prenuptial agreement between Allison and Lucille Mussett Allison provided for Lucille Allison to receive $1,000 per month. Myra Allison, his mother, received 90 percent of the estate. The other heirs to the estate were Allison's siblings, Noel Cornelius Allison, his brother, and Helena May Adkinson, his sister, and various nieces and nephews.[19]

31

The Indianapolis Motor
Speedway Thereafter

If the four founders of the Indianapolis Motor Speedway were to visit the racetrack today, they would be astounded by the technological improvements in the automobile, which was their original goal. The one hundred years of racing at this venue is a tribute to Allison and his friends Fisher, Newby and Wheeler as well as to the stewards of the track, Eddie Rickenbacker and Anton Hulman, who kept the vision alive despite the difficult times during the Great Depression as well as during and after World War II.

Rickenbacker, who purchased the Indianapolis Motor Speedway in 1927, was not content to be back in the automobile business. His heart was in the aeronautical industry. He encouraged General Motors to purchase a 40 percent interest in the Fokker Aircraft Corporation of America in May 1929. With the appointment as vice president of sales by General Motors, Rickenbacker moved to New York and turned over the operation of the Speedway to Pop Myers.[1]

Rickenbacker's association with General Motors started with the purchase of a Sheridan dealership in 1921. When General Motors unveiled the LaSalle in March 1927, it was selected as the pace car for the 1927 Indianapolis 500. Rickenbacker, who drove the car for the pace lap, was impressed with the vehicle. With a new brand to promote, General Motors wanted to kick off a major marketing campaign for the LaSalle. Lawrence P. Fisher, the head of the Cadillac division of General Motors, hired Rickenbacker to direct the marketing campaign.[2]

During the first year of operations under Rickenbacker's ownership, improvements to the Speedway were focused on improving the safety of the Speedway, including the rebuilding of the retaining walls and changing the angles of the curves.[3] Thinking of having the race broadcast on the radio,

Rickenbacker invited Merlin H. Aylesworth, the president of NBC, to the 1929 race.[4]

As part of the activities for winter visitors to Miami Beach, Fisher had introduced golf and polo.[5] With golf becoming a national pastime, and based upon the success of golf in Miami Beach, Fisher and Allison encouraged Rickenbacker to install a golf course during the negotiations for the purchase of the Speedway.[6] It was a logical use of the land in the center of the race-course. And like the previous ill-fated attempt of polo matches, a golf course would provide an income source other than the race and auto testing. Rickenbacker hired William H. Diddel to design the golf course, which opened in 1929 with nine holes inside the racetrack and another nine holes on the outside of the backstretch.[7] The golf course was barely opened when the October 1929 stock crash occurred. Although not immediately apparent at the time of the initial crash, the events over the next decade would be a great test of the famed track.

After the running of the 1929 contest, Rickenbacker announced changes to the format of the race for the 1930 event. His goal was to lower the cost of buying and maintaining race cars which prohibited automobile manufacturers' participation in the race. The knowledge of engine design had resulted in a race car engine running 6,000 to 8,000 revolutions per minute, which was too fast for use in a passenger automobile. As a result, automobile manufacturers had stopped entering cars in the race in 1920.[8]

Primary changes made by Rickenbacker for the race included banning the use of superchargers and raising the minimum cubic inches of displacement. Additionally, the dimensions of the race cars included raising the minimum weight to 1,750 pounds, increasing the vehicle width to 31 inches[9] and increasing the wheelbase from 100 inches to 135 inches.[10] The field was also expanded from 33 positions to 40 positions with the hope of increasing the number of entries by semi-stock cars.[11] These changes had the desired impact as there was a greater diversity of race cars than had participated in the 1929 race.

Rickenbacker also decided to reestablish the requirement for a riding mechanic for the first time since 1922.[12] This action was not well received. Wilbur Shaw, who was the first to win back-to-back 500-mile classics, later expressed his opinion on the reinstatement of the requirement in his book *Gentlemen, Start Your Engines*. In the early days of racing the racing mechanics provided information to the driver by hand signals and monitored the oil pressure. By the time of reinstatement, Shaw saw no benefit of a riding mechanic. He was not aware of any instance in which a riding mechanic prevented an accident. Rather, when a wreck occurred, two people were usually injured, with the more serious injuries frequently being to the riding mechanic. Additionally, the riding mechanic added unneeded weight to the cars and also the cost of the racing team since he was generally on the payroll.[13]

The decision by Rickenbacker to encourage participation of semi-stock cars in the 500-mile race had a positive impact during the Depression. During the early 1930s, familiar names were racing at the Speedway, including Buick, Chrysler, Ford, Packard and Studebaker. The number of entrants also soared and ranged from 45 to 72.[14]

The flags used to signal information to the drivers also changed for the 1930 race. The United States had adopted the now familiar signal lights with green meaning go, yellow meaning caution and red meaning stop. It made sense for the signaling flags for the race to correspond to the traffic lights.[15]

Among the seventy-two entries in the 1931 race was a diesel-powered car from Cummins Engine Company of Columbus, Indiana, a manufacturer of diesel engines. The company's owner, Clessie Cummins, hoped to prove that a diesel powered car could go the distance.[16] Driven by Dave Evans, the Cummins car completed the 500 miles without a single pit stop and finished the race in 13th position.[17] The entire race was run on 31 gallons of diesel with a cost of $2.55.[18]

By 1932, the impact of the Depression was taking its toll on the Speedway. As unemployment soared, thousands of seats remained unoccupied on race day. An earlier decision by Rickenbacker to increase the consolation awards for those finishing out of the top ten was honored but increased the financial stress. The continuation of the lap prize money was possible only from the generosity of Henry Ford, who provided $5,000 for this purpose.[19] Despite the financial difficulties, Rickenbacker was determined to continue the race. By again lowering the ticket prices and the prize purse, the track continued to operate. By 1933, the Indianapolis Motor Speedway was the only major racetrack in the United States continuing to operate.[20]

Oil on the racetrack caused by leaking automobiles had been a safety issue since the opening of the Speedway. In 1933, the Speedway limited the amount of oil for the race to six and one half gallons.[21] This action forced the automobile builders to solve the leaking oil problems.

During the early 1930s, the track became a much more dangerous racing venue. In the six year period between 1930 and 1936, nine drivers and six riding mechanics died, compared to a total of four drivers and two mechanics for the eighteen years between 1911 and 1929. In an effort to curb the fatalities, the field was once again limited to 33 vehicles for the 1934 race.[22]

An analysis of the underlying cause pointed to inexperience of first-time drivers. Rookie participants in the race had been involved in the wrecks which led to the deaths. In 1936, the track instituted the rookie driver test, which required the driving of 100 miles prior to being allowed to practice and qualify for the race.[23]

Another outcome of the deaths was a major reworking of the four corners of the track. When originally built, the Speedway had an outer lip curved at approximately 45 degrees on the corners. After the completion of the 1935 race, the outer lip was removed and a second retaining wall was built at a 90 degree angle to the roadway. Hoping to eliminate cars that hit the interior retaining wall bouncing back into the oncoming traffic, the inner retaining wall in the corners was removed and a safety apron was installed.[24] After twenty-five years of racing, some of the bricks were badly deteriorated. At first, the turns were paved. In 1939, the backstretch was paved. By 1940, the remainder of the track was paved with the exception of 650 linear feet in front of the grandstand, which remained unpaved until 1961.[25]

Watchers of the Indianapolis 500-Mile Race are familiar with the tradition of the winner drinking milk. It started in 1936 when Louis Myers won his third race. After a long, hot drive, he wanted his favorite drink since childhood, buttermilk. As he was drinking the buttermilk, he was photographed. The tradition of the winner drinking milk continues to this day, with a hiatus between 1947 and 1955.[26]

The 1937 race was the last with a requirement for a riding mechanic.[27] Driving an Offenhauser, Wilbur Shaw, who had driven his first race at Indianapolis in 1927, won the classic, setting a new course record at 113.580 miles per hour.[28] Shaw placed second in 1938 before winning the 1939 contest in a Maserati.[29] The 1939 victory was the first by a foreign made vehicle since 1919 when the race was won by a Peugeot owned by Allison.[30]

After winning the race in 1939, Shaw visited friends in Akron, Ohio. He was well known to Firestone management as he had previously represented them on a safety tour. While in Akron, Shaw was approached by Leonard Firestone to organize an aviation division for the company. Not yet ready to give up auto racing, Shaw tentatively accepted subject to Firestone's giving him a leave of absence in May so that he could continue to participate in the Indianapolis 500.[31] Firestone agreed to the leave of absence. With the exception of participating in the 500-mile race in 1940 and 1941, Shaw had retired from auto racing.[32]

In the 1940 race, Shaw was again victorious in the Maserati. The average speed was 114.277 miles per hour, with the final 125 miles being driven under a caution flag due to rain. With the 1940 victory, Shaw joined Louis Myers in having won three Indianapolis 500 races and became the first to win back-to-back contests.

On Memorial Day 1941, as the crowd started to enter the gates at 7:00 A.M., a tremendous explosion rocked the garage area. A welder's torch ignited fumes from gasoline being used to fill George Barringer's car in a nearby stall.[33] With the race crowd blocking access to the garage area, the flames quickly spread out of control, engulfing the southern half of the garage area. Racing teams worked feverishly to move their cars, spare parts, tires and tools to safety as 55-gallon drums of fuel exploded. Due to the quick action of the racing teams, all but one car in the starting lineup was saved. The fire destroyed the southern half of the garage area. Those with cars housed in the northern garages offered spare equipment to the affected racing teams' equipment. The fire delayed the start of the race by an hour.[34]

With the attack by Japan on the United States on December 7, 1941, and Germany's declaring war on the United States four days later, Rickenbacker believed there would be shortages of critical materials to the war effort, including aluminum, steel, rubber and fuel.[35] Deducing that this war could go on for a protracted time, Rickenbacker announced on December 29[36] that there would be no racing until the conclusion of the war. Just as Allison and Fisher had done in World War I, Rickenbacker immediately offered the use of the Indianapolis Motor Speedway to the federal government. Unfortunately, the aircraft used in World War II required more space than the Speedway could provide. With no racing planned, the racetrack was shuttered by Pop Myers, the Speedway's general manager.

Many years before the beginning of World War II, Firestone had established a racing division to develop tires that could take the punishment of a 500-mile race, which many felt was equivalent to 50,000 miles of normal driving. The company was able to use the information gained through the racing efforts to improve the tires used on passenger cars. One of the innovations was a tire with an inner tube that during a blowout maintained about one half of its air.[37]

By 1944, the Allies had gained momentum in World War II. When it appeared that the war was coming to a conclusion, Firestone Tire was anxious to test a synthetic tire for passenger cars. Who better to test the tires than Wilbur Shaw, the three-time winner of the Indianapolis 500 races? With the permission of the federal government, Shaw returned to the track on November 29 in a Firestone test car. The ravages of time and weather on the Speedway's physical plant were stunning to him. Before the tire test could begin, it was necessary to patch the large crevices which had formed in the pavement on the corners and to cut the grass growing up between the bricks on the straightaways. The wooden stands which had held spectators watching his victories at the Speedway appeared as if they could collapse at any moment.

Shaw reported that the Speedway "reminded me of a dilapidated back house on an abandoned farm." Focusing on the task at hand, Shaw drove 500 miles in the test car at an average speed of 100.34 mph.[38]

With an emotional attachment to the Speedway, Shaw worried about its future. As a driver, he understood the contributions the Speedway had made to the development and improvement of the automobile. Shaw also knew that the condition of the track would require extensive funds to return to racing conditions.[39]

By the conclusion of World War II, Rickenbacker was the president of Eastern Airlines and an absentee owner of the track. He had turned responsibility for it over to his brother, Al, after the track was shuttered. Many in the town of Speedway believed the track would be turned into a housing development. There had been some efforts to save it from this fate, including one by the American Legion. There was also speculation that Rickenbacker would continue to own the track but that the management of it would be turned over to Seth Klein, the former chief starter of the race.[40]

Over the last months of World War II, Shaw talked with Rickenbacker about the track on several occasions. From these conversations, he knew that Rickenbacker didn't want the expense of restoring the track and was willing to sell. Shaw felt strongly that the track was "the world's last great speed shrine which must be preserved at any cost."[41] Based upon his conviction, Shaw decided to actively pursue a purchaser for the track. He visited Rickenbacker at his Eastern Airlines offices in New York, inquiring about the cost to purchase the track. Rickenbacker responded that he would sell it for what he had in it. He would not, however, give Shaw an option for the purchase of the track.

Returning to Indianapolis, Shaw approached Indiana National Bank about how much money could be borrowed using the property as collateral. He also prepared detailed estimates of the cost to make the needed improvements. Preparing a formal prospectus hoping to raise $750,000 in cash, he sent the prospectus to approximately thirty firms and individuals that he thought might be willing to make an investment in increments of $25,000.[42]

The response appeared encouraging, with eighteen firms and individuals wishing to make an investment, some of which were for more than the $25,000. Unfortunately some of those wishing to invest envisioned the Speedway as an opportunity to promote their particular product to the exclusion of competitors' products.[43] This was in contradiction to the founding principals of Fisher, Allison, Newby and Wheeler, who wanted the track to be a testing ground for the automobile industry.

Shaw backed away from the potential investors but continued his work to find a buyer for the Speedway — someone who would have the same vision as those who had founded the racetrack. Homer Cochrane, an Indianapolis investment banker, encouraged Shaw to meet with Anton ("Tony") Hulman. Hulman was the head of Hulman & Co., a Terre Haute, Indiana, firm that owned Clabber Girl. Cochrane advised Shaw that Hulman was a very capable businessman and had the financial resources to purchase the track. He was also active in civic affairs. The fact that Hulman did not have a connection to the automobile industry was a positive to Shaw, as his only interest would be what was best for the Speedway.[44]

Hulman had first attended the 1914 race with his father and had been in regular attendance in the intervening years. Coincidentally, Hulman's father knew Carl Fisher.[45]

A meeting between Shaw and Hulman and his associates focused initially on the operations of the Speedway. After approximately two hours of conversation, Shaw returned the conversation to the potential profits which could be made from the Speedway. Hulman indicated he would not enter into this transaction solely to make a profit, although he wanted to make sure that the racetrack could be self supporting as well as provide for its improvements — that he wouldn't need to make additional capital contributions on an annual basis. Hulman reportedly said, "The Speedway always has been a part of Indiana, as the Derby is part of Kentucky."[46]

About ten days after Shaw met with Hulman and his associates, they inspected the property. Hulman could envision the severely dilapidated Speedway with double-decked grandstands of concrete and steel replacing the wooden grandstands. On November 14, 1945, in a private room at the Indianapolis Athletic Club, ownership of the Indianapolis Motor Speedway was transferred to Hulman.[47] Hulman, who became chairman of the board, hired Shaw as the president of the Indianapolis Motor Speedway. Pop Myers became vice president, a position he held until his death in 1954 at age 80.[48]

With the transfer of the Speedway, preparations began immediately to ready the racetrack for a Memorial Day contest in 1946. Superintendent Jack Fortner was very familiar with the track, as he had been responsible for its maintenance prior to World War II. He had the task of bringing the track back to life in a very short five months. The Pagoda and one of the grandstands needed to be replaced for safety purposes and several other grandstands needed significant repairs. Two new concrete and steel grandstands were planned, one to replace a grandstand which was beyond salvage. Complicating construction were restrictions on the type of steel desired. Upon learning from Harry Tousely that a substitute type of steel could be utilized, Hulman agreed and construction of new grandstands commenced.

With an already tight construction schedule which began in the midst of winter, the completion of the improvements was slowed when the track was opened on May 1 for practice laps and time trials. The workmen would stop their work when a race car roared down the track.[49]

An obstacle to the running of the 500-mile race in 1946 was a lack of race drivers. Many of those who had participated prior to World War II had retired, creating a shortage of experienced drivers.[50] Shaw was also worried about the quality of the racing machines since the majority were between five and eight years old.[51]

The response to the reopening of the Speedway was immense. By the close of registration for participating in the race, 56 entries had been received.[52] There was a full complement of thirty-three drivers which took the green flag beginning the race.[53] Ticket sales were brisk. Donations for the lap prize fund were fully subscribed for the first time since 1927.[54]

On Memorial Day 1946, those who had entered the Speedway grounds by 10:00 A.M. heard James Melton, a friend of Hulman's and a leading tenor for the New York Metropolitan Opera, sing "Indiana."[55] This was the first time the song had been heard at the racetrack since it was played in 1919 with the victory by Howdy Wilcox. Driving the Lincoln pace car on the renewal of the race was Henry Ford II, who had been named the nation's "outstanding young man of the year" by the United States Junior Chamber of Congress.[56]

In 1947, Hulman faced a crisis that could have ended the storied history of the Indianapolis Motor Speedway. Drivers had organized the American Society of Professional Automobile Racing (ASPAR). After collectively bargaining with race promoters of 100 mile championships on dirt tracks for 40 percent of the gate receipts, the group approached Speedway management for the same deal. But there was an underlying difference. The race promoters leased racetracks which were frequently state-owned for a nominal fee or a small percentage of the gate receipts. This was a different operating model than the Indianapolis Motor Speedway, which had the ongoing costs of maintenance, improvements, staffing and taxes. Shaw promised the drivers association to increase the guaranteed purse from $60,000 to $75,000. But this was not satisfactory to the drivers, who threatened to strike at the 1947 race. When time trials started in mid–May, the resolve of the members of ASPAR started to waiver. They indicated a willingness to drop their demands if they could participate in the time trials. Unfortunately, the deadline for entries had passed. Just as with the late entry by Ralph DePalma for the 1915 race, all of the entrants would have to agree for the ASPAR drivers to participate in the time trials. The ensuing negotiations resulted in

ASPAR members being allowed to participate in the time trials. The crisis was averted.[57]

There were two other issues which Shaw needed to address prior to the 1947 Indianapolis 500. The first was additional grandstand seating for the crowds and the second was improving the traffic flow into the track. In order to accommodate the automobile traffic, the Speedway was modified so that twenty-one lanes of traffic could enter the track simultaneously.[58]

The first television broadcast of the 500-mile race occurred in 1949. Indianapolis' first television station, WFBM, went on the air on Memorial Day with coverage of the race.[59] Since the mid–1930s, race coverage had been broadcast by WLW of Cincinnati, Ohio, an affiliate of the Mutual Radio Network. The coverage format consisted of a 30 minute prerace show, a 30 minute postrace wrap-up and three fifteen minute updates during the race. When racing resumed in 1946, an Indianapolis station, WIBC, which was a Mutual Radio Network affiliate, took the responsibilities for race coverage. Although Mutual Radio Network decided not to broadcast the race in 1951, race fans were able to listen to coverage through WIBC's efforts. To ensure broadcast coverage in future years, during the winter of 1951-1952, the Speedway formed the Indianapolis Motor Speedway Radio Network, with 26 stations participating. It initially was going to follow the established format; however, the three other Indianapolis stations were unhappy, as they had all been planning to make proposals to cover the race. The solution arrived at by Hulman and Shaw was that all four Indianapolis stations would participate in the race. This allowed for continuous coverage of the race from the prerace show to the postrace wrap-up. The Indianapolis Motor Speedway Radio Network was an immediate success and coverage quickly expanded to 135 networks. Ultimately, coverage of the race expanded to over 1,000 networks and to the Armed Forces Network in both Europe and the Far East on a delayed basis.[60]

Unexpectedly, on August 3, 1955, the Automobile Association of America disbanded the Contest Board, which had been the governing body for the Indianapolis Motor Speedway since its founding in 1909. The question became who would assume the responsibilities for governance. Hulman spearheaded a group which included George M. Ober, judge of magistrate's court at Speedway, Indiana, and Colonel A.W. Herrington, a former Contest Board chairman. Also selected were members of the racing community, including Duane Carter, a driver; Bob Estes, a car owner; Herb Porter, a mechanic; and Tom Marchese, a promoter. This working group established the United States Auto Club, Inc., on September 16, 1955.[61]

In the 1960s, racing at the Indianapolis 500 changed. Throughout the

1950s, the races were dominated by front-engine roadsters. Hulman predicted in 1960 that by 1970 there would be turbine powered vehicles racing at the Speedway.[62] The 1961 race included the first rear-engine car. By the end of the decade, all racers were rear-engine vehicles.[63] In 1967, another innovation had race cars changing again. The Granatelli brothers introduced a turbocharged car. This car's power plant was a Pratt-Whitney turbine engine normally used in helicopters with a reported horsepower of 550 mph.[64] A broken transmission on lap 197 prevented this car from winning the race.[65] Concerned about speed, the United States Auto Club began instituting rules governing the use of turbocharged cars, beginning in 1968.[66] Despite the rules, adaptation of the turbocharged car was rapid. By 1970, all thirty-three of the racers were powered by a turbocharged engine.[67]

In 1971, the United States Congress mandated that Memorial Day would be celebrated on the last Monday of May. This changed the running of the race, which traditionally had been on Memorial Day (May 30) with the exception of any Memorial Day that fell on Sunday. In 1971, with Memorial Day being on Monday, the race was held on Saturday, May 29.[68] So as to not conflict with the Indianapolis 500 parade, which was held on Saturday, the 1973 race was to be held on Monday, May 28.

The race was delayed by early morning rains. On the first lap of the race, there was a pile-up stopping the race. Then the skies opened up and rain came down in torrents. With the track soaked, the race was stopped for the day. Tuesday was reminiscent of Monday. The racers had started the pace lap when the skies opened again. The race was again postponed, this time until Wednesday. The green flag starting the race on Wednesday occurred at 2:10 P.M. After 58 laps of racing, a crash occurred that stopped the race. After the track was cleared, the race was restarted. With 133 laps completed, the skies opened up again. Race officials declared the race over with 332.5 miles having been run.[69] After the multiple delays in the 1973 race, Speedway management decided to run subsequent races on the Sunday preceding Memorial Day.[70]

With the increase in speed came an increase in the number of serious accidents, which all too often resulted in fatalities both during the races and during practice. After two fatalities during the 1973 race, modifications to the racetrack were completed to make it safer, including raising the outside retaining wall to 54 inches from 36 inches and changing the inside retaining wall so that it paralleled the track, which enabled racers to enter the pits immediately after turn four.[71]

After thirty-two years of owning the Indianapolis Motor Speedway, Hulman died in 1977. Through his leadership, the Indianapolis 500 had continued as the premier racing event throughout the world. The world of auto racing had changed from the vision of Allison, Fisher, Newby and Wheeler. Their foresight of improving the American auto through auto racing had achieved their desires. Today, the Hulman family continues the one-hundred year tradition of racing at the Indianapolis Motor Speedway.

32

Allison Engineering in the Aftermath

When Allison died, the company he founded had developed a reputation for high quality engineering work involving engines and gear reduction. Unfortunately for the company, they had not developed a sustainable product line. Since the company was operated as the personal project of its founder, it also had not developed consistent profitability or cash flow. Without Allison's deep pockets, the company's future was dependent upon finding a buyer who did not need an immediate payback on their investment and establishing a viable product line.

Shortly after Allison's death, the estate administrators began working on finding a buyer. They understood that the value of this company was in the reputation it had developed for engineering excellence, not in the value of the machines, tools and building. Throughout his lifetime, Allison shared with close friends and business associates his dreams for his various business interests. Thomas Pancoast and those from Indiana National Bank administering his estate were made aware of his preferences for the disposition of Allison Engineering.

Allison had expressed to his friends that he wanted Allison Engineering to remain in Indianapolis. This stipulation limited its marketability. Two companies, Wright Aeronautical and Consolidated Aircraft, made proposals to buy Allison Engineering but in both cases, the purchase would have meant the closing of the Indianapolis plant and a transfer of the assets to other locations. In late 1928, interest in the operation was expressed by Fisher & Company of Detroit, Michigan.[1]

Fisher & Company was owned by Lawrence P. Fisher and E.J. Fisher, who also owned Fisher Body. Of significance, the brothers also were on the executive committee for General Motors. Fisher & Company was willing to pay $500,000 for Allison Engineering and to agree to leave the operations in Indianapolis.[2] At the time of the purchase, the company had 200 employees and approximately 50,000 square feet of manufacturing space.[3] Upon purchasing it on January 1, 1929, Fisher & Company named Eddie Rickenbacker as the president.[4]

On April 1, 1929, Fisher & Company sold Allison Engineering to General Motors for "the price paid by them plus 6% interest during the time they have held the investment."[5] The sale to General Motors wasn't announced until May 24, 1929. General Motors documents reflect a willingness to spend $800,000 for the acquisition of Allison Engineering, which consisted of $592,000 for the original purchase of the company, the two Speedway, Indiana, buildings and fourteen adjacent acres. General Motors had also purchased an additional eleven acres and had allocated $200,000 for improvements to the operation.[6] Throughout the transition to Fisher & Company and General Motors, Norman Gilman had remained as the general manager.

General Motors management had determined that the airplane industry was the growth area for the 1930s, just as the automobile had been at the beginning of the century. Alfred P. Sloan, Jr., president of General Motors explained the entrance into the aviation industry: "The development of such a plane would have large, unfavorable consequences for the automobile industry, and we felt that we had to gain some protection by 'declaring ourselves in' the aviation industry."[7] General Motors management also believed that the expertise they had developed in manufacturing the automobile could be transferred to aircraft.

The purchase of Allison Engineering by General Motors was part of their push into the aviation industry. Also in 1929, General Motors bought a 24 percent interest in Bendix Aviation and a 40 percent interest in Fokker Aircraft Corporation. Over time General Motors invested in companies involved in aircraft manufacturing, aircraft engine manufacturing and airlines, including Fokker, General Aviation, North American Aviation, Eastern Air Transport (which became Eastern Airlines), Transcontinental Air Transport and Western Air Express.[8]

World War I had transformed aviation from the days of a small core of people being involved to an activity that had a larger appeal to the general public. The growth of the airplane's acceptance was similar to the growth in the acceptance of the automobile. At first, aviation was limited to the rich and then, as the technology improved, it became affordable and broad based.

The General Motors Operations Committee focused on the types of aviation engines which Allison Engineering should design and build. As part of the Operations Committee, Gilman had already been thinking about the future of this company and had decided that the future lay in the development of an engine to replace the now obsolete Liberty engine. This would build upon Allison Engineering's knowledge of water-cooled engines and the stresses upon engines when they are manufactured from aluminum and steel.[9]

In his oral history of Allison, John Goldthwaite told of Gilmore's insight into the need for a larger engine:

> About this time —1927, 1928 — the aircraft transport business was beginning to grow up and the army was beginning to re-equip after World War I. Gilman, watching the increasing speeds of airplanes — because year after year, when the airplanes got faster, they needed a little more power. Now, looking at the military, every year the army would introduce a new plane with a little more power and a little more speed. And he drew that curve and extended it up for several years, and he decided in several years they'd be requiring engines much, much larger than they had.[10]

In the development of this engine, Gilman believed the company should strive for more horsepower than had ever been developed. The company's goal became the development of a 1,000 horsepower engine.[11]

In May 1929, Gilman hired Harold Cominez, an aircraft engine designer, to develop the prototype for a more powerful engine. Using the best features of the Liberty engine and a Rolls-Royce V1650 engine, the V1710 engine was designed. Responding to an order from the United States Navy, the prototype for a 750 horsepower engine was delivered in March 1932.[12]

The United States Navy ultimately wanted to increase the power of the engine to 1,000 horsepower.[13] Initially, everything looked positive for the engine at 750 horsepower. As the engine capacity was increased to 800 horsepower, however, the engine started experiencing a variety of failures, including cracked crankcases and fatigued crankshafts.[14]

By 1936, there was increased speculation about war with the rise of fascism. Ronald Hazen, who had joined Allison in 1933, was named chief engineer and put in charge of the task of identifying and fixing the underlying problems with the V-1710 engines. He focused on two requirements by the Air Corp which he felt led to the engine failure. Even though a satisfactory fuel injector had not been built, the contract required fuel injection rather than a carburetor. The second issue was the requirement for lightweight engines, which resulted in their being unable to bear the stress of high revolutions.[15]

After identifying the issues, Allison engineers redesigned the V-1710 engine with a standard carburetor and strengthened the weak points through additional metal and improved castings. The redesigned engine prototype was ready for testing in thirteen weeks, in June 1936. In a 150 hour test, the engine performed well until the 140 hour mark, when a crack developed in the cylinder head. Despite this setback, the results of the test led to an order for eight of the engines. On a cold December day at the Wright Airfield outside of Dayton, Ohio, the V-1710 was attached to an aircraft and made its first flight. In April 1937, the V-1710 engine passed its 150 hour trial, becoming the first United States built engine to generate 1,000 horsepower.[16]

This engine was chosen by Lockheed Aircraft Corporation for its XP-38 aircraft, which was entered into a Army Air Corps design competition for planes with speeds up to 360 miles per hour. The twin engine plane delivered speeds in excess of 400 miles per hour on a run from Riverside, California, to Dayton, Ohio. Unfortunately, on the final leg of the trip to Long Island, New York, the plane crashed while landing. The speed obtained during the flight was of great interest to those in England and France. Germany's Messerschmitt B-109 had set a world's speed record of 469 mph using a 1,000 horsepower Daimler-Benz engine. Neither England nor France had an engine which could approach the power of the Messerschmitt B-109 engine. As a result, orders poured in from England and France in addition to the United States for over 4,000 V-1710 engines.[17]

With war breaking out in Europe, the specter of the United States being drawn into the fighting increased. Even though funding had not been procured for engines, assistant secretary of war Louis Johnson asked General Motors to construct a plant for the mass production of V-1710 engines. Although General Motors did not have a contract to produce the engines, they built a unique 360,000 square foot facility in Speedway, Indiana.[18]

The plant design was influenced by the sensitivity of key materials used in the engine, aluminum and magnesium, which were sensitive to humidity and fluctuations in temperature. As a result, the plant was designed without windows. In order to light the plant, the fluorescent light, which had been first displayed at the 1939 World's Fair, was used. In the first large scale use of fluorescent lighting, the plant required 20,000 five-foot long lighting fixtures, which were manufactured by Westinghouse.[19] In order to keep the temperature stable, the plant was air conditioned.[20]

By the time the production began at this facility, General Motors had procured a contract from the United States for the V-1710 engine.[21] Additional orders were received from France, Great Britain and China.[22] Prior to the construction of the new plant, Allison Engineering, with a payroll of approximately 600, produced on average of 200 engines per year. In 1940, Allison produced 1,153 engines, a number which grew to 6,433 in 1941. By December 1941, there were over 12,000 employees dedicated to the production of the V-1710 engine.

As the war continued, the production demands outstripped the capacity of the Allison manufacturing facilities. In response, a 200,000 square foot building was constructed. One of the challenges encountered during the construction project was the inability to use steel, as this material was needed for military hardware. The plant was built using wood for the beams, struts, and braces for the structural components. One of the side effects of the construction was that wood warps, which required it to be straightened on a regular basis.[23]

By 1943, when production of the V-1710 peaked, Allison had more than 23,000 employees producing over 3,000 aircraft engines monthly. Between 1939 and 1945, approximately 70,000 V-1710 engines and 10 million aircraft engine bearings were produced at Allison.[24]

While Allison ramped up the production of the V-1710 to support the war effort, the Allison engineers were focused on improvement in the engine. This resulted in the V-1710 engine's horsepower increasing from 1,000 in 1937 to 1,600 horsepower during take-off and 2,000 horsepower during combat by the end of World War II.[25]

The V-1710 was developed for the military market. With World War II drawing to a close, the need for the V-1710 engine would decrease significantly. The question facing the management of Allison Engineering and General Motors was the long-term future of the company.

In the early 1940s, Germany, England and Italy had developed a jet propulsion engine. Great Britain had tested a jet engine developed by Frank Whittle in flight in May 1941.[26] Refinement and production of this engine in Great Britain was by Rolls-Royce.[27] The United States had not developed this capability, which was of a concern to military officials. Under an agreement between Britain and the United States, the technology behind the jet engine was made available to the United States, with the engine to be built by General Electric. The first flight of a United States produced jet engine occurred in October 1942.

In 1944, Allison's general manager, Ed Newill, was visiting the Air Material Command located at Wright Field outside of Dayton, Ohio. While at Wright Field, Newill was summoned by Colonel Orville MacNamara, a senior procurement officer. Newill, in his oral history, told the following story:

> When I got to Colonel MacNamara's office, he closed his door and made sure nobody was within earshot, and he said, "Can Allison manufacture jet engines?" I said, "Well, Orv, I never saw a jet engine nor the design of one, but if anybody can make them, we can make them." And he said, "Well, General Electric is beginning to build some J-33 engines. We need a lot of them, and with Allison's declining piston engine production we're considering Allison to build jet engines." So I said, "That's fine. Could we get two or

three of these engines to put in a test cell and operate them and learn something about them?" And he said, "There's never one of them been built." And so I said, "How about giving me three sets of drawing so that we can at least study the paper work?" He says, "The drawings aren't finished." So I said, "Orv, are you kidding me, or what's going on here?" And he said, "I was never more serious in my life, and we want you to build jet engines, and we want a lot of them. I'd like you to have you back in this office one week from today with a bid on what it will cost you to get into this jet engine business and what the price of the engine is going to be." So I said, "Well, Orv, what can you tell me about the engine? Do you know what it weighs?" He says, "Yes, I do know what it's going to weigh." And he gave me a figure. He also had a small drawing showing half of a cross section and half of an external view of this J-33 engine. He says, "I can give you a copy of that, but that's absolutely all I can give you." So I took the copy, of course, and the next morning had a meeting of our staff, as soon as I got back into Indianapolis, and we discussed what we could do to meet his request of a quotation of building this engine at a price and with a promised delivery date, and what it would cost to revise our plant to get into it. Well, we had changed the piston engines enough to have a pretty good idea of what it would cost to go from one type of a model to another type of the same model. And so did a "guesstimate" of what that cost would be. We didn't know a thing about the parts of the jet engine that we were going to be asked to build, so finally I said, "Well, we know what the weight of the engine is; it can't cost more than $20 a pound, so that's the price." So, adding the preparations costs in as a burden cost over and above the engine manufacturing cost, we said to each other, "Well, why do we wait for a week from now — I'll go back to Wright Field tomorrow morning and give them this quotation?" We did. And we came within about four percent of what the cost of it actually turned out to be after we had built two or three hundred of the engines.[28]

Allison engineers worked with General Electric on the development of the jet propulsion engine and delivered it on time and within 10 percent of the pricing. Allison successfully transitioned from production of turboprops to jet engines. The first jet engine produced was the J-33, which was delivered in February 1945. Over the succeeding years, Allison manufactured 15,525 of the J-33 engines for Lockheed, Grumman, Chonce Vought and Martin. The second generation of jet engines, the J-35, was also jointly developed with General Electric and produced by Allison.[29] By 1948, the military application of the J-33 jet engine was expanded to include commercial aircraft.[30] As the United States adapted to jet propulsion, first for military and then for commercial aircraft, Allison became the largest producer of jet engines in the United States.[31]

World War II also brought an opportunity to Allison to manufacture an improved battle tank transmission. General Motors was initially approached in 1941 to develop the transmission. The transmission had been developed by 1944 and in early 1945 Allison gained the prime contract for manufacturing of it.

As World War II drew to a close, General Motors was already manufacturing engines for trucks, construction equipment and marine applications through its Detroit Diesel Engines subsidiary. With Detroit Diesel operating at 100 percent capacity and unable to meet the need, Allison, with excess manufacturing capacity, became involved in the production of transmissions for commercial purposes.[32] Allison also began production of automotive shocks, hydraulic lifts, and diesel blowers for General Motors' automotive and diesel locomotive businesses.[33]

Despite the successes Allison Engineering had with both the Liberty and V-1710 engines, the large engine makers, General Electric and Pratt & Whitney, had the financial resources to make the investment in new engines that might or might not be needed. General Motors management made the decision not to play the high stakes game.[34] They were willing to develop engines for the military market providing the government paid for the development costs.[35]

Rather than focusing on jet engines, Allison became focused on the turboprop engine. They developed the T-56 turboprop that was used by Lockheed Aircraft Corporation for the Hercules C130 aircraft. Lockheed was also developing a commercial aircraft in response to a need by American Airlines for an airplane which could fly at speeds of more than 400 mph, have the flexibility to fly short routes (100 miles) and long routes (2,700 miles) profitably, and land and take off from a variety of airports.[36]

Allison was selected to provide the engines for this aircraft, known as the Electra. Initial orders for the engines were strong, with American Airlines ordering 35 planes and Eastern Airlines ordering 40 planes. Soon, other airlines followed suit, as the plane could cruise at 370 miles per hour and the cabins were relatively quiet when compared to the piston driven engines. The first deliveries of the Electra were made in 1959. Lockheed Aircraft stopped production of the Electra aircraft in 1961 after producing only 170 due to two factors. Boeing had introduced the 707 jet aircraft in December 1958. The second factor was the disintegration of two Electra aircraft during flight. Allison continued to supply turboprop engines to the military and freight carriers and charter operators, primarily in Latin America.[37]

In 1960, the U.S. Army decided to put out a request for proposals on a new generation of rotary wing helicopters. Some twenty proposals were submitted by a variety of helicopter manufacturers. Allison developed the T63 engine. Despite its light weight of 109 pounds the T63 could deliver

250 horsepower. Ultimately, Hughes Aircraft won the contract and, as the engine supplier, Allison initially produced engines for 1,413 army helicopters. Allison provided an additional 2,200 engines for the second round of army helicopters, which were manufactured by Bell. With the success of the new generation of helicopter in military action, it wasn't long before the helicopter manufacturers adapted their lightweight helicopters to commercial aviation. The Allison T-63 engine has been used by sixty helicopter manufacturers.[38]

Allison teamed with Rolls-Royce for the development of an engine for the F-111 military aircraft as well as an engine for the Boeing 727 aircraft. Both of these engines were ultimately awarded to Pratt & Whitney. A collaboration with Rolls-Royce was awarded to Allison for an engine used in the A-7, which was the most used aircraft during the Vietnam War.[39] As the United States entered the space race, Allison was involved in the development of rocket motor cases that were used on the Minuteman missiles, as well as in the development of fuel tanks for the Apollo Lunar Excursion Model.[40]

In 1970, Allison became part of Detroit Diesel, with headquarters in Detroit. This new entity combined three different businesses — the diesel engines manufactured by Detroit Diesel and the gas turbines and heavy-duty transmissions manufactured by Allison. At the time of the combination of the entities, there was such a strong demand for the diesel engines it outstripped the ability of Detroit Diesel to manufacture, while the gas turbine business had excess capacity. Unfortunately for Allison, there was a conflict between what was necessary to propose in the jet engine business and the automobile business. The jet engine business requires continuous research and superior technology, while the automotive industry requires manufacturing skill.[41]

In 1981, when Garrett AiResearch approached General Motors about a joint venture for new military engines, the idea came up to sell the division. In 1982, General Motors put Allison up for sale and had seven interested parties. During the process, Morgan Stanley, the investment bank hired by General Motors to manage the sale, told General Motors management that if they were going to stay in the gas turbine business, they "should hire someone who knows something about the turbine engine business to run it."[42]

General Motors listened to what Morgan Stanley said. Rather than sell the business, they separated Allison from Detroit Diesel and hired Blake Wallace, who had worked at the other major jet engine makers — Pratt & Whitney, Garrett AiResearch and General Electric. General Motors also let the management team led by Wallace develop their own strategy and run the business. By the late 1970s, Allison was facing increasing global competition for gas turbine engines. The goals for Allison were to strengthen their three existing markets (light helicopters, large turboprops and industrial and marine engines), as well as to work towards commercial transport engines and to reenter the military engine business.[43] Allison began selling turboprop engines to Embraer, the Brazilian aircraft manufacturing company. Allison also produced the engines for Cessna's Citation X. When Embraer transitioned to a jet for its regional aircraft, Allison was selected as the exclusive supplier of the engines.[44]

In the early 1990s, General Motors again reviewed the contribution of Allison to their business. General Motors decided that they were not crucial to the core business, the result being that Allison was again put up for sale, in 1992. They received offers from General Electric, Pratt & Whitney, Rolls-Royce and Allied Signal but all offers were rejected. Allison management, Blake Wallace and Mike Hudson also made an offer for $500 million, which was rejected. Wallace and Hudson made a second proposal to General Motors for $325 million in 1993, which was accepted. Financial support for this transaction was provided by investment firm Clayton, Dubilier & Rice.[45]

Rolls-Royce and Pratt & Whitney continued to be interested in buying Allison. Since the purchase was by a financial buyer who was interested in their return on investment, both parties felt that Clayton, Dubilier & Rice would be wanting to find a strategic buyer. After conducting a due diligence review of Allison, Pratt & Whitney backed off on making an offer over antitrust concerns. Rolls-Royce saw synergies to be gained from the purchase of Allison. Rolls-Royce would benefit from a broadened business base, an expansion of its United States sales, better access to U.S. governmental contracts and expansion of Allison's research and development. On November 21, 1994, the sale of Allison to Rolls-Royce was announced; the price was $525 million.[46]

Rolls-Royce continues the helicopter legacy at the Rolls-Royce Helicopter facility in Indianapolis. In excess of 28,500 of the 250 model turboprop helicopter engines have been produced since the first production; more than 16,000 are flying today. In aggregate, this engine has logged more than 194 million flying hours. Also based in Indianapolis is Rolls-Royce North American Technologies, Inc., which continues the tradition of engine research. This division of Rolls-Royce pays homage to the Allison heritage, as it is known as LibertyWorks.

The Allison heritage continues today with Allison Transmissions, which is also based in Indianapolis. The company was divested by General Motors in August 2007 and is currently owned by the Carlyle Group and Onex. The transmissions produced are found in a variety of commercial vehicles, including fire trucks, buses, delivery trucks, and off-road dump trucks. They have also developed hybrid electric drives. The company has over 2,700 employees and a presence in eighty countries.[47]

Epilogue

Sara Cornelius Allison maintained a residence at the Marott Hotel in Indianapolis and also had a home in Asheville, North Carolina. She died in 1938 in Asheville.

Myra Allison ultimately received the majority of Jim Allison's estate, including both Riverdale Springs and the home on Star Island, Miami Beach. She died in 1931 and is buried with other members of the Allison family, including James Allison, at Crown Hill Cemetery in Indianapolis. The Star Island house was sold in 1932 and Riverdale Springs was sold in 1936 by the estate of Myra Allison.

Lucille Mussett Allison returned to Miami Beach and lived in the "bachelor" home built by Allison until 1929. She never remarried and died in Coral Gables, Florida, in 1971.

Carl Fisher was not successful in the development of Montauk, New York. Development was underway in New York when the 1926 hurricane hit Miami, causing significant damage to Miami Beach. Fisher and other major developers of Miami Beach quickly began the rebuilding in Florida. Unfortunately, the speculation which had ramped up the values of the properties not only in Miami Beach but throughout the United States came rapidly to an end about the same time as the September hurricane. Miami Beach would take years to recover from this reversal and Montauk Point never took off as a summer resort. Speculation money moved from real estate into the stock market, which collapsed in 1929. Fisher returned to Miami Beach. After years of heavy drinking, he experienced liver damage and slowly deteriorated. He died in Miami Beach and is buried at Crown Hill Cemetery in Indianapolis.

George O. Curme, Jr., found that with the acquisition of Prest-O-Lite by Union Carbide, a cheaper source of acetylene was no longer needed. Curme continued his research focusing on the by-products of artificial acetylene and discovered ethylene glycol, which was the first "permanent" antifreeze distributed under the trade name of Prestone. In his later research he discovered butadiene, a key component of synthetic rubber manufacturing. The ability to separate the gases also resulted in low-cost propane. Dr. Curme became the head of organic chemistry at Union Carbide.[1]

Howard Wilcox, approximately two weeks after the running of the 12th Indianapolis 500 in 1923, was killed in a racing accident on the wooden track at Altoona, Pennsylvania. Wilcox had been involved with the Indianapolis 500 since the inception of the race and was a race car driver and friend of Allison. As part of the National team, Wilcox had driven to 14th place in 1911 and 9th place in 1912. In 1913 and 1914, he drove a Gray Fox to 6th place and 22nd place respectively. By 1915, he was driving for Harry Stutz and placed seventh after having started on the pole position. He returned to driving a car with an Allison/Fisher connection in 1915 and 1916 when he drove a Premier to 7th place in both years. He was Allison's choice for driving the Peugeot that won the Indianapolis 500 in 1919.

Louis Mowbray, after the closing of the Miami Aquarium, returned to the New York Aquarium. In 1926, he returned to Bermuda and founded the Bermuda Aquarium, which opened in February 1928. In 1933, he brought penguins and tortoises back from the Galapagos Islands and was successful in breeding both species in captivity. He suffered a stroke in 1943 and died in 1952.[2]

Chapter Notes

Introduction

1. "J.A. Allison Dies in Indiana of Pneumonia," *Miami Herald*, August 4, 1928, p. 1.
2. "Allison, Speedway Promoter, Dies Here," *Indianapolis Star*, August 4, 1928, p. 1.
3. "Carl Fisher and Others Paid Homage to Allison," *Indianapolis Star*, August 6, 1928, p. 1.
4. Clymer, *Indianapolis 500 Mile Race History*, 2.
5. *Ibid.*, 259, 296.

Chapter 1

1. Allison: The Man and His Legacy, 1.
2. Sonnenberg and Schoneberger, *Allison: The Power of Excellence*, 12.
3. Hale, *Growth and Change*, 6.
4. *Ibid.*, 79.
5. Sonnenberg and Schoneberger, *Allison: Power of Excellence*, 12.
6. *Ibid.*, 12, 13.
7. Bennett, *History of the Panama Canal*, 421.
8. Hyman, *Hyman's Handbook*, 246.
9. Lewis, *Eddie Rickenbacker*, 17.
10. Hale, *Growth & Change*, 62–66.

11. Kalleen, "Raceway History House," 110.
12. Hale, *Growth & Change*, 95.
13. *Ibid.*, 83, 84.
14. Allison, "Sara," 57.
15. Nolan, *Barney Oldfield*, 23.
16. Hale, *Growth & Change*, 85.
17. Bodenhamer, Barrows and Vanderstel, *The Encyclopedia of Indianapolis*, 277.
18. Ritchie, *Major Taylor*, 27.
19. Bodenhamer, Barrows and Vanderstel, *The Encyclopedia of Indianapolis*, 320.
20. Hale, *Growth & Change*, 86, 87.

Chapter 2

1. Bird, *The Motor Car*, 16.
2. *Ibid.*, 25.
3. *Ibid.*, 26.
4. *Ibid.*, 26, 27.
5. *Ibid.*, 37, 38.
6. *Ibid.*, 39.
7. *Ibid.*, 35.
8. *Ibid.*, 37.
9. *Ibid.*, 47, 48.
10. *Ibid.*, 49.
11. *Ibid.*, 50
12. *Ibid.*, 55.
13. *Ibid.*, 56.
14. *Ibid.*, 57.

15. *Ibid.*, 59.
16. *Ibid.*, 60.
17. *Ibid.*, 60, 61.
18. *Ibid.*, 63.
19. *Ibid.*, 64.
20. *Ibid.*, 82.
21. *Ibid.*, 84.
22. *Ibid.*
23. *Ibid.*, 85.
24. *Ibid.*, 84, 85.

Chapter 3

1. Authors of *Automotive Quarterly*, "General Motors: The First 75 Years," 8.
2. *Ibid.*
3. *Ibid.*, 10.
4. *Ibid.*
5. *Ibid.*, 11.
6. *Ibid.*, 12.
7. *Ibid.*
8. Watts, *The People's Tycoon*, 19.
9. *Ibid.*, 23, 24.
10. *Ibid.*, 28, 29.
11. *Ibid.*, 34, 40.
12. *Ibid.*, 57.
13. Nolan, *Barney Oldfield*, 31, 32.
14. *Ibid.*, 32, 33.
15. *Ibid.*, 32.
16. Lewis, *Eddie Rickenbacker*, 30.
17. Nolan, *Barney Oldfield*, 36.
18. *Ibid.*, 37.
19. Davidson and Shaffer, *Autocourse*, 14.

Chapter 4

1. Watts, *The People's Tycoon*, 66.
2. *The Motor Car*, 173, 174.
3. Watts, *The People's Tycoon*, 65–67.
4. *Ibid.*, 67.
5. *Ibid.*, 68, 69.
6. *Ibid.*, 72.
7. *Ibid.*, 77.
8. *Ibid.*, 79.
9. Nolan, *Barney Oldfield*, 17–19.
10. *Ibid.*, 49.
11. *Ibid.*, 52, 53.
12. Bloemker, *500 Miles to Go*, 22.
13. Watts, *The People's Tycoon*, 86.
14. *Ibid.*, 80.
15. Shaw, *Gentlemen, Start Your Engines*, 153.
16. *Ibid.*, 78.
17. *Ibid.*
18. Georgano, *The Beaulieu Encyclopedia of the Automobile*, 1106.
19. Nolan, *Barney Oldfield*, 110, 112.
20. "Clemens Sets New 100 Mile Record," *Indianapolis Morning Star*, November 5, 1905, p. 18.
21. *Ibid.*
22. "24 Hours of Indianapolis," FirstSuperspeedway.com, 1.
23. *Ibid.*
24. Bloemker, *500 Miles to Go*, 32.
25. "Many New Records Set in 24 Hour Race," *Indianapolis Morning Star*, p. 7.
26. Nolan, *Barney Oldfield*, 114.
27. *Ibid.*, 115.
28. Lewis, *Eddie Rickenbacker*, 56.
29. *Ibid.*

Chapter 5

1. Bloemker, *500 Miles to Go*, 24.

2. Foster, *Castles in the Sand*, 49.

Chapter 6

1. Dunn, *Greater Indianapolis*, vol. 1, p. 595.
2. Allison, "Sara," 1.
3. *Ibid.*, 150.
4. *Ibid.*, 132.

Chapter 7

1. "Spectacular Fire and Explosion Wreck Business Building," *Indianapolis Morning Star*, August 18, 1907, p. 1.
2. *Ibid.*
3. "Prest-O-Lite Lets Go Again," *Indianapolis Morning Star*, December 21, 1907, pp. 1, 3.

Chapter 8

1. "No Deaths but Another Explosion," *Indianapolis News*, June 6, 1908, p. 3.
2. *Ibid.*, pp. 1, 3.
3. "Force Jars Hospital," *Indianapolis Star*, June 7, 1908, p. 1.
4. "No Deaths but Another Explosion," *Indianapolis News*, June 6, 1908, p. 3.
5. *Ibid.*
6. "City Jolted Again by Prest-O-Lite," *Indianapolis Morning Star*, June 7, 1908, p. 1.
7. *Ibid.*
8. "No Deaths but Another Explosion," *Indianapolis News*, June 6, 1908, p. 3.
9. "City Jolted Again by Prest-O-Lite," *Indianapolis Star*, June 7, 1908, p. 1.
10. "City Jolted by Prest-O-Lite," *Indianapolis News*, June 7, 1908, p. 1.
11. "No Deaths but Another Explosion," *Indianapolis News*, June 6, 1908, p. 3.
12. "City Jolted by Prest-O-Lite," *Indianapolis News*, June 7, 1908, p. 1.
13. "Frame Law to Bar Prest-O-Lite Plant," *Indianapolis Morning Star*, June 8, 1908, p. 1.
14. "City Jolted Again by Prest-O-Lite," *Indianapolis News*, June 7, 1908, p. 1.
15. *Ibid.*
16. "Prest-O-Lite to Go," *Indianapolis Morning Star*, June 16, 1908, p. 1.
17. "Frame Law to Bar Prest-O-Lite Plant," *Indianapolis Morning Star*, June 8, 1908, p. 1.

Chapter 9

1. Davidson and Shaffer, *Autocourse*, 16, 17.
2. *Ibid.*, 17.
3. Brooklands Society, "And Darkness Was upon the Face of British Motor Racing."
4. Davidson and Shaffer, *Autocourse*, 20.
5. *Ibid.*
6. Clymer, *Indianapolis 500 Mile Race History*, 9.
7. Bloemker, *500 Miles to Go*, 38.
8. Kimes, "The Rise & Fall of the Empire," *Automotive Quarterly*, 68.
9. *Ibid.*

Chapter 10

1. Bloemker, *500 Miles to Go*, 38, 39.
2. *Ibid.*, 39.
3. *Ibid.*, 36.
4. Fisher, *The Pacesetter*, 47.
5. *Ibid.*
6. Bloemker, *500 Miles to Go*, 44.
7. *Ibid.*, 40, 41.

8. Scott and Gray, *Indy Racing Before the 500*, 29.
9. *Ibid.*, 13.
10. Davidson and Shaffer, *Autocourse*, 22.
11. Bloemker, *500 Miles to Go*, 41.
12. *Ibid.*, 45, 46.
13. Scott and Gray, *Indy Racing Before the 500*, 22.
14. *Ibid.*, 25.
15. *Ibid.*, 26.
16. *Ibid.*, 27.
17. *Ibid.*
18. Bloemker, *500 Miles to Go*, 41.
19. Scott and Gray, *Indy Racing Before the 500*, 29.
20. *Ibid.*, 31.
21. Bloemker, *500 Miles to Go*, 48.
22. *Ibid.*
23. *Ibid.*, 49.
24. *Ibid.*, 51.
25. Scott and Gray, *Indy Racing Before the 500*, 32.
26. *Ibid.*, 33.
27. *Ibid.*, 34.

Chapter 11

1. Scott and Gray, *Indy Racing Before the 500*, 37, 39.
2. *Ibid.*
3. *Ibid.*, 39.
4. Fisher, *The Pacesetter*, 51.
5. Scott and Gray, *Indy Racing Before the 500*, 42.
6. Bloemker, *500 Miles to Go*, 57.
7. Scott and Gray, *Indy Racing Before the 500*, 40.
8. *Ibid.*, 39.
9. Bloemker, *500 Miles to Go*, 58.
10. Scott and Gray, *Indy Racing Before the 500*, 42.
11. Georgano, *The Beaulieu Encyclopedia*, 1517.
12. Rosenberg, *America at the Fair*, 272.
13. Scott and Gray, *Indy Racing Before the 500*, 43.
14. *Ibid.*, 47.

15. Nolan, *Barney Oldfield*, 58, 59.
16. Scott and Gray, *Indy Racing Before the 500*, 47, 49.
17. Bloemker, *500 Miles to Go*, 59, 60.
18. Scott and Gray, *Indy Racing Before the 500*, 47, 49.
19. Bloemker, *500 Miles to Go*, 60.
20. *Ibid.*, 61.
21. Scott and Gray, *Indy Racing Before the 500*, 47, 49.
22. Bloemker, *500 Miles to Go*, 62.
23. *Ibid.*
24. Scott and Gray, *Indy Racing Before the 500*, 65, 66, 70.
25. *Ibid.*
26. Bloemker, *500 Miles to Go*, 63.
27. *Ibid.*
28. Scott and Gray, *Indy Racing Before the 500*, 65, 66, 70.
29. *Ibid.*
30. Fisher, *The Pacesetter*, 52.
31. Bloemker, *500 Miles to Go*, 67.
32. Fisher, *The Pacesetter*, 52, 53.
33. Scott and Gray, *Indy Racing Before the 500*, 73.
34. *Ibid.*
35. *Ibid.*
36. *Ibid.*, 75, 76, 77.
37. "Speedway Paving Example for City," *Indianapolis Morning Star*, July 19, 1910, p. 3.
38. Scott and Gray, *Indy Racing Before the 500*, 75, 76, 77.
39. Fisher, *Fabulous Hoosier*, 20, 21.
40. Scott and Gray, *Indy Racing Before the 500*, 74.
41. Bloemker, *500 Miles to Go*, 71.
42. *Ibid.*
43. Fisher, *The Pacesetter*, 54.

44. Kimes, "The Rise & Fall of the Empire," 68.
45. Fisher, *The Pacesetter*, 54.

Chapter 12

1. Speedway Civic Committee, *The Story of Speedway*, 39.
2. *Ibid.*, 95.
3. Bodenhamer, Barrows and Vanderstel, *The Encyclopedia of Indianapolis*, 1284, 1285.
4. Speedway Civic Committee, *The Story of Speedway*, 77.

Chapter 13

1. Davidson and Shaffer, *Autocourse*, 26.
2. Hanley and Hanley, *Marmon Heritage*, 317.
3. *Ibid.*
4. Scott and Gray, *Indy Racing Before the 500*, 97.
5. *Ibid.*, 101, 103.
6. *Ibid.*, 110.
7. Bloemker, *500 Miles to Go*, 76.
8. Fisher, *The Pacesetter*, 54.
9. Scott and Gray, *Indy Racing Before the 500*, 112.
10. Fisher, *The Pacesetter*, 54.
11. Scott and Gray, *Indy Racing Before the 500*, 115.
12. Fisher, *The Pacesetter*, 54.
13. Scott and Gray, *Indy Racing Before the 500*, 115.
14. Davidson and Shaffer, *Autocourse*, 26.
15. Kimes "The Rise & Fall of the Empire," *Automotive Quarterly*, 68.
16. Davidson and Shaffer, *Autocourse*, 27.
17. Scott and Gray, *Indy Racing Before the 500*, 183.
18. Hanley and Hanley, *Marmon Heritage*, 318.

Chapter 14

1. Bloemker, *500 Miles to Go*, 78, 79.
2. *Ibid.*, 79.
3. *Ibid.*, 79, 80.
4. *Ibid.*, 79.
5. Davidson and Shaffer, *Autocourse*, 28.
6. *Ibid.*
7. Fisher, *The Pacesetter*, 55.
8. Bloemker, *500 Miles to Go*, 84.
9. Hanley and Hanley, *Marmon Heritage*, 323.
10. Bloemker, *500 Miles to Go*, 84.
11. Nolan, *Barney Oldfield*, 105, 106.
12. *Ibid.*, 106–108.
13. *Ibid.*, 108, 109, 115.
14. Hanley and Hanley, *Marmon Heritage*, 323.
15. *Ibid.*
16. *Ibid.*
17. *Ibid.*
18. Fisher, *The Pacesetter*, 58.
19. *Ibid.*
20. Bloemker, *500 Miles to Go*, 89.
21. Davidson and Shaffer, *Autocourse*, 31.
22. *Ibid.*, 33.
23. Fisher, *The Pacesetter*, 58.
24. Clymer, *Indianapolis 500 Mile Race History*, 256.
25. Shaw, *Gentlemen, Start Your Engines*, 62.
26. Kimes, "The Rise and Fall of the Empire," *Automotive Quarterly*, 68.
27. Hanley and Hanley, *Marmon Heritage*, 324.
28. *Ibid.*
29. Bloemker, *500 Miles to Go*, 91.
30. Lewis, *Eddie Rickenbacker*, 47.
31. *Ibid.*, 46–48.
32. *Ibid.*, 59.
33. Bloemker, *500 Miles to Go*, 92.
34. Hanley and Hanley, *Marmon Heritage*, 325.
35. *Ibid.*
36. Bloemker, *500 Miles to Go*, 95.
37. Hanley and Hanley, *Marmon Heritage*, 325.
38. Clymer, *Indianapolis 500 Mile Race History*, 26, 27.

Chapter 15

1. "8th Man Dies, Causes to Be Studied by Grand Jury," *Indianapolis Morning Star*, December 8, 1911, pp. 1, 7.
2. "Around Noon, Building Still Under Construction Collapsed," *Indianapolis News*, December 6, 1911, p. 1.
3. "7 Dead, 21 Injured, Search Continues for More," *Indianapolis Morning Star*, December 7, 1911, pp. 1, 6.
4. *Ibid.*
5. *Ibid.*
6. *Ibid.*
7. *Ibid.*
8. *Ibid.*
9. "8th Man Dies, Causes to be Studied by Grand Jury," *Indianapolis Morning Star*, December 8, 1911, pp. 1, 7.
10. *Ibid.*
11. *Ibid.*
12. *Ibid.*
13. "Building Code Revision Asked by Carpenters," *Indianapolis Morning Star*, December 30, 1911, pp. 1, 3.

Chapter 16

1. The Prest-O-Lite Company, Inc., *The Prest-O-Liter*. Indianapolis: Prest-O-Lite Co., n.d.
2. National Academy of Sciences, *Biographical Memoirs*, 123–128.
3. Dodson, *The Work of Jens Jensen*, 13.
4. Clymer, *The Treasury of Early American Automobiles*, 129.
5. Bodenhamer, Barrows and Vanderstel, *The Encyclopedia of Indianapolis*, 1134.
6. "Prest-O-Lite Plant Opened in Speedway," *Indianapolis Star*, May 25, 1913, p. 4.
7. Letter from James P. Carney to Carl Fisher, October 1, 1917.

Chapter 17

1. Dodson, *The Work of Jens Jensen*, 16, 17.
2. Grese, *Jens Jensen*, 22.
3. *Ibid.*, 1.
4. *Ibid.*, 63.
5. *Ibid.*, 95.
6. *Ibid.*, 98, 99.
7. *Ibid.*, 69.
8. *Ibid.*, 200.
9. *Ibid.*, 168, 172, 174.
10. *Ibid.*
11. Marian University, "The Mansions of Marian," 5.
12. *Ibid.*, 13.
13. Dodson, *The Work of Jens Jensen*, 20.
14. *Ibid.*, 20, 21.
15. Grese, *Jens Jensen*, 172.
16. *Ibid.*, 168.
17. Dodson, *The Work of Jens Jensen*, 29, 31.
18. Allison, "Sara," 57.
19. *Ibid.*, 175.
20. Thomas and Venturi, *William L. Price*, 35.
21. *Ibid.*, 42.
22. *Ibid.*, 48.
23. *Ibid.*, 65.
24. *Ibid.*, 157, 158.
25. "Marian College to Open September 8, 1937," *Indianapolis Star*, August 22, 1937, section 1, p. 5.
26. Allison, "Sara," 177.
27. "Former Allison Mansion Open for Public Tours," *Indianapolis Star*, August 28, 1977, section 7, pp. 1, 11.

28. Allison, "Sara," 176.
29. "Marian College to Open September 8, 1937," *Indianapolis Star*, August 22, 1937, section 1, p. 5.
30. Allison, "Sara," 177.
31. *Ibid.*, 259.
32. *Ibid.*, 178.
33. "Marian College to Open September 8, 1937," *Indianapolis Star*, August 22, 1937, section 1, p. 5.
34. "Decorating for Dollars," *Indianapolis Star*, April 26, 1991, p. 1.
35. Latham, "Houses and Horses the Old-Fashioned Way," *Circular* 10, pp. 1, 2.
36. "Former Allison Mansion Open for Public Tours," *Indianapolis Star*, August 28, 1977, section 7, pp. 1, 11.
37. "Mogul Built Wonder House," *Indianapolis News*, May 28, 1969, p. 19.
38. Dodson, *The Work of Jens Jensen*, 15.

Chapter 18

1. Fisher, *The Pacesetter*, 98.
2. *Ibid.*, 98.
3. *Ibid.*, 98, 99.
4. *Ibid.*, 98.
5. *Ibid.*, 99.
6. Shaw, *Gentlemen, Start Your Engines*, 140, 186.
7. Bloemker, *500 Miles to Go*, 101, 102.
8. *Ibid.*, 100, 101.
9. *Ibid.*, 101, 102.
10. Stutz Motor Car Company, *The Splendid Stutz*, 40.
11. Clymer, *Indianapolis 500 Mile Race History*, 33.
12. Bloemker, *500 Miles to Go*, 103, 104.
13. Davidson and Shaffer, *Autocourse*, 35.
14. Bloemker, *500 Miles to Go*, 104, 105.
15. *Ibid.*, 106–108.
16. *Ibid.*, 108.

17. *Ibid.*, 110, 111.
18. *Ibid.*, 111.
19. *Ibid.*, 112, 113.
20. *Ibid.*, 113.
21. *Ibid.*, 114.
22. *PSA Peugeot Citron*, "Jules Goux — A French Victory at Indianapolis," April 25, 2002.
23. Clymer, *Indianapolis 500 Mile Race History*, 47.
24. Bloemker, *500 Miles to Go*, 114, 115.
25. *Ibid.*, 116.
26. *Ibid.*, 115, 116.
27. Clymer, *Indianapolis 500 Mile Race History*, 52.
28. Bloemker, *500 Miles to Go*, 118.
29. *Ibid.*, 120.
30. Clymer, *Indianapolis 500 Mile Race History*, 60.
31. Bloemker, *500 Miles to Go*, 120, 121.

Chapter 19

1. Davidson and Shaffer, *Autocourse*, 38.
2. Bloemker, *500 Miles to Go*, 123.
3. Nolan, *Barney Oldfield*, 155.
4. *Ibid.*, 154.
5. *Ibid.*, 117, 118, 119.
6. *Ibid.*, 121.
7. *Ibid.*, 157.
8. Bloemker, *500 Miles to Go*, 123.
9. Lewis, *Eddie Rickenbacker*, 61.
10. Bloemker, *500 Miles to Go*, 124.
11. Davidson and Shaffer, *Autocourse*, 39.
12. Bloemker, *500 Miles to Go*, 124.

Chapter 20

1. Lincoln Highway Association, *The Lincoln Highway*, 2.
2. *Ibid.*, 4.
3. *Ibid.*, 10.
4. *Ibid.*

5. *Ibid.*, 29.
6. *Ibid.*, 30.
7. *Ibid.*, 35.
8. *Ibid.*, 43, 44.
9. *Ibid.*, 46.
10. *Ibid.*, 48.
11. *Ibid.*, 52, 53, 54.
12. *Ibid.*, 67.
13. *Ibid.*, 72.
14. *Ibid.*, 78.
15. *Ibid.*, 80, 81.
16. *Ibid.*, 150.
17. *Ibid.*, 108.

Chapter 21

1. Nolan, *Barney Oldfield*, 183.
2. Clymer, *Indianapolis 500 Mile Race History*, 77.
3. *Ibid.*
4. Bloemker, *500 Miles to Go*, 126.
5. Clymer, *Indianapolis 500 Mile Race History*, 84.
6. *Ibid.*, 78.
7. *Ibid.*, 79.
8. Bloemker, *500 Miles to Go*, 128.
9. Lewis, *Eddie Rickenbacker*, 70.
10. *Ibid.*, 80.
11. Marion County, Indiana Clerk's Office, Miscellaneous Record Book 88, p. 375.
12. Lewis, *Eddie Rickenbacker*, 80.
13. *Ibid.*, 76, 77.
14. Bloemker, *500 Miles to Go*, 132.
15. Davidson and Shaffer, *Autocourse*, 44.
16. *Ibid.*, 44.
17. Nolan, *Barney Oldfield*, 190, 191.
18. Davidson and Shaffer, *Autocourse*, 41.
19. Bloemker, *500 Miles to Go*, 135.
20. *Ibid.*, 136.
21. Nolan, *Barney Oldfield*, 192, 193.
22. *Ibid.*, 193, 194.
23. Davidson and Shaffer, *Autocourse*, 43.

24. *Ibid.*, 42, 43.
25. Lewis, *Eddie Rickenbacker*, 83.
26. Davidson and Shaffer, *Autocourse*, 43.
27. Bloemker, *500 Miles to Go*, 138.
28. *Ibid.*
29. Bosler, interoffice memo, August 28, 1952.
30. Lewis, *Eddie Rickenbacker*, 86.
31. Bloemker, *500 Miles to Go*, 139.
32. Pugh, *The Magic of A Name*, 96.
33. Nolan, *Barney Oldfield*, 208.
34. Bloemker, *500 Miles to Go*, 139.
35. Davidson and Shaffer, *Autocourse*, 43.
36. Bloemker, *500 Miles to Go*, 139.

Chapter 22

1. "183-Inch Type is Likely to Prove Leader," *Indianapolis Star*, June 1, 1919, section 3, pp. 25, 26.
2. Pugh, *The Magic of a Name*, 97.
3. Davidson and Shaffer, *Autocourse*, 45.
4. Nolan, *Barney Oldfield*, 211, 212.
5. Bloemker, *500 Miles to Go*, 141.
6. *Ibid.*, 142.
7. Clymer, *Indianapolis 500 Mile Race History*, 98.
8. Davidson and Shaffer, *Autocourse*, 44.
9. *Ibid.*
10. Bloemker, *500 Miles to Go*, 143.
11. *Ibid.*, 143, 144.
12. *Ibid.*, 144.
13. Rolls-Royce Heritage Trust, Allison Branch, records.
14. "183-Inch Type Is Likely to Prove Leader," *Indianapolis Star*, June 1, 1918, section 3, p. 25.

15. Songwriters Hall of Fame Website.
16. Davidson and Shaffer, *Autocourse*, 104.
17. Songwriters Hall of Fame Website.
18. Lavender, *Miami Beach in 1920*, 122–123.
19. *Ibid.*, 127.
20. Fisher letter to Allison, March 20, 1920.
21. Allison letter to Fisher, March 24, 1920.
22. Fisher letter to Allison, March 27, 1920.
23. *Ibid.*
24. Clymer, *Indianapolis 500 Mile Race History*, 97.
25. *Ibid.*
26. *Ibid.*
27. Davidson and Shaffer, *Autocourse*, 46.
28. Bloemker, *500 Miles to Go*, 145.
29. Davidson and Shaffer, *Autocourse*, 46.
30. Bloemker, *500 Miles to Go*, 146, 148.
31. Clymer, *Indianapolis 500 Mile Race History*, 107.
32. Bloemker, *500 Miles to Go*, 149.
33. *Ibid.*
34. *Ibid.*
35. *Ibid.*
36. Davidson and Shaffer, *Autocourse*, 46.
37. *Ibid.*, 48.
38. Clymer, *Indianapolis 500 Mile Race History*, 108.
39. *Ibid.*
40. Bloemker, *500 Miles to Go*, 149.
41. Davidson and Shaffer, *Autocourse*, 48.
42. *Ibid.*
43. Bloemker, *500 Miles to Go*, 154.
44. Davidson and Shaffer, *Autocourse*, 48.
45. Bloemker, *500 Miles to Go*, 155, 156.
46. Clymer, *Indianapolis 500 Mile Race History*, 111.
47. *Ibid.*, 118.
48. *Ibid.*, 119.

49. Davidson and Shaffer, *Autocourse*, 49.
50. *Ibid.*, 50.

Chapter 23

1. Kleinberg, *Miami Beach: A History*, 1.
2. *Ibid.*, 5.
3. *Ibid.*, 6.
4. Lavender, *Miami Beach in 1920*, 10.
5. Kleinberg, *Miami Beach: A History*, 9, 10.
6. *Ibid.*, 10.
7. Lavender, *Miami Beach in 1920*, 10–13.
8. Kleinberg, *Miami Beach: A History*, 19.
9. Lavender, *Miami Beach in 1920*, 12.
10. Kleinberg, *Miami Beach: A History*, 22.
11. *Ibid.*, 24, 25.
12. Lavender, *Miami Beach in 1920*, 11, 12.
13. Kleinberg, *Miami Beach: A History*, 26.
14. *Ibid.*, 27.
15. *Ibid.*, 28.
16. Bloemker, *500 Miles to Go*, 109.
17. Nash, *The Magic of Miami Beach*, 105.
18. Lavender, *Miami Beach in 1920*, 10, 11, 12, 13.

Chapter 24

1. Bloemker, *500 Miles to Go*, 110.
2. Allison, "Sara," 181.
3. Lavender, *Miami Beach in the 1920*, 15.
4. Fisher letter to Allison, January 2, 1920.
5. Lavender, *Miami Beach in 1920*, 96.
6. Allison, "Sara," 182.
7. Lavender, *Miami Beach in 1920*, 14.
8. *Ibid.*, 13.
9. *Ibid.*, 27–29.
10. Ibid 34–36.
11. *Ibid.*, 122.
12. *Ibid.*, 130, 131.

13. Dinn, *Boats by Purdy*, 135.
14. Lavender, *Miami Beach in 1920*, 69–71.
15. *Ibid.*, 87.
16. "Miami Aquarium Doors to Swing Closed for All Time at 6 P.M.," *Miami Herald*, April 1, 1923, p. 1.
17. Lummus letter to Fisher, March 26, 1919.
18. Allison letter to Fisher, March 29, 1919.
19. "Louis Mowbray," Bermuda Biographies, www.bermudabiographies.bm (accessed August 26, 2008).
20. Allison letter to Mowbray, May 26, 1919.
21. LaGorce, "Miami's Aquarium Opened to Public for First Time," *Miami Metropolis*, January 1, 1921, p. 1.
22. Lavender, *Miami Beach in 1920*, 53.
23. Floyd, "Report of the Collapse of the Water Reservoir at the Miami Aquarium Association."
24. Powers, "Report to McLanahan & Bencker."
25. Lavender, *Miami Beach in 1920*, 80.
26. *Ibid.*, 46, 47.
27. *Ibid.*, 44, 45.
28. *Ibid.*, 47–49.
29. "Opening of Aquarium Drew a Large Crowd of Lovers of Nature," *Miami Metropolis*, January 4, 1921, p. 4.
30. Nichols, "The Modern Aquarium," *Natural History*, 357.
31. LaGorce, "Miami's Aquarium Opened to Public for First Time," *Miami Metropolis*, January 1, 1921, p. 1.
32. "Open Aquarium Makes Miami 'Naples and Monaco' of America," *Miami Herald*, January 2, 1921, p. 1.; LaGorce, "Miami's Aquarium Opened to Public for First Time," *Miami Metropolis*, January 1, 1921, p. 1.

33. Kleinberg, *Miami Beach: A History*, 78.
34. *Ibid.*, 61, 62.
35. Fisher letter to Deering, December 17, 1917.
36. Miami Aquarium & Laboratory, "If You Drive Over Today, You'll Enjoy Yourself," *Miami Herald*, March 23, 1923, p.13.
37. Kleinberg, *Miami Beach: A History*, 90.
38. "Fish In Miami Waters," *Miami Herald*, March 16, 1923, p. 1.
39. "Hundreds of Baby Sea-Horses Born to Proud Parents in Aquarium Tank," *Miami Herald*, March 22, 1923, p. 8.
40. "Miami Aquarium Doors to Swing Closed for All Time at 6 PM," *Miami Herald*, April 1, 1923, pp. 1, 11.
41. Fisher letter to Allison, March 30, 1923.
42. "Miami Aquarium Doors to Swing Closed for All Time at 6 PM," *Miami Herald*, April 1, 1923, pp. 1, 11.
43. *Ibid.*
44. *Ibid.*
45. "Miami Aquarium, Emptied of Sea Life, Now Mute Testimonial to Its Founder," *Miami Herald*, April 7, 1923, p. 7.
46. "Miami Aquarium Doors to Swing Shut for All Time at 6 PM," *Miami Herald*, April 1, 1923, pp. 1, 11.
47. *Ibid.*
48. "County Publicity Tax Urged for Aquarium," *Miami Herald*, April 5, 1923, p. 3.
49. Fisher letter to Mahoney, August 5, 1928.

Chapter 25

1. Dunn, *Greater Indianapolis*, 447.
2. *Ibid.*

3. Ogle, *Ambitious Brew*, 145.
4. *Ibid.*, 146–148.
5. *Ibid.*, 147.
6. *Ibid.*, 151.
7. Behr, *Prohibition: 13 Years*, 59.
8. Ogle, *Ambitious Brew*, 151.
9. Behr, *Prohibition*, 65.
10. *Ibid.*, 67.
11. Allen, *Only Yesterday*, 185, 186.
12. Behr, *Prohibition*, 80.
13. *Ibid.*, 81.
14. Lavender, *Miami Beach in 1920*, 88.
15. Allen, *Only Yesterday*, 187.
16. *Ibid.*, 188.
17. *Ibid.*, 190.
18. Allison letter to Fisher, April 5, 1920.
19. "Liquor Found at the Aquarium," *Miami Herald*, April 28, 1921, p. 13.
20. Fisher letter to Allison, April 25, 1920.

Chapter 26

1. Bloemker, *500 Miles to Go*, 163.
2. *Ibid.*
3. Davidson and Shaffer, *Autocourse*, 52.
4. Clymer, *Indianapolis 500 Mile Race History*, 121.
5. Bloemker, *500 Miles to Go*, 158.
6. Clymer, *Indianapolis 500 Mile Race History*, 130.
7. Bloemker, *500 Miles to Go*, 163.
8. Allison letter to Fisher, June 14, 1923.
9. "James A. Allison New Speedway President," *Indianapolis News*, June 12. 1923, p. 1.
10. "Resolution to Fix Capital and Surplus at $3,300,000 to be Submitted for Stockholders' Approval," *Indianapolis Star*, May 19, 1923, p. 1.

11. "Fletcher American Bank Absorbs National City," *Indianapolis Star*, March 1, 1924, p. 1.

12. Clymer, *Indianapolis 500 Mile Race History*, 135.

13. *Ibid.*, 145.

14. *Ibid.*, 157.

15. *Ibid.*, 138.

16. *Ibid.*, 179.

17. *Ibid.*, 173.

18. Bloemker, *500 Miles to Go*, 169, 170.

19. Clymer, *Indianapolis 500 Mile Race History*, 179.

20. *Ibid.*, 182.

21. Lewis, *Eddie Rickenbacker*, 289, 290.

22. Bloemker, *500 Miles to Go*, 174, 175.

23. *Ibid.*, 175.

Chapter 27

1. Sonnenberg and Schoneberger, *Allison: Power of Excellence*, 22.

2. *Ibid.*, 57.

3. Goldthwaite oral history, 2.

4. Sonnenberg and Schoneberger, *Allison: Power of Excellence*, 60.

5. Leyes and Fleming, *The History of North American Small Gas Turbine*, 520.

6. *Ibid.*, 520, 521.

7. Goldthwaite Oral History, 2.

8. Nolan, *Barney Oldfield*, 205.

9. Leyes and Fleming, *The History of North American Small Gas Turbine*, 520, 521.

10. Goldthwaite Oral History, 2.

11. Leyes and Fleming, *The History of North American Small Gas Turbine*, 520, 21.

12. Pugh, *The Magic of a Name*, 96, 97.

13. Goldthwaite Oral History, 4.

14. *Ibid.*, 5, 10.

15. Dinn, *Boats by Purdy*, 34.

16. *Ibid.*

17. *Ibid.*

18. Fisher Letter to Allison, September 15, 1922.

19. Dinn, *Boats by Purdy*, 34.

20. Goldthwaite Oral History, 2, 3.

21. *Ibid.*, 9.

22. *Ibid.*, 10.

23. Leyes and Fleming, *The History of North American Small Gas Turbine*, 521.

24. Goldthwaite Oral History, 12.

25. *Ibid.*, 3, 4.

26. "Jim Allison's Fame Still Growing," *The Guide*, 5.

27. Goldthwaite, Interoffice Memo, February 1, 1950.

28. Goldthwaite Oral History, 3, 4.

29. Goldthwaite, Inter-Office Memo, February 1, 1950.

30. Sonnenberg and Schoneberger, *Allison: Power of Excellence*, 43.

31. Rolls-Royce Corporation-Allison Branch, Untitled History of Allison Engineering, December 1962, 5.

32. Sonnenberg and Schoneberger, *Allison: Power of Excellence*, 22, 43.

33. Leyes and Fleming, *The History of North American Small Gas Turbine*, 522.

34. Goldthwaite Oral History, 4.

35. Leyes and Fleming, *The History of North American Small Gas Turbine*, 522.

36. Goldthwaite Oral History, 5.

37. Sonnenberg and Schoneberger, *Allison: Power of Excellence*, 44.

38. "Jim Allison's Fame Still Growing," *The Guide*, May 22, 1972, 6.

39. Sloan, *My Years with General Motors*, 362, 363.

40. "Jim Allison's Fame Still Growing," *The Guide*, May 22, 1972, 6.

41. Allison Letter to Fisher, August 20, 1924.

42. Goldthwaite Oral History, 6.

Chapter 28

1. Allison, "Sara," 179.

2. LaGorce letter to Fisher, April 6, 1921.

3. Western Union telegram from Allison to Fisher, April 5, 1921.

4. Langston letter to Fisher, Sept. 13, 1923.

5. Allison, "Sara," 277.

6. Ash, "Well Done, St. Francis, Both the Hospital and the Steak," *Miami News*, June 28, 1964, p. 14.

7. Kleinberg, *Miami Beach: A History*, 53, 93, 112.

8. Ash, "Well Done, St. Francis," *Miami News*, June 28, 1964, p. 14.

9. Kleinberg, *Miami Beach: A History*, 89, 90.

10. *Ibid.*, 93.

11. *Ibid.*, 96.

12. Moore and Jones, *Men of the South*, 348.

13. Kleinberg, *Miami Beach: A History*, 128, 129.

14. "Fisher to Build Clubhouse to Cost $1,500,000," *The Illustrated Tab*, October 13 1925, p. 16.

15. Allison letter to Fisher, July 24, 1924.

16. Allison letter to Fisher, July 25, 1925.

17. Fisher letter to Allison, August 4, 1925.

18. Kleinberg, *Miami Beach: A History*, 95.

19. *Ibid.*, 104.

20. *Ibid.*, 98.

21. *Ibid.*, 106.

22. *Ibid.*

23. Ash, "Well Done, St. Francis," *Miami News*, June 28, 1964, pp. 14, 15.

24. *Ibid.*, 15.

Chapter 29

1. Allison, "Sara," 278.
2. Redford, *Billion Dollar Sandbar*, 116.
3. Elwood, *Rough Guide to Miami*, 49.
4. Derr, *Some Kind of Paradise*, 187.
5. John Levi letter to Carl Fisher, April 30, 1919.
6. *Ibid.*
7. Allison, "Sara," 278.
8. "J.A. Allison Dies in Indiana of Pneumonia," *Miami Herald*, August 5, 1928, p. 2.
9. Allison, "Sara," 278.
10. Pancoast letter to Fisher, Oct. 17, 1928.
11. Allison, "Sara," 281.
12. *Ibid.*, 327, 328.

Chapter 30

1. Allison, "Sara," 179, 180.
2. Western Union telegram from Adkins to Fisher, August 3, 1928.
3. "James A. Allison, Capitalist, Dies," *Indianapolis News*, August 4, 1928, p. 1.
4. "Allison, Speedway Promoter, Dies Here," *Indianapolis Star*, August 4, 1928, p. 1.
5. "Ex Wife Asks 2 Million of Allison Widow," *Indianapolis Star*, August 7, 1928, pp. 1, 2.
6. Rolls-Royce Heritage Trust, Allison Branch, Untitled History of Allison Engineering, December 1962, 6.
7. Levi letter to Snowden, Undated.
8. Western Union telegram from Fisher to Shutts and Stout, September 28, 1928.
9. Stout letter to Fisher, October 8, 1928.
10. "J.A. Allison Estate in Florida $1,250,000," *Miami Herald*, September 5, 1928, p. 1.
11. Levi letter to Foley, October 20, 1928.
12. Stout letter to Fisher, October 8, 1928.
13. Fisher letter to Davis, October 18, 1928.
14. Lewis, *Eddie Rickenbacker*, 285–296.
15. Pugh, *The Magic of a Name*, 100.
16. Western Union telegram from Stout to Fisher, April 15, 1929.
17. Davis and Foley letter to Fisher, October 16, 1928.
18. "Allison Fortune Goes to Mother," *Indianapolis Star*, April 7, 1929, section 3, p. 21.
19. *Ibid.*

Chapter 31

1. Lewis, *Eddie Rickenbacker*, 296.
2. Bloemker, *500 Miles to Go*, 175.
3. Lewis, *Eddie Rickenbacker*, 295.
4. *Ibid.*
5. Lavender, *Miami Beach in 1920*, 131.
6. Davidson and Shaffer, *Autocourse*, 65.
7. Bloemker, *500 Miles to Go*, 176.
8. Clymer, *Indianapolis 500 Mile Race History*, 200.
9. *Ibid.*
10. *Ibid.*
11. Bloemker, *500 Miles to Go*, 178.
12. *Ibid.*
13. Shaw, *Gentlemen, Start your Engines*, 129, 130.
14. Bloemker, *500 Miles to Go*, 178.
15. *Ibid.*, 180.
16. Davidson and Shaffer, *Autocourse*, 71.
17. Bloemker, *500 Miles to Go*, 179.
18. Davidson and Shaffer, *Autocourse*, 71.
19. Bloemker, *500 Miles to Go*, 183.
20. *Ibid.*
21. Shaw, *Gentlemen, Start Your Engines*, 186.
22. Bloemker, *500 Miles to Go*, 185.
23. *Ibid.*, 187.
24. *Ibid.*
25. Davidson and Shaffer, *Autocourse*, 83, 84.
26. *Ibid.*, 85, 86.
27. Bloemker, *500 Miles to Go*, 193.
28. Clymer, *Indianapolis 500 Mile Race History*, 252.
29. *Ibid.*, 268.
30. *Ibid.*
31. Shaw, *Gentlemen, Start Your Engines*, 256, 257.
32. Davidson and Shaffer, *Autocourse*, 102.
33. Clymer, *Indianapolis 500 Mile Race History*, 294, 295.
34. Bloemker, *500 Miles to Go*, 200, 201.
35. Lewis, *Eddie Rickenbacker*, 385.
36. Davidson and Shaffer, *Autocourse*, 101.
37. Shaw, *Gentlemen, Start Your Engines*, 252.
38. Davidson and Shaffer, *Autocourse*, 102.
39. Shaw, *Gentlemen, Start Your Engines*, 274.
40. Davidson and Shaffer, *Autocourse*, 102.
41. Shaw, *Gentlemen, Start Your Engines*, 275.
42. *Ibid.*
43. Shaw, *Gentlemen, Start Your Engines*, 276.
44. *Ibid.*, 276, 277.
45. Davidson and Shaffer, *Autocourse*, 103.
46. Shaw, *Gentlemen, Start Your Engines*, 279.
47. Bloemker, *500 Miles to Go*, 206–209.
48. Davidson and Shaffer, *Autocourse*, 103.
49. Shaw, *Gentlemen, Start Your Engines*, 285.
50. Bloemker, *500 Miles to Go*, 209–210.

51. Shaw, *Gentlemen, Start Your Engines*, 287.
52. Davidson and Shaffer, *Autocourse*, 104.
53. Bloemker, *500 Miles to Go*, 209, 210.
54. Davidson and Shaffer, *Autocourse*, 104.
55. *Ibid.*
56. Shaw, *Gentlemen, Start Your Engines*, 285.
57. Bloemker, *500 Miles to Go*, 213, 216.
58. Shaw, *Gentlemen, Start Your Engines*, 288.
59. Davidson and Shaffer, *Autocourse*, 115.
60. *Ibid.*, 127, 128.
61. Bloemker, *500 Miles to Go*, 241, 242.
62. *Ibid.*, 269.
63. Davidson and Shaffer, *Autocourse*, 193.
64. *Ibid.*, 183.
65. *Ibid.*, 185.
66. *Ibid.*, 186.
67. *Ibid.*, 195.
68. *Ibid.*, 198.
69. *Ibid.*, 204, 205.
70. *Ibid.*, 208.
71. *Ibid.*, 207.

Chapter 32

1. Sonnenberg and Schoneberger, *Allison: Power of Excellence*, 40.
2. *Ibid.*
3. *Ibid.*, 41.
4. *Ibid.*, 40.
5. *Ibid.*, 41.
6. *Ibid.*
7. Sloan, *My Years with General Motors*, 363.
8. Sonnenberg and Schoneberger, *Allison: Power of Excellence*, 41.
9. *Ibid.*, 44, 45.
10. Goldthwaite Oral History, 22.
11. Sonnenberg and Schoneberger, *Allison: Power of Excellence*, 44, 45.
12. *Ibid.*
13. Pugh, *The Magic of a Name*, 101.
14. Sonnenberg and Schoneberger, *Allison: Power of Excellence*, 45, 48, 49.
15. *Ibid.*, 49, 50.
16. *Ibid.*, 50, 51.
17. *Ibid.*, 55.
18. *Ibid.*, 55, 56, 57, 62, 81.
19. "Allison Plant Features Bared," *Indianapolis Star*, December 31, 1939, p. 5.
20. Goldthwaite Oral History, 37, 142.
21. Sonnenberg and Schoneberger, *Allison: Power of Excellence*, 55.
22. Pugh, *The Magic of a Name*, 101.
23. *Ibid.*, 102.
24. Sonnenberg and Schoneberger, *Allison: Power of Excellence*, 55, 56, 57, 62, 81.
25. Pugh, *The Magic of a Name*, 102.
26. Sonnenberg and Schoneberger, *Allison: Power of Excellence*, 92, 93, 95, 104.
27. Pugh, *The Magic of a Name*, 102.
28. *Ibid.*
29. Sonnenberg and Schoneberger, *Allison: Power of Excellence*, 92, 93, 95, 104.
30. Pugh, *The Magic of a Name*, 105.
31. Sonnenberg and Schoneberger, *Allison: Power of Excellence*, 92, 93, 95, 104.
32. *Ibid.*, 100.
33. Pugh, *The Magic of a Name*, 106.
34. Sonnenberg and Schoneberger, *Allison: Power of Excellence*, 144–147.
35. Pugh, *The Magic of a Name*, 106.
36. *Ibid.*, 107.
37. Sonnenberg and Schoneberger, *Allison: Power of Excellence*, 144–147.
38. *Ibid.*, 150–153.
39. Pugh, *The Magic of a Name*, 110, 111.
40. Sonnenberg and Schoneberger, *Allison: Power of Excellence*, 168, 171.
41. *Ibid.*, 174, 175.
42. *Ibid.*, 179.
43. *Ibid.*, 180, 182.
44. Pugh, *The Magic of a Name*, 121.
45. *Ibid.*, 113.
46. *Ibid.*, 113–116.
47. Allison Transmissions Inc. Website.

Epilogue

1. Moore and Jones, *Biographical Memoirs*, 123–128.
2. "Louis Mowbray," *Bermuda Biographies*, www.bermudabiographies.bm (accessed August 26, 2008).

Bibliography

Allen, Frederick Lewis. *Only Yesterday: An Informal History of the Nineteen-twenties.* New York: Harper, 1957.

Allison, Sara Cornelius. "Sara." Marian University Archives: Unpublished manuscript, 1938.

Automotive Quarterly. General Motors: The First 75 Years of Transportation Products. General Motors Corporation.

Behr, Edward. *Prohibition: 13 Years That Changed America.* London: BBC Books, 1997.

Bennett, Ira Elbert. *History of the Panama Canal: Its Construction and Builders.* Washington, DC: Historical Publishing, 1915.

Bird, Anthony. *The Motor Car, 1765–1915.* New York: Taplinger, 1961.

Bloemker, Al. *500 Miles to Go: The History of the Indianapolis Speedway.* New York: Coward-McCann, 1961.

Bodenhamer, David J., Robert G. Barrows, and David Gordon Vanderstel. *The Encyclopedia of Indianapolis.* Bloomington: Indiana University Press, 1994.

The Brooklands Society. "And Darkness Was Upon the Face of British Motor Racing." www.brooklands.org.uk.

Clymer, Floyd. *Indianapolis 500 Mile Race History: A Complete Detailed History of Every Indianapolis Race Since 1909.* Los Angeles: Floyd Clymer, 1946.

_____. *Treasury of Early American Automobiles 1877–1925.* New York: McGraw Hill, 1950.

Davidson, Donald, and Rick Shaffer. *Autocourse: Official History of the Indianapolis 500.* Silverstone, Northants, UK: Crash Media, 2006.

Derr, Mark. *Some Kind of Paradise: A Chronicle of Man and the Land in Florida.* New York: W. Morrow, 1989.

Dinn, Allan E. *Boats by Purdy.* St. Michaels, MD: Tiller, 2003.

Dodson, Kenneth. "Work of Jens Jensen at the James A. Allison Estate." Thesis, Ball State University, 1998.

Dunn, Jacob Piatt. *Greater Indianapolis: The History, the Industries, the Institutions, and the People of a City of Homes.* Chicago: Lewis, 1910.

Elwood, Mark. *Rough Guide to Miami.* New York: Rough Guides, 2005.

First Superspeedway.com. "24 Hours at Indianapolis: The Birth of the Brickyard."

Fisher, Jane. *Fabulous Hoosier: A Story of American Achievement.* New York: R.M. McBride, 1947.

Fisher, Jerry M. *The Pacesetter: The Untold Story of Carl G Fisher.* Ft. Bragg, CA: Lost Coast, 1998.

Foster, Mark S. *Castles in the Sand: The Life and Times of Carl Graham Fisher.* Gainesville: University Press of Florida, 2000.

Georgano, G.N. *The Beaulieu Encyclopedia of the Automobile.* Chicago: Fitzroy Dearborn, 2000.

Grese, Robert E. *Jens Jensen: Maker of Natural Parks and Gardens.* Baltimore: Johns Hopkins University Press, 1992.

Hale, Hester Ann. *Growth and Change: Indianapolis 1820–1920.* H.A. Hale, 1982.

Hanley, George Phillip, and Stacey Pankiw Hanley. *The Marmon Heritage: More Than 125 Years of American Production of World Renowned Products.* Rochester, MI: Doyle Hyk, 1985.

Hyman, Max Robinson. *Hyman's Handbook of Indianapolis: An Outline History.* M.R. Hyman, 1907.

Kalleen, James L. "Raceway History House." *Indianapolis Home & Garden.* May 1979, p. 110.

Kimes, Beverly Rae. "The Rise and Fall of the Empire." *Automotive Quarterly* 12, no. 1, pp. 68–77.

Kleinberg, Howard. *Miami Beach: A History.* Miami, FL: Centennial, 1994.

LaGorce, John Oliver. "Miami's Aquarium Opened to Public for First Time." *Miami Metropolis,* January 1, 1921, p. 1.

Latham, Charles, Jr. "Houses & Horses the Old-Fashioned Way," *Circular* 10, no. 1 (June 1989), 1, 2. Marion County/Indianapolis Historical Society.

Lavender, Abraham D. *Miami Beach in 1920: The Making of a Winter Resort.* Charleston, SC: Arcadia, 2002.

Lewis, David A. *Eddie Rickenbacker: American Hero in the 20th Century.* Baltimore: Johns Hopkins University Press, 2005.

Leyes, Richard A., and William A. Fleming (National Air and Space Museum). *The History of North American Small Gas Turbine Aircraft Engines.* Reston, VA: Smithsonian Institution, 1999.

Lincoln Highway Association. *The Lincoln Highway: The Story of a Crusade That Made Transportation History.* New York: Dodd Mead, 1935.

Marian University. "The Mansions of Marian." Indianapolis (privately published; 1st printing 1985, 2nd printing 1991).

Miller, Wanda Lou. *Allison: The Man and His Legacy.* Rolls-Royce Heritage Trust — Allison Branch archives (n.p., n.d.).

Moore, Daniel Decatur, and James O. Co. Jones. *Men of the South: A Work for the Newspaper Reference Library.* New Orleans: Southern Biographical Association, 1922.

Nash, Charles Edgar. *The Magic of Miami Beach.* Philadelphia: David McKay, 1938.

National Academy of Sciences. *Biographical Memoirs.* Washington, DC: National Academy Press, 1994.

Nichols, John T. "The Modern Aquarium." *Natural History* 21, American Museum of Natural History, 1921.

Nolan, William F. *Barney Oldfield: The Life and Times of America's Legendary Speed King.* New York: G.P. Putnam's Sons, 1961.

Ogle, Maureen. *Ambitious Brew: The Story of American Brew.* Orlando: Harcourt, 2006.

Pugh, Peter. *The Magic of a Name: The Rolls-Royce Story.* Part 3, *A Family of Engines.* Cambridge, England: Icon, 2002.

Redford, Polly. *Billion Dollar Sandbar: A Biography of Miami Beach.* New York: Dutton, 1970.

Ritchie, Andrew. *Major Taylor: The Extraordinary Career of a Champion Bicycle Racer.* San Francisco: Bicycle, 1988.

Rosenberg, Chaim M. *America at the Fair: Chicago's 1893 World's Columbian Exposition.* Charleston, SC: Arcadia, 2008.

Scott, D. Bruce, and Hetty Gray. *Indy Racing Before the 500.* Batesville, IN: Indiana Reflections, 2005.

Shaw, Wilbur. *Gentlemen, Start Your Engines.* New York: Coward-McCann, 1955.

Sloan, Alfred P., Jr. *My Years with General Motors.* Garden City, NY: Doubleday, 1964.

Sonnenburg, Paul, and William A. Schoneberger. *Allison: Power of Excellence 1915–1990.* Malibu: Coastline, 1990.

Speedway Civic Committee, History Committee. *The Story of Speedway.* s.l.: s.n, 1976.

Stutz Motor Car Company. *The Splendid Stutz.* Indianapolis: Stutz Motor Car Company, 1930.

Thomas, George E., and Robert Venturi. *William L. Price: Arts & Crafts to Modern Design.* New York: Princeton Architectural Press, 2000.

Watts, Steven. *The People's Tycoon: Henry Ford and the American Century,* New York: Alfred A. Knopf, 2005.

Letters and Telegrams

Adkins, E.H. Western Union Telegram to Carl Fisher, August 3, 1928, Historical Museum of South Florida, Carl G. Fisher Collection.

Allison, James. Letter to Fisher, March 29, 1919, Historical Museum of South Florida, Carl G. Fisher Collection.

_____. Letter to Louis Mowbray, May 26, 1919, Private Collection.

_____. Letter to Fisher, March 24, 1920, Historical Museum of South Florida, Carl G. Fisher Collection.

_____. Letter to Fisher, April 5, 1920, Historical Museum of South Florida, Carl G. Fisher Collection.

_____. Western Union Telegram to Fisher, April 5, 1921, Historical Museum of South Florida, Carl G. Fisher Collection.

_____. Letter to Fisher, June 14, 1923, Historical Museum of South Florida, Carl G. Fisher Collection.

_____. Letter to Fisher, July 24, 1924, Historical Museum of South Florida, Carl G. Fisher Collection.

_____. Letter to Fisher, August 20, 1924, Historical Museum of South Florida, Carl G. Fisher Collection.

_____. Letter to Fisher, July 25, 1925, Historical Museum of South Florida, Carl G. Fisher Collection.

_____. Letter to Fisher, August 4, 1925, Historical Museum of South Florida, Carl G. Fisher Collection.

Carney, James P. Letter to Carl Fisher, November 1, 1917, Historical Museum of South Florida, Carl G. Fisher Collection.

Davis, Paul, and M.E. Foley. Letter to Carl Fisher, October 16, 1928, Historical Museum of South Florida, Carl G. Fisher Collection.

Fisher, Carl G. Letter to John Deering, December 17, 1917, Historical Museum of South Florida, Carl G. Fisher Collection.

_____. Letter to James Allison, January 2, 1920, Historical Museum of South Florida, Carl G. Fisher Collection.

_____. Letter to Allison, March 20, 1920, Historical Museum of South Florida, Carl G. Fisher Collection.

_____. Letter to Allison, March 27, 1920, Historical Museum of South Florida, Carl G. Fisher Collection.

_____. Letter to Allison, April 25, 1920, Historical Museum of South Florida, Carl G. Fisher Collection.

_____. Letter to Allison, September 15, 1922, Historical Museum of South Florida, Carl G. Fisher Collection.

_____. Letter to Allison, March 30, 1923, Historical Museum of South Florida, Carl G. Fisher Collection.

_____. Letter to Dan Mahoney, August 5, 1928, Historical Museum of South Florida, Carl G. Fisher Collection.

_____. Western Union Telegram to Frank B. Shutts and Elmer W. Stout, September 28, 1928, Historical Museum of South Florida, Carl G. Fisher Collection.

_____. Letter to Paul Y. Davis, October 18, 1928, Historical Museum of South Florida, Carl G. Fisher Collection.

LaGorce, John O. Letter to Carl Fisher, April 6, 1921, Historical Museum of South Florida, Carl G. Fisher Collection.

Langston, Lou. Letter to Carl Fisher, September 13, 1923, Historical Museum of South Florida, Carl G. Fisher Collection.

Levi, John. Letter to Carl Fisher, April 30, 1919, Historical Museum of South Florida, Carl G. Fisher Collection.

_____. Letter to James Snowden, Undated, Historical Museum of South Florida, Carl G. Fisher Collection.

_____. Letter to M.E. Foley, October 20, 1928, Historical Museum of South Florida, Carl G. Fisher collection.

Lummus, J.N. Letter to Carl Fisher, March 26, 1919, Historical Museum of South Florida, Carl G. Fisher Collection.

Pancoast, Thomas. Letter to Carl Fisher, October 17, 1928, Historical Museum of South Florida, Carl G. Fisher Collection.

Stout, Elmer. Letter to Carl Fisher, October 8, 1928, Historical Museum of South Florida, Carl G. Fisher Collection.

_____. Western Union telegram to Fisher, April 15, 1929, Historical Museum of South Florida, Carl G. Fisher Collection.

Newspaper Articles

"Allison, Capitalist, Dies Here." *Indianapolis Star*, August 4, 1928, p. 1.

"Allison Fortune Goes to Mother." *Indianapolis Star*, April 7, 1929, sec. 3, p. 21.

"Allison Plant Features Bared." *Indianapolis Star*, December 31, 1939, p. 5.

"Allison, Speedway Promoter, Dies Here." *Indianapolis Star*, August 4, 1928, p. 1.

"Around Noon, Building Still Under Construction Collapsed." *Indianapolis News*, December 6, 1911.

Ash, Agnes. "Well Done, St. Francis, Both the Hospital and the Steak." *Miami News*, June 28, 1964, p. 14.

"Building Code Revision Asked by Carpenters." *Indianapolis Morning Star*, December 30, 1911, pp. 1, 3.

"Carl Fisher and Others Paid Homage to Allison." *Indianapolis Star*, August 6, 1928.

"City Jolted by Prest-O-Lite." *Indianapolis News*, June 7, 1908, p. 1.

"Clemens Sets New 100 Mile Record." *Indianapolis News*, November 5, 1905, p. 18.

"County Publicity Tax Urged for Aquarium." *Miami Herald*, April 5, 1923, p. 3.

"8th Man Dies, Causes to Be Studied by Grand Jury." *Indianapolis Morning Star*, December 8, 1911, pp. 1, 7.

"Ex Wife Asks 2 Million of Allison Widow." *Indianapolis Star*, August 7, 1928, p. 1.

"Fish in Miami Waters." *Miami Herald*, March 16, 1923, p. 1.

"Fisher to Build Clubhouse to Cost $1,500,000." *The Illustrated Tab*, October 13, 1925, p. 16.

"Fletcher American Bank Absorbs National

City." *Indianapolis Star*, March 1, 1924, p. 1.

"Force Jars Hospital." *Indianapolis Star*, June 7, 1908, p. 1.

"Former Allison Mansion Open for Public Tours." *Indianapolis Star*, August 28, 1977, sec. 7, pp. 1, 11.

"Frame Law to Bar Prest-O-Lite Plant." *Indianapolis Morning Star*, June 8, 1908, p. 1.

Frank, Sally. "Decorating for Dollars." *Indianapolis Star*, April 26, 1991 (Clipping file, Indiana State Library).

"Hundreds of Baby Sea-Horses Born to Proud Parents in Aquarium Tank." *Miami Herald*, March 22, 1923, p. 8.

"If You Drive Over Today, You'll Enjoy Yourself." *Miami Herald* (Aquarium Ad) March 23, 1923, p. 13.

"J.A. Allison Dies in Indiana of Pneumonia." *Miami Herald*, August 4, 1928, p. 1.

"J.A. Allison Estate in Florida $1,250,000." *Miami Herald*, September 5, 1928, p. 1.

"James A. Allison New Speedway President." *Indianapolis News*, June 12, 1923, p. 1.

"Jim Allison's Fame Still Grows." *The Guide*, May 22, 1974, p. 5.

"Jules Goux — A French Victor at Indianapolis." *PSA Peugeot Citron*, April 25, 2002. www.psa-peugeot-citroen.com.

"Liquor Found at Aquarium Seized." *Miami Herald*, April 28, 1921, p. 13.

"Many New Records Set in 24 Hour Run." *Indianapolis Morning Star*, November 18, 1905, p. 7.

"Marian College to Open September 8, 1937." *Indianapolis Star*, August 22, 1937, sec. 1, p. 5.

"Miami Aquarium Doors to Swing Closed for All Time at 6 PM." *Miami Herald*, April 1, 1923, p. 1.

"Miami Aquarium, Emptied of Sea Life, Now Mute Testimonial to Its Founder." *Miami Herald*, April 7, 1923, p. 7.

"Miami's Aquarium Opened to Public for the First Time." *Miami Metropolis*, January 1, 1921, p. 1.

"Mogul Built Wonder House." *Indianapolis News*, May 28, 1969, p. 19.

"No Deaths but Another Explosion." *Indianapolis News*, June 6, 1908, p. 3.

"183-Inch Type Is Likely to Prove Leader." *Indianapolis Star*, June 1, 1919, sec. 3, pp. 25, 26.

"Opening Aquarium Makes Miami 'Naples and Monaco of America.'" *Miami Herald*, January 2, 1921.

"Opening of Aquarium Drew a Large Crowd of Lovers of Nature." *Miami Metropolis*, January 4, 1921, p. 1.

"Prest-O-Lite Lets Go Again." *Indianapolis Morning Star*, December 21, 1907, pp. 1, 3.

"Prest-O-Lite Plant Opened in Speedway." *Indianapolis Star*, May 25, 1913, p. 4.

"Prest-O-Lite to Go." *Indianapolis Morning Star*, June 16, 1908, p. 1.

"Resolution to Fix Capital and Surplus at $3,300,000 to Be Submitted for Stockholders' Approval, May 19." *Indianapolis Star*, April 17, 1923, p. 1.

"7 Dead, 21 Injured, Search Continues for More." *Indianapolis Morning Star*, December 7, 1911.

"Spectacular Fire and Explosion Wreck Business Building." *Indianapolis Morning Star*, August 18, 1907, p. 1.

"Speedway Paving Example for City." *Indianapolis Morning Star*, July 19, 1910, p. 3.

Miscellaneous

Allison Transmissions. www.allisontransmissions.com.

Bosler, T.C. Interoffice Memo. Rolls-Royce Heritage Trust, Allison Branch, August 28, 1952.

Floyd, C.B. "Report of the Collapse of the Water Reservoir at the Miami Aquarium Association." Winterthur Library: Joseph Downs Collection of Manuscripts and Printed Ephemera, Col. 41.

Goldwaithe, John. Oral History. Center for the Study of History and Memory, Indiana University, 1979.

_____. Interoffice Memo, February 1, 1950. Rolls-Royce Allison Heritage Trust.

"Louis Mowbray." *Bermuda Biographies*. www.bermudabiographies.bm.

Marion County, Indiana, Clerk's Office. Miscellaneous Record Book 88, page 375.

Powers, Eugene S. "Report to McLanahan & Bencker on Failure of Reinforced Concrete Tank at the Aquarium Building of the Miami Aquarium Association, July 28, 1920." Winterthur Library: Joseph Downs Collection of Manuscripts and Printed Ephemera, Col. 41.

Prest-O-Lite. *The Prest-O-Liter*. Indianapolis: Prest-O-Lite Co., [191–?].

Rolls-Royce Corporation — Allison Branch. Untitled History of Allison Engineering. n.p., December 1962.

Songwriters Hall of Fame. www.songwritershalloffame.org.

Index

Numbers in **bold italics** indicate pages with photographs.